From the library of

*"But when the fulness
of the time was come,
God sent forth his Son..."*

St. Paul to the *Galatians*

BEFORE THE TIMES

BEFORE THE TIMES

Priscilla and Rebecca Patten

Foreword by Merrill C. Tenney
Introduction by Bebe Patten,
Afterword by Gary R. Moncher

Strawberry Hill Press

Strawberry Hill Press
2594 15th Avenue
San Francisco, California 94127

Manufactured in the United States of America

Edited by Diane Sipes
Book design by Carlton C. Herrick
Typesetting: Nina Bredt

Library of Congress Cataloging in Publication Data

Patten, Priscilla, 1950-
   Before the times.

   Bibliography: p.
   1. Judaism—History—Post-exilic period, 586 B.C.-
210 A.D.—Addresses, essays, lectures. 2. Jews—
History—586 B.C.-70 A.D.—Addresses, essays, lectures.
3. Jewish sects—Addresses, essays, lectures.
4. Music in the Bible—Addresses, essays, lectures.
I. Patten, Rebecca, 1950-   joint author.
II. Sipes, Diane. III. Title.
BM176.P27   930'.04924   80-36848
ISBN: 0-89407-047-9
ISBN 0-89407-038-X (pbk.)

Dedication
to

Dr. Bebe Patten

Acknowledgments

We want to express our appreciation to some of the many people who helped to make this book possible: to our mother, Dr. Bebe Patten, who first inspired us to study the New Testament, and who always believed in us; to Dr. Merrill C. Tenney, who introduced us to deeper study of the backgrounds of the New Testament era; to our brother, Thomas Patten, and Hannah Karajian for research work on Music and on Alexander the Great; to Gary Moncher who contributed the work on the Afterword; to Dr. Glenn Kunkel who spent many hours in editing this manuscript; to our typists, Mildred Waring and Esther Carlson; to Eva Freeman for her research and assistance; and finally, to our students whose interest in the subject helped us to continue in this project.

Contents

LIST OF MAPS

LIST OF ILLUSTRATIONS

Foreword

Between the last of the prophets of the Old Testament, whose ministry closed with the restoration at the time of the Second Temple about 450 B.C., and the advent of Christ recorded in the Gospels lies a period virtually unknown to many students of the Bible. No account of it exists in the current canonical text, although fragmentary relics appear in the Old Testament Apocrypha. Yet the events of this period are important because they formed the political and religious environment in which the earliest Christian faith developed. The Jewish and Gentile cultures of that time, the expectations of a Messiah, and the spiritual roots of the revelation of God in the New Testament can be understood better by a knowledge of that period.

This book is an attempt to present briefly and clearly the major factors that determined the cultural background of the life and work of Christ as described in the Gospels. The complexity of its political history and the significance of its religious parties are lucidly explained. The final chapter on musical instruments will enable one to appreciate better the orchestral aids that were used in public praise, both in the Temple and, to some extent, in the early Church. This volume should be a helpful guide and introduction to further study of the intertestamental period. The chapter on the Dead Sea Scrolls explains the origin of the discovery that has revealed much that was unknown in the past.

The authors are to be commended for producing this handbook for readers of the Bible. It will set much of their study in a new perspective.

Merrill C. Tenney

Wheaton College, Illinois
February 1980

17

Introduction

For almost 2,500 years—from Alexander's consolidation of his conquests in the Middle East, the birth, death and resurrection of Jesus Christ, through the ensuing history of concomitant development of religious, political, philosophical, social and creative human endeavor—diverse peoples at once both schismatically divided yet historically empathetic have shaped our complex world of today. As we approach the twenty-first century, perhaps it is more than ever imperative that we attempt to appreciate just how our questioning and seeking forebears still inform our present day thinking.

In their study Rebecca and Priscilla Patten succinctly synthesize the progression of some of the most important data available at this time and the way in which it has shaped and is shaping the world's way today. For example, no comprehension of modern-day politics in the Middle East is possible without a knowledge of the Biblical, historical and ethnological progressions of the past three millennia. The present tensions in the Middle East have as much root in the "Biblical" past as they do in the "Islamic." In the following pages, an essential overview of the Greek-Roman-Judaic-Christian bases of our Western World today is presented with scholarly impartiality and insight.

When the young genius of Alexander brought an eastern empire under the sway of Grecian influence, the Jews of his empire were long established in their monotheistic conviction as opposed to the Greeks' pantheistic beliefs and observances. Still, as the Doctors Patten remark, so great was Alexander's desire to bring the very best of his Hellenic culture to all his empire, and to absorb the very best of the cultures under his dominion that a transcultural melding occurred that is to this very day in evidence. It is significant that *Before the Times* opens on this observation which serves as a backdrop then for the following examination of the further developments in history, society, philosophy and the Judeo-Christian ethic.

Whereas the Grecian influence seems more or less benign, and their political influence more concentrated on military and political (in the sense of a city/state responsibility rather than a tribal concept), in the greater concept they were to provide a background for Jesus' universal appeal: "Love thy neighbor as thyself."

The death of Alexander was to throw the Jewish peoples into oppression from his successors. In so doing, the most sacred beliefs of the Jews were threatened. Under Judas Maccabeus, revolt against the oppressors served to focus their nation upon theoretical and theological imperatives as well as survivalistic identity.

It would be interesting to speculate on how our twentieth century might be today had Rome not "conquered the world," including Israel. If anything is truly apparent in history, it must be that all Rome worshiped Rome itself and all the panoply and all the "circus" of its conceit. In its excesses, the Jews sustained their abuses and blasphemies; in effect, it hardened their steel. If Judea suffered the Romans, then Jesus becomes one of the most representative examples of that suffering, and it is in this context we must observe this period. The Doctors Patten studiously examine it and, I think, offer an entirely inspired correlative discussion of its importance to present day thinking.

Following these rather well known historical episodes, there is an invaluable but little known sequence of events and developments among the Jews themselves. Here, Rebecca and Priscilla bring to us a long-overdue evaluation of the development of Jewish and Christian theology and philosophy. At this point, the *Torah* was perhaps overstudied. Still, the fact is that erudite commentary was the life of Jewish belief and argument amongst diversive Jews. Little known amongst Jews themselves are the various sects whose beliefs and interpretations of the "Old Testament" as expounded in the *Torah* varied greatly. Historically and basically, the ensuing chapters bring to cognitive significance how the ministry of Jesus was both a continuation of the precepts found in Judaism, and a fulfillment of "the Times" promised by the Jewish prophets.

There follows a most pertinent comment on the importance of the Dead Sea Scrolls—a heritage we may not yet fully appreciate. Had any of us ever doubted the validity of our Biblical dedication and study, the discovery of these unquestionably authentic attestations to our fidelity in Christ and the eternal promise of our dedication are here confirmed.

The final chapter of this book is devoted to Musical Instruments. To some, we suspect, that may seem a bit out of context. Still, I am never prayerful without thinking of Jubal's lyre or of Handel's incredibly Holy inspirations. *The music of Faith is the music of the spheres!*

May all who read this book find direction and guidance for a better understanding of the Times of our Lord.

Dr. Bebe Patten
Oakland, California

Chapter I

THE INFLUENCE OF ALEXANDER THE GREAT ON THE LATE FOURTH AND EARLY THIRD CENTURIES B.C.

Chapter I

THE INFLUENCE OF ALEXANDER THE GREAT ON THE LATE FOURTH AND EARLY THIRD CENTURIES B.C.

Alexander the Great! Great in his impact on world civilization. Great in his vision of a unified world that blended the best cultural values of the West and the East in the most humane and enlightened empire the world had ever known. His policies of cultural assimilation, education and world commerce worked for the good of all the nations comprising his empire. His rule gave new thrust to the concept of the importance of the individual as envisioned by Plato, Aristotle and, later, by the Epicureans and the Stoics. This was a world that in language, philosophy, and general culture provided the seed bed for early Christianity and helped to make possible its widespread acceptance and rapid extension in the first century.

Alexander the Great, son of Philip of Macedon, probably made more changes in the world of his time than did any other universal figure. His influence can still be seen in the world of today. He gave the world new concepts of armies and of government. He made possible universal world trade, and he successfully blended the Greek and Asiatic cultures. He made education in many fields blossom through his personal discoveries and through exchange of world knowledge made possible by his world empire. Alexander's philosophical ideas triggered the minds of men, instilling new thoughts which prepared the world for the message of Christianity.

Alexander was an invincible military genius. He conquered the known world of his day, using a nationalistic army with no mercenaries, relying solely on the ties holding his men to their own land. He knew that the spirit of his fellow Macedonians would be stronger than that of the mercenary armies of the other nations because they were fighting for their own soil.[1] Unlike earlier armies, the Macedonians spent enough time in rigid training to consider soldiering a true profession. Yet at heart they were still farmers. Other armies of the time were either mercenary, caring only for money, not their homeland, or they were quickly assembled in times of emergency without any previous training.[2]

One of Alexander's great contributions to the world was the refining of this nationalistic army. Founded by his father Philip, the Macedonian phalanx reached its peak under Alexander and lasted beyond the coming of Rome to world power.[3] Alexander introduced the heavy use of cavalry, new organization for the army, and ingenious strategies that enabled him to conquer the world at the age of thirty-two. The army was made up of the phalanx of infantry in the center and two side wings, one of infantry and one of cavalry. The phalanx, the army's heartbeat, consisted of 1,000 footmen in rank and sixteen in file—16,000 men armed with sixteen-foot iron spears and iron shields.[4] Alexander used light and heavy cavalry of different types. He opened, and sometimes closed, the battles with his cavalry. (From 333-222 B.C. cavalry was an important feature in world armies.) Between his phalanx and his cavalry Alexander's army was almost invincible.[5]

Alexander organized new military groups. He instituted the *agema,* or Royal Guard, composed of the Royal Pages, boys training for military tasks, and the Bodyguards, made up of his staff of officers. These groups continued throughout the fourth century, B.C. and into the reigns of the Ptolemies and Seleucids[6] of the third and second centuries.

Tracing some of his battles we can easily see the new tactics introduced by Alexander. In the attack on the North, in Thrace, the Macedonians had to climb steep mountains. The Thracians sent loaded wagons over the mountains to roll onto and crush Alexander's army. Alexander had the men lock their shields over their heads so the wagons would roll over the shields. Only a few were crushed.[7]

Other tactics were introduced in the siege of Tyre, where for the first time the Greeks learned to attack a walled city.[8] Alexander had battering rams made—long, heavy beams headed with iron or brass and suspended by a chain. These were swung into the wall until a breach was made. Alexander taught the men to build a huge causeway from the mainland of what is now Lebanon to the island of Tyre. As they worked on this ramp they erected machines for throwing stones and darts onto the Tyrian galleys that tried to approach them.[9] The siege at Tyre with the powerful stone-throwing machines and catapults was made possible because of Alexander's earlier experience at Halicarnassus, where for the first time in world history catapults were used to hurl objects over a city wall. Alexander built siege sheds to cover the battering rams, thus enabling them to reach the walls of Halicarnassus. Later, at Tyre, the catapults actually threw the objects directly at the walls until they gave way. These machines were tremendously complementary to the battering rams.[10]

In his battle against Darius, Alexander introduced a procedure to defeat the fearsome Persians, who drove their elephants and chariots with scythes

Illus. 1

Alexander, on horseback, at the battle of Issus. This mosaic, found at Pompeii, is thought to be a copy of an original painting of c. 330 B.C.

attached to the axles straight into the enemy lines. First, Alexander would frighten the elephants; then his footmen would seize the horses of the chariots. After this they would step back, let the Persians march through, and then attack them from the rear.[11] Never before had the armies of the world been able to defeat the terrible Persians.

Along with military improvements, Alexander introduced new ideas of government, which had as a partial basis his self-concept as a deity. He established himself as the son of the god, Jupiter-Ammon,[12] when he marched through Egypt. From his birth it was rumored that Alexander was the product of his witch-mother and a god.[13] Many believed this, and the public announcement of it in an Egyptian temple appeared to confirm Alexander as a monarch god. As W. W. Tarn has shown, Alexander set the example for the Ptolemies and Seleucids:

> The worship that gave the precedent to the world was the official worship of the great Macedonian instituted in Egypt by Ptolemy I, probably soon after he took the crown in 305. Soon after 280 Ptolemy II instituted at Alexandria a great festival in worship of his father, Ptolemy I, and Antiochus I followed by deifying Seleucus as Zeus Nikator; and therewith was established the further principle that the kings, like Alexander, officially became gods after death.[14]

The Ptolemies traced their lineage directly to Heracles and Dionysus, while the Seleucids were supposedly descended from Apollo.[15] Alexander was especially worshiped in Alexandria because he had founded the city. As might be expected, his army worshiped him greatly after his death.

Alexander's purpose in deifying himself was not so much to start an official cult for his personal glorification as it was to unify his subjects under him as a god, as well as a king. The political advantage of this policy was quickly seized upon by his successors Antigonus I, Demetrius I, Lysimachus, Seleucus I, Ptolemy I, and Cassanders—all of whom worshiped in different places. Thus, the old Hellenic democratic city-states were quickly formed into monarchies headed by power-hungry despots claiming divinity for themselves.

The military colony was established under Alexander; before his time the Greeks had known only the *polis,* "city," or the *kome,* "village," (Alexander personally founded over seventy cities.[16]) All of the Alexandrias were of his own making. These Alexandrias were not as formally structured as the Greek *poleis,* each of which was characterized by the division of citizens into tribes, a council chosen from the tribes, magistrates, separate city-lands belonging only to its citizens, laws, a budget, an Assembly, and city subdivisions. Only a king could found a city. The king would have to find land and settlers, build the walls, and supply food and cattle for the people. Taxation, of course, would not be enforced at the beginning. It was the king's responsibility to provide housing and a city code, and to establish the political and social life of

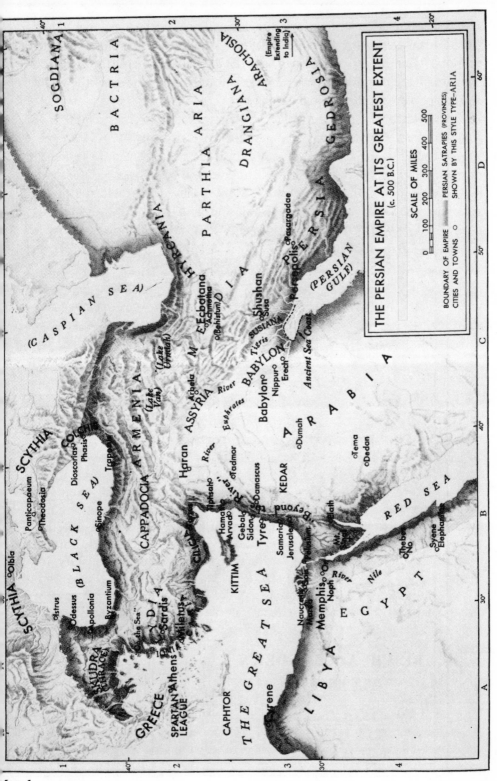

THE PERSIAN EMPIRE AT ITS GREATEST EXTENT
(c. 500 B.C.)

SCALE OF MILES

0   100   200   300   400   500

BOUNDARY OF EMPIRE ▬▬▬   PERSIAN SATRAPIES (PROVINCES)
CITIES AND TOWNS o   SHOWN BY THIS STYLE TYPE–ARIA

Map 1

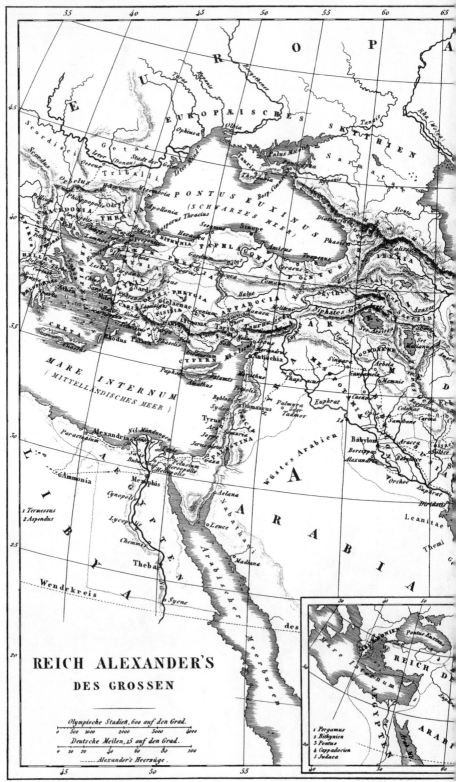

28   *Map 2*   The Kingdom of Alexander the Great.

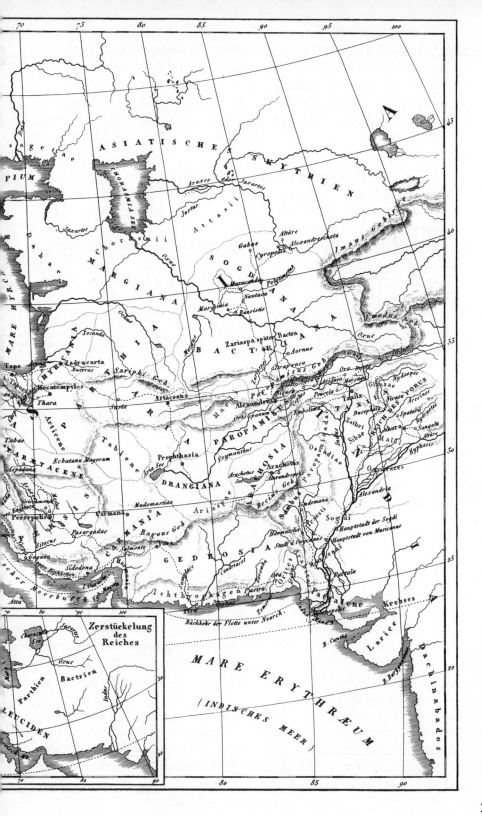

29

the city.[17] Although many of Alexander's military colonies eventually became cities under the Seleucids and Ptolemies, they were not founded for that purpose. Neither was the military colony like a *kome,* or village, simply a collection of houses without the orders of the city—the *kome* could be very large or very small. To the Greeks, cities as large as Jerusalem, Babylon, and Memphis were only villages because they did not have the systematized government of the Greek *poleis.*

In keeping with Alexander's policy, the purposes of the military colony were to infiltrate the newly conquered Asian peoples with Greeks to spread Greek culture, to provide military defense, and to establish reserves for Alexander's army. It was not necessary to set up the military colony as the king would set up the *polis;* it could be founded by the monarch and then given to subordinate governors to finish.[18]

Alexander appointed a commander of troops, a tax collector, and a general administrator with orders to make Greek centers out of the Asian settlements.[19] He imposed Greek law on the colonies and encouraged Greeks to settle in them. This idea was taken up by the Seleucids, who designed an even better way to accommodate both foreigners and Greeks within one city.[20]

The main purpose of the military colony was to provide defense. Alexander set up some colonies in Bactria-Sogdiana (Asia Minor) for protection against the nomads, and in Media to defend his land from attack by native tribes. Later the Seleucids made a chain of such settlements across Asia Minor to protect their coastal area from the Galatians.[21].

Reserves for the Macedonian army were organized in the colonies. Each colonist was given a *kleros,* a piece of land, in return for military service. Colonists were to be available any time they were needed, as the obligation to serve went along with the property. If the land was sold, the obligation to serve was transferred to the buyer. In this way, the Macedonians increased their ranks. The *kleros* system originated with Alexander and was widely used after his death to augment the Seleucid armies. One could find military colonies beside any city or village.[22]

Alexander's policies also affected the opening of world trade. Merchants from the Far East could exchange goods with those of the ports of Corinth, Tyre, and Alexandria without fear of crossing hostile territorial boundaries along the trade routes. Now that the whole world was under one regent, no nation could interrupt the flow of commerce. When trade increased, opportunities opened up and money flowed more freely, encouraging the growth of interesting new trade developments.

International trade began to enlarge the coffers of the world while Alexander's empire set a precedent for the efficient Roman road system to come. Few appear to have noticed that this evolved from the former Hellenistic system. Before Alexander, the Persians had excluded the Greeks from trading with inner Asia, but now the territories of Asia and Egypt were flourishing with new wealth. New cities and towns had sprung up, a primitive form of credit and banking was introduced, and the standard of living was improved for the upper classes. Contracts were signed, and usually the demand for most products was greater than the supply. W. W. Tarn notes that the city of Delos made retail profits of 100 percent, although the usual percentage was more like twenty or thirty.[23] The influence of this new boom in trade on the Hellenistic kings resulted in all of them becoming merchants, with the possible exception of the Antigonids.

To accommodate the increase in world trade, new ports and bigger ships had to be built. Merchant ships were built with a capacity of 4,200 tons, and a new method of sailing was introduced enabling ships to sail directly from one point to another instead of hugging the coast from point to point—one could, for example, now sail directly from Tyre to Alexandria in Egypt without following the Palestinian coast line. Tarn says, "The book of Timosthenes of Rhodes, *On Harbours,* filled the place now held by the *Mediterranean Pilot*" as a guide to navigation.[24]

Alexander's own currency became international, and the amount of money in circulation increased tremendously. Fortunately, the Alexander-drachma was equivalent to the Attic currency which had been used by Athens, Macedonia, cities in the Black Sea area, the Far East, Pergamum, Bithynia, Cappadocia and Epirus. The Romans made their denarii equal to the Attic drachma, the equivalent of the Alexander-drachma. During the third century B.C. the Alexander-drachma was still used, and it outlasted even the coming of Rome as a world power.[25]

The role of the city in the economic system changed with Alexander. Instead of small-scale production, competition on a larger basis had begun.[26] In former days one city could provide most of its own needs and be relatively independent, but this was only because trade laws with surrounding countries were never certain and relations were often strained. With the opening of trade between the countries, however, the cities specialized in certain products because they knew they could depend on other cities to supply them with the rest of their needs.[27] Important cities with their specialties included:

Alexandria	—	papyrus, glass, linens, perfumes
Antioch	—	textiles
Corinth	—	bronze
Delos	—	slaves
Miletus	—	wool
Rhodes	—	pottery
Cnidus	—	pottery
Priene	—	salt
Uruk	—	salt

Because most of the Hellenistic cities were situated in fertile lands that produced their own food supplies, their trade was mostly in manufactured goods.[28] Trade and economic developments were vast, and were constantly expanding. This sudden burst of commerce was due directly to the success of Alexander in unifying the nations and cultures of the world.

As already stated, Alexander encouraged the blending of Asiatic and Greek cultures. He did this, in part, by instigating marriages between his own soldiers and Oriental women and by combining in various ways the luxury and easy life of the East with the simplicity and energetic life of the West.

From his childhood Alexander had been enchanted by the East. He believed that the true gods dwelt in the East (as suggested by the sunrise). As a student of Aristotle, Alexander studied for hours, reading stories of the East after completing Aristotle's endless laboratory experiments.[29]

He would question ambassadors from the East who visited his father concerning the habits of their kings and the geography of their lands.[30]

When Alexander finally conquered the East he took a wife from the barbarian Bactrian tribe, Rushanak (Roxana), a girl who knew no Greek and had no education. He encouraged his soldiers to marry Oriental brides also. At Susa he invited his officers to a mass wedding where he took another wife, Darius' eldest daughter. Eighty of his officers followed his example.[31]

One writer says that perhaps as many as 10,000 soldiers followed Alexander's example, for he gave each of them dowries and listed them in a special roster.[32] These marriages between Greeks and Asiatics produced an influential upper class in the Hellenized areas. They were continued during the fourth and third centuries B..C.because few women immigrated to the East during or after Alexander's lifetime. Such marriages were encouraged everywhere, be it with Egyptian, Macedonian or barbarian.[33]

The easy life of the East was in direct contrast to the hard life of the Macedonians. Asia was made up of splendid palaces, vast cities, and enormous armies. The Greeks led disciplined lives, encouraging hard work, courage, genius and skill. They built strong citadels and compact towns. In conquering Persia and becoming the owner of these elegant luxuries, Alexander's habits changed drastically, and a large part of his army followed his example. The old, simple, Hellenic life was soon tainted with the corruptions and the ostentatious gaudiness of the East. The wealth of the East was sent back to Greece.[34] As Edward Burns states, "The Hellenic devotion to simplicity and the golden mean gave way to extravagance in art and to a love of luxury and riotous excess."[35]

But despite this, an educational revolution occurred as a result of Alexander's success in blending the knowledge of the two worlds of East and

West. He supported private and community educational institutions everywhere, and was responsible for the development of Alexandria, the great learning center of the ancient world, with its vast library and university, where Jews and Greeks were brought together in the first translation of the Old Testament into Greek.

Alexander's study under Aristotle was marked by a great interest in science, an interest that led him to take along with his army two surveyors, a mineralogist, a weather expert, scientists of animal and plant life, physicians and musicians. The discoveries made on his Asian campaigns opened the way to further discovery and advancement. Alexander's surveyors formed a geography of Asia, and laid the foundations for Dicaearchus' map of the world, drawn in 300 B.C. and in which time the heights of Greek mountains, and even the world's circumference, were calculated. His scientists proved that India was not connected to Africa. (This had been an insurmountable obstacle for Aristotle.) Eratosthenes of Cyrene (275-200 B.C.) discovered that all the oceans were one and that one could sail eastward from Spain around Africa and arrive in India.[36] Theophrastus (372-287 B.C.) compiled the discoveries of Alexander's expeditions in his famous *History of Plants*.[37] Alexander supplied scientists with information on botany, zoology, geography, ethnography, and hydrography,[38] and because of the political unity in the world created by Alexander's policies, Chaldeans, Egyptians, and Greeks were able to exchange their knowledge.[39]

Alexander gave financial aid to the development of learning and financed Aristotle's work in Greece. Aristotle has been credited with establishing the first private library of any means, a library made possible by Alexander. As a result of Alexander's help, libraries began forming in cities everywhere, including Antioch, Pergamus, Rhodes, and Smyrna.[40] Not only did he encourage the development of libraries, but he established theatres and temples in the new cities he built.[41]

Of all the cities built by Alexander and his successors, Alexandria, in Egypt, is the most famous. This city was responsible for the preservation of much valuable research. Ptolemy I, one of Alexander's generals, established a museum or school there.[42] Its library grew to over 500,000 manuscripts. Alexandria rivaled Athens in knowledge and was more integrated with different races than was Athens. Alexandria is important not only for the preservation of highly valued manuscripts, but for the diffusion of Hellenic literature throughout the world.[43] W. H. McNeill comments:

> Though we have no explicit record telling us the fact, there must have been some regular permission to copy books in the library, and multiplying them by slave hands, to disperse them by way of trade all over the Greek-speaking world.[44]

The Alexandrian scholars also systematized Greek grammar and edited and preserved the famous literary works of the Greeks.[45]

The contribution to world knowledge included records and traditions dating back to pre-Hellenic times, and their scientific observations added much to the knowledge of the Greeks.[46] In exchange Greece gave the East her art, literature, games, and philosophy. The technological inventions of the fourth and third centuries are so numerous that a separate study of Hellenistic civilization would be needed to enumerate them. The sciences of mechanics and astronomy were completely revamped; geometry and trigonometry were introduced; steam power was discovered, and hundreds of new theories and products were invented.[47]

One source describes the situation in a nutshell:

> The civilization of modern times has come from the blending of East and West—not from Greece alone. And all of this was made possible by the work of Alexander. "He grafted the new West upon the old East, and from this graft sprang the plant of our later civilization". . . He did more than any single man up to this day to make one part of the world known to the other . . .[48]

Alexander's policy of promoting a unified world based on Hellenistic philosophy and culture strongly influenced the development of the pre-Christian world; he sought to establish:

1. One *lingua franca*
2. One fusion of the gods[49]
3. One empire
4. One monarch-god
5. One blend of culture

With the expansion of thought, two major philosophies began to develop in about the year 300 B.C.—Stoicism and Epicureanism. Man stopped thinking of himself as merely another stone in the wall of the city. He began to realize his own emotional and intellectual needs as an individual. He was no longer merely an instrument of the State. The Stoics enlarged upon Alexander's idea of human brotherhood and the ideal state. Before Alexander, the Greeks had looked upon the barbarians as inferior people, but Alexander rejected this view.[50] The Stoics also believed, like Alexander, that the souls of barbarians were not inferior.[51] William Tarn well describes the situation:

> Man as a political animal, a fraction of the *polis* or self-governing city-state, had ended with Aristotle; with Alexander begins man as an individual . . . At a banquet at Opis, Alexander prayed for a union of hearts (*homonoia*) among all peoples and a joint commonwealth of Macedonians and Persians; he was the first to transcend national boundaries and to envisage, however imperfectly, a brotherhood of man in which there should be neither Greek nor barbarian.[52]

The Stoics also rejected the idea of separate city-states. They wanted one great city, or world state, under one law.[53] All citizens would be willingly bound together in unity.

Epicurus (342-270 B.C.), the father of Epicureanism, adopted Alexander's concept of individualism in another way. He, too, said that man was not just a political being, that he had intellectual and practical needs as well. The main aim of Epicureanism was to avoid pain. The type of pleasure he advocated was not sensual but intellectual, one in which the mind is quiet and free from all anxiety. Happiness is the goal, and it is achieved by friendship, virtue, and living apart from the world. With the development of a world empire in which the emphasis shifted from the city-state to the individual, Epicureanism became popular.[54]

In the third century B.C. education became more widespread and many private philosophies developed. Foreigners established various clubs among the Greeks with the purpose of promoting their special philosophies or religions.

By opening men's minds through the diffusion of education and culture, Alexander in no small way prepared the world for the coming of Christianity. As we have seen, he stressed unity,[55] attempting to unite everyone under himself as a god. This policy was followed up by the Caesars of the New Testament era.

Philosophical discussions current in Alexander's time often centered on such questions as, "How many gods are there?" "How was the world and man formed?" "Why are we here?" "Is there a second life?" "Are souls immortal?" Various philosophers tried without success to answer these questions. Thus, when Christianity began to develop, the concepts that defined it were already being discussed by the non-Christian world, giving the early Christians a responsive audience. Many found it to be the answer to their mental struggle as well as to their soul's salvation. Plato had said that souls are immortal, and Epicurus stressed virtue as a means of achieving happiness. These truths are found in Christianity. Of course, there were ethical limits to the foundational supports provided by pre-Christian philosophies: None of them, for example, stressed the Christian message, "Love thy neighbor as thyself."[56]

With Alexander promoting Oriental ideas, many mystery religions of the East came into the Western world. To some extent at least, such cults met personal needs that many began to realize. People were becoming dissatisfied with the remoteness of the pantheon. They could no longer relate to a carved god(dess) of stone. McNeill states that the decline of the Greek gods as the sole religion came about with the decline of the city-states.[57] Mystery religions like the cults of Isis and Serapis, Attis, and the Great Mother Goddess of Asia Minor provided personal involvement for the individual.

35

While the educated upper classes were impressed with the new philosophies, the mystery religions, featuring many licentious rites, appealed to the lower classes.[58] Christianity supplied the answers to both classes: A religion with both strong ethics and truths that provided a personal experience with a deity. The idea held by some that Christianity evolved from the ethical philosophies and mystery religions has no support in fact. These ideas merely paved the way, and in one way or another made the world receptive to the message of Christ and the Church.

The educational developments mentioned earlier aided the spread of Christianity. When Alexander founded Alexandria in Egypt, scholarship advanced, leading Ptolemy II (Philadelphus, 284-247 B.C.) to ask for Jewish rabbis to come from Palestine to translate their sacred scriptures into Greek. This was probably a unifying measure, for theirs was a powerful Jewish sect in his kingdom. Thus, through the translation of the Greek Septuagint, men were provided with the Jewish Bible in the Greek tongue long before Christianity actually came into being.[59]

Certainly, the systematization of the Greek language into specific declensions, etc., provided a basis for the writings of the New Testament authors. All of the New Testament is in Greek—the universal language of the first century—because of the Hellenistic influence.

In summary, Alexander of Macedon effected a profound change in world culture during the fourth and third centuries before Christ. Although he is still known primarily as a conqueror, perhaps his greatest work is seen in the extent of his influence on almost every facet of human life. He introduced major changes in the conduct of military engagements, including a nationalistic army with better machines, organization, and new strategies. In government, he established in the world consciousness the concept of the monarch-god, military colonies, and Greek law. He promoted world trade and internationalized world commerce. He promoted stability by encouraging specialization in production. He facilitated the blending of world cultures through encouragement of integrated marriages. He promoted education through his personal discoveries and through the exchange of world knowledge so important to the strength of the empire. He encouraged the development of new philosophies based on the concept of brotherhood and the world State. The expansion of human ideas and the development of the Greek language set the scene for the mission of Jesus and the establishment of the Church.

Chapter II

THE MACCABEAN REVOLT

Chapter II

THE MACCABEAN REVOLT

Some of the changes promoted by Alexander were not well received. When Hellenism began to interfere with Hebrew religion and culture, the Jews revolted in an effort to bring about religious and political freedom. This revolt was led by the courageous and intensely dedicated Maccabees. Their religious zeal and heroic self-sacrifice were the determining factors in the Jewish defeat of Antiochus Epiphanes and other Syrian monarchs who sought to destroy Judaism and impose idolatrous worship on the Jews. The heroic faith of a father and his five sons united a divided and seemingly defeated people and led them to religious and political independence and the restoration of their Temple worship. Their faith and courage were keys to the recovery and strengthening of Jewish religious identity and unity. Without the exploits of the Maccabees, Judaism would have perished and the foundation of Christianity would have been destroyed.

After the death of Alexander the Great in 323 B.C. the Jewish state of Judea became a vassal of Egypt until 198 B.C. The fortunes of war, however, later made it a part of the Syrian Empire. (The Syria concerning us here is not the Syria of today or the Assyria of antiquity, but the Greek Seleucid Empire.) At that time an empire was composed of any number of petty kingdoms and principalities that paid tribute to an overlord and owed him loyalty. In exchange for tribute money they were often allowed to set up their own local governments and were seldom interfered with, politically or religiously. Usually, however, vassals of this sort were commanded to worship the pagan gods of their overlords, and in most cases the subjugated peoples never minded adding a few more gods to their list of local deities.[1]

The Jews were different. We know that they worshiped one god—the God of Israel—refusing to recognize any others. As a vassal nation they were willing to pay taxes, work as government officials, etc., but they would not burn incense to the king's image. This, of course, suggested treason,[2] but as long as the Jews were allowed their freedom of religion they were submissive to their rulers. Indeed, this was the situation under Antiochus III, of the Seleucid Empire, 223-187 B.C. The Jews were permitted to establish their own community and to govern themselves with their own officials. Their High Priest could act as their natural ruler.

Under this system, the Jews lived comfortably for quite some time. They even accepted certain elements of the Greek culture (I Macc. 1:10-15). Even the most liberal of the Jews, however, were not ready to throw out their laws and traditions, expecially those concerning eating unclean food or desecrating the Sabbath day.[3]

As Hellenism and the Greek culture began to permeate the Jewish way of life, their government also changed. What once was a spiritual leadership by the high priest was combined with a civil leadership, which carried with it the more democratic Greek ideas and methods of government. Thus, the office of High Priest became a matter of venal competition and dispute (Jos., *Ant.* xii. 4, 1ff.; cf. xii. 5, 1).

Under Antiochus III the Jews were favored; they were exempted from taxes for three years, supplied with timber from Lebanon for the rebuilding of the walls of Jerusalem, given money for temple sacrifices, and given political freedom as already mentioned (Jos., *Ant. xii, 3, 3*). Thus for a number of years the Jews lived in relative peace and prosperity.

In 190 B.C. Antiochus was defeated by the Romans at the Battle of Magnesium and forced to give twenty hostages to Rome, one of which was his son, Antiochus IV (Epiphanes). After this, Antiochus III was a broken man, dying three years later. He was succeeded by another son, Seleucus IV (187-175 B.C.), who during an uneventful reign was murdered by his high priest Heliodorus. Heliodorus then proclaimed Seleucus' young son king of Syria. Antiochus Epiphanes, hearing the news, returned from Rome, murdered his nephew and set himself up as king (175 B.C.).[4] With Epiphanes began the period that was to culminate in the Maccabean revolt.

Antiochus Epiphanes was a controversial figure, whom Polybius (a pagan writer who lived around the time described in I Maccabees) calls a "madman." He associated with the common people in their festivals and baths, yet loved pomp and glory and spent much time in erecting statues and temples. The latter practice led him to proclaim himself a god and to demand worship. The Syrians agreed to worship, but the Jews resisted his demand, and thus began an era of inner turmoil in the country between the Hellenistic and anti-Hellenistic factions.[5]

Had Antiochus IV left the Jews to choose their own leaders and run their own affairs the Jews might never have given him any trouble, despite their revulsion against Hellenism and the Greek culture. To most Jews, the Greek culture was odious since it involved worship of foreign deities, eating of food

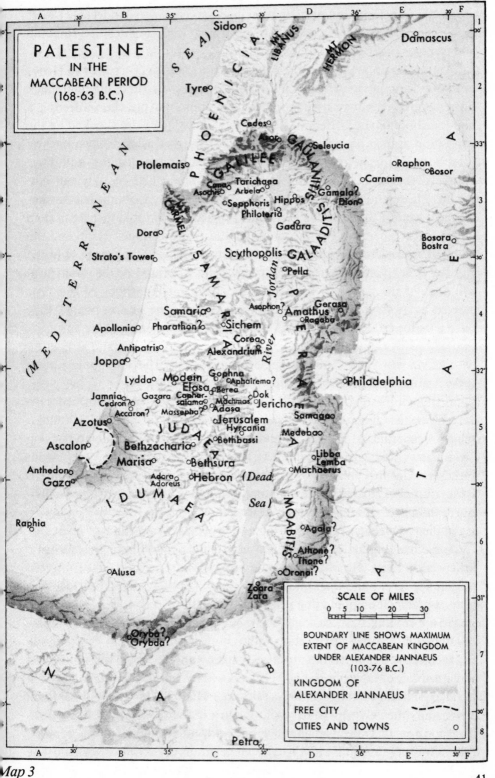

PALESTINE
IN THE
MACCABEAN PERIOD
(168-63 B.C.)

(MEDITERRANEAN SEA)

Sidon
Damascus
Tyre
Cedes
Seleucia
Ptolemais
Raphon
Bosor
Carnaim
Cana
Tarichaea
Asochis
Arbelo
Gamala
Sepphoris
Hippos
Dion
Philoteria
Dora
Gadara
Bosora
Bostra
Strato's Tower
Scythopolis
GALAADITIS
Pella
Samaria
Asophon?
Amathus
Gerasa
Ragaba
Pharathon
Sichem
Apollonia
Corea
Antipatris
Alexandrium
Joppa
Gophna
Lydda
Modein
Aphairema?
Elasa
Berea
Jamnia
Gazara
Capher-
Dok
Cedron
salama
Machmas
Jericho
Accaron?
Adasa
Massepha?
Samaga
Azotus
Jerusalem
Hyrcania
Medeba
Ascalon
Bethzacharia
Bethbassi
Marisa
Bethsura
Libba
Lemba
Anthedon
Adora
Hebron
(Dead
Machaerus
Gaza
Adoreus
IDUMAEA
Sea)
MOABITIS
Raphia
Agala?
Athone?
Thone?
Alusa
Oronai?
Zoara
Zara

PHOENICIA
MT LIBANUS
MT HERMON
GALILEE
GAULANITIS
MT CARMEL
SAMARIA
Jordan River
JUDAEA
Philadelphia

Oryba?
Orybda?

Petra

SCALE OF MILES

0 5 10   20   30

BOUNDARY LINE SHOWS MAXIMUM
EXTENT OF MACCABEAN KINGDOM
UNDER ALEXANDER JANNAEUS
(103-76 B.C.)

KINGDOM OF
ALEXANDER JANNAEUS

FREE CITY

CITIES AND TOWNS   o

Map 3

41

regarded as unclean, and participation in games considered indecent. Under the Seleucids, the Greek language prevailed and Greek architecture, thinking and customs had become common.

Antiochus Epiphanes deposed the high priest Onias, successor to Heliodorus, and appointed in his stead his brother Jason, who had turned his back on religious orthodoxy and supported the aims of Antiochus, offering a higher tribute to the coffers of his Majesty. The Jews were shocked by the deposition of their high priest. They rejected this royal ascendancy over their priesthood, bitterly resenting interference with their leaders and their religion. Having their leaders selected for them was bad enough, but Antiochus chose those who were essentially Hellenist. Committing further outrages against the Jews, he outlined a program that would turn Jerusalem into a Hellenistic city. This program was carried out under Jason and the name of Jerusalem was changed to Antioch. A gymnasium was built in the city for Greek games in which the participants appeared naked. Sacrificial offerings to the gods preceded the games. Since gymnasiums of this type exerted a powerful attraction on the young men of the subject people, they were a major establishment for the promotion of Hellenism. The introduction of the gymnasium to Jerusalem—with its naked exercises and assocation with pagan worship—shocked the Jews most of all. The Jews looked upon these heathen practices with gross repugnance.

Although Jason had greatly intensified the Hellenistic influence in Jerusalem he still showed compassion for Jewish traditionalists, permitted religious separation, respected the sanctity of the Temple, made no bans on Jewish laws and customs, and did not coerce the community to adopt Hellenism. Jason's policy proved too moderate to satisfy Antiochus, who, to further his aims, dismissed Jason, appointing Menelaus, an extreme Hellenist, to the office of High Priest in Jerusalem.

Under Menelaus, Hellenism spread. Whereas Jason did not coerce or force the traditional Jews, Menelaus actively sought to impose Hellenistic practices on them. He would not tolerate religious separation. He subjected the Jews to taunts and flagrant acts of contempt for Jewish customs. He persuaded young Jews, including priests, to enter the Greek games. Since they had to appear naked, these young men sought to eradicate the sign of circumcision by undergoing a painful operation.

Menelaus committed other outrages against the Jews. He was implicated in the murder of Onias, who had been deposed by Antiochus and had been in hiding. Onias was still regarded as the true High Priest by the traditional Jews, and when the Jews heard of his murder they rose up in angry demonstration against the Hellenistic group. An additional, if not foremost, reason for their uprising was a raid by Menelaus on the precious vessels of the

Temple to help pay the heavy tribute he had promised to the king. Menelaus had gone too far. The Jews discovered the violation of the Temple treasury at the same time they heard the news of Onias' murder.

A rift was now developing among the Jews. Some were pious and refused to accept Hellenism while others gave in to it, and still others accepted it voluntarily. For the most part, the Jews were God-fearing, however, following the Torah and the customs and traditions of their religion. They spurned the material benefits of Hellenism when the price was religious abdication. Still, a few wealthy upper class Jews were attracted by the commercial opportunities offered by the Greeks and succumbed to the new fashions and worldly ideals of Hellenism, while some of the younger Jews were attracted to the Greek games. These few adopted the characteristics of the conquerors—their diversions, social and domestic habits, costumes, architecture and language.

To this point Hellenism had not been forced upon the Jews; Menelaus had taken no overt action against the traditionalits, made no mandatory laws regarding the acceptance of Hellenism. The Jews were allowed to accept or refuse, and many left the city, going out to the villages and towns that were as yet untouched by the abhorred Hellenism. One of them was Mattathias who took his family and went back to his native village, Modin, where they could worship and live as Jews (II Macc. 3:1-6; I Macc. 2: 1-5, 15-31). The Hellenization of Jerusalem under Menelaus was already bad enough to spark rebellion; but the real explosion was yet to come.

During this time of stress in Judea, Antiochus invaded Egypt, trying to unite Syria and Egypt, and was rebuffed by the Romans, His unification scheme collapsed, leaving him angry and frustrated (Jos., *Ant. xii.* 5, 2; I Macc. 1:16-64).

To make matters worse, news came to Judea that Antiochus had been killed, and immediately there was an armed conflict between the Hellenistic and the anti-Hellenistic Jews. Many Hellenistic Jews were killed, being thrown from the wall of the Temple, a height of over 100 feet. Antiochus, hearing of the revolt, rushed back from Egypt, doubly incensed, and senselessly slaughtered 10,000 Jews. It was a terrible time of butchery and plunder, for the Syrian army that he sent in behaved as though they were in a rebellious country. This injustice could possibly have been forgotten in time, but Antiochus heaped more insults upon the heads of the Jews. He issued an edict forbidding the keeping of the Sabbath, religious festivals, and the rite of circumcision. He also forbade them to offer sacrifices to God and compelled them to worship idols. He entered Jerusalem and plundered the Temple, setting up a statue of Jupiter in the Holy of Holies, the most sacred part of the Temple. Pigs, which were abominable to the Jews, were sacrificed on the

THE SELEUCID KINGS
IN THE TIME OF THE MACCABEES

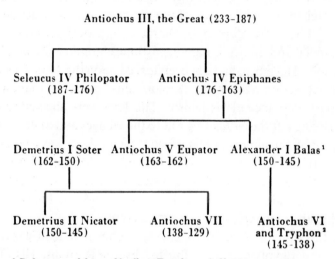

Antiochus III, the Great (233–187)

Seleucus IV Philopator (187–176)

Antiochus IV Epiphanes (176–163)

Demetrius I Soter (162–150)

Antiochus V Eupator (163–162)

Alexander I Balas[1] (150–145)

Demetrius II Nicator (150–145)

Antiochus VII (138–129)

Antiochus VI and Tryphon[2] (145–138)

[1] Balas passed himself off as Epiphanes' illegitimate son.

[2] Antiochus VI, while still a minor, was elevated to the throne by a man named Tryphon, who then waged war against Demetrius II in Antiochus' name.

Illus. 2

THE HOUSE OF THE MACCABEES (HASMONEANS)

(167–29 B.C.E.)

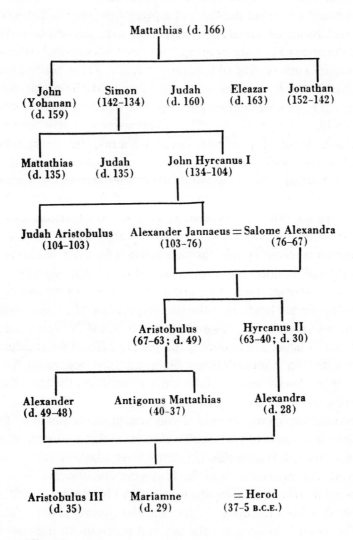

Mattathias (d. 166)

John (Yohanan) (d. 159)   Simon (142–134)   Judah (d. 160)   Eleazar (d. 163)   Jonathan (152–142)

Mattathias (d. 135)   Judah (d. 135)   John Hyrcanus I (134–104)

Judah Aristobulus (104–103)   Alexander Jannaeus (103–76) = Salome Alexandra (76–67)

Aristobulus (67–63; d. 49)   Hyrcanus II (63–40; d. 30)

Alexander (d. 49–48)   Antigonus Mattathias (40–37)   Alexandra (d. 28)

Aristobulus III (d. 35)   Mariamne (d. 29)   = Herod (37–5 B.C.E.)

Illus. 3

Temple altars and their blood sprinkled on the Holy Scriptures. He compelled the priests to eat unclean flesh and burned the Books of the Law.

All Jews were ordered to renounce the laws of their God and to offer sacrifices to the Greek deities. Under penalty of death it was prohibited for Jews to congregate in prayer, to observe the Sabbath and the religious festivals, to have sacred writings in their possession, to be circumcised or to follow the dietary laws. Death was also the penalty for refusing to follow idolatrous practices, to eat the flesh of a pig, or to join in sacrificial pagan rituals. Cruel forms of torture and execution were devised to serve as examples of the price to be paid by all who refused to conform.[6] An example is seen in Eleazar, a ninety-year-old, learned friendly, warm-hearted man, who was respected by the Jewish community and even by the Seleucids. Antiochus chose to use him as an example, knowing full well that Eleazar would not comply with his orders. He ordered him to eat swine's flesh; when he refused the guards seized him, stripped him, bound his arms, and scourged him with whips. He was then broken on the rack and his maimed body was taken to the flames. They burned him with wickedly devised instruments and poured into his nostrils a hot, strong fluid. In the midst of these torments, he died.[7] Neither before nor since the time of Eleazer has the spiritual existence of Israel been so imperiled.[8] (Jos., *Ant.* xii. 5, 4; *Wars* i. 1, 2; II Macc. 6:1-7:42).

The sudden persecution was almost too much for the Jews. Small groups of them gathered together to try to resist, but were unequal to their oppressors, and many were martyred. One group hid in caves, where they continued to observe the dietary laws, the Sabbath, and the law of circumcision. Their hiding place was discovered, however, and Phillip, the Phrygian, led a group against them. It being the Sabbath, the people offered no resistance, and most were killed when soldiers threw firebrands into their caves. This led to the decree of the Jewish leaders that in extreme necessity the Holy Day might be broken by resistance to the enemy.

The persecution increased until it culminated in the revolt of the Maccabees. The main reason for the revolt was to gain religious freedom. According to I Maccabees 2:1ff, an elderly priest named Mattathias first raised the flag of revolt. During a meeting of the Jews a commissioner of the king compelled a priest to offer a sacrifice at a local altar. This was too much for Mattathias. He slew both the apostate Jew and the commissioner, and then he said, "Whosoever is zealous for the law and maintaineth the covenant, let him come forth after me!" (I Macc. 2:27; Jos., *Ant.* xii, 6, 2). As he was speaking, his five sons attacked the rest of the troops. The sons, led by Judas Maccabaeus, then went throughout the cities, inciting the people to revolt. They would attack suddenly, destroying temples and altars. Though small in number, they had such a thorough knowledge of the terrain that they were almost impossible to defeat.

Seen through the eyes of worldly power, Mattathias' deed was an act of political terrorism, and Mattathias and his five sons, John, Simon, Judas, Eleazar, and Jonathan, fled from punishment, accompanied by the people of Modin.[9] They took essential belongings, food, and the uniforms and weapons of the slain troops, and headed for the hills above Gophna, just beyond the Judean border in southern Samaria, thirteen miles northeast of Modin. The band numbered 200 in all, of which forty or fifty were men.

For whatever reason, the Seleucid authorities left the group unmolested for about a year. In that year, they accomplished four main objectives: 1) They trained Jews in guerrilla warfare; 2) they roused the spirit of resistance among the Jews of Judea, recruiting as many as possible to their ranks; 3) they restored a respect for the Law of Moses and the "maintenance of the covenant" wherever this had been weakened by the Hellenistic process; 4) they gave battle whenever they encountered the enemy, but did not initiate military action until they were ready.[10] In addition, they established their base of operations in the hills of Gophna; they organized an intelligence network, supply system, and messenger service through friends in the villages; they arranged for reliable contacts in all villages to gather information on activities of Seleucid troops in their areas; they spread the news, by relay from village to village, of what had happened at Modin; and reported on their resistance aims. Young villagers volunteered to join the rebels, and Jews hiding in the hills and wilderness of Judea, mostly Hasidim, made their way to the rebels' base at Gophna.

Mattathias knew that the Seleucid troops would attack on the Sabbath, thinking that the Jews would not fight on that day. Therefore, having seen and heard of massacres of pious Jews on the Sabbath, he rallied his followers to defend themselves, saying, "If we all do as our brethren have done, and do not fight against the Gentiles for our lives and our ordinances, they will soon destroy us from off the earth." They resolved not to attack, but to defend themselves on the Sabbath. They prepared themselves to violate the Torah for the sake of the Torah.[11]

In 166 B.C. Mattathias died, and his place as leader was taken by his third son, Judas, who was described as "a mighty warrior from his youth"(I Macc. 2:66) and "like a lion in his deed, like a lion's cub roaring for a prey" (I Macc. 3:4). He was given the nickname "Maccabee," meaning "hammer" or "hammer-headed," in token of his military exploits. The name was continued by his brothers, who escalated the revolt. Under Judas' leadership the struggle turned into a full-scale war, with well-planned battles.

The first two battles were fought northwest of Jerusalem, in Modin. In the first, Apollonius, general of the Samaritan forces, attacked the Jews and was defeated. In the second, when Seron, the "strategus" of Coele-Syria, came, Judas exhorted his people to remember that God could save them. And, suddenly attacking the Syrians, they drove them down the pass at Bethhoron, where Joshua had destroyed the army of the five kings (I Macc, 3:27-4:25 and Jos., *Ant.* xxi. 7, 3-4).

Antiochus Epiphanes, who was in Syria while these battles were being fought, decided that decisive action was necessary and sent out 40,000 infantry and 7,000 cavalry troops. But Judas and his band of 3,000 surprised and defeated them, pursuing them into the plains of Philistia. By this time more Jews were being recruited, and soon the army numbered 10,000. Judas was then able to defeat Lysias in Beth-zur so that the Syrian general had to return to Syria (I Macc. 3:27-4:25 and Jos., *Ant.* xii. 7, 5).

Judas proved to be a great leader of his people. He had piety, valor, resourcefulness and good sense. By making the best use of these attributes, with God's help he was able to defeat the Syrians with a small army of untrained warriors.

Now that their enemies were crushed, their task was to purify the Temple and rededicate the Sanctuary, and in 164 B.C. Judas marched on Jerusalem and occupied Mt. Zion, shutting up the Syrian troops and their Jewish sympathizers in the Akra. Then he chose new priests and set up the altar, once again dedicating it to the God of Israel. In the month of Kislev (i.e., December) 164 B.C., exactly three years after its desecration by Antiochus, the Temple was restored to its former service. (The day is still commemorated at the Feast of Hanukkah, or "Dedication.") To ensure the Temple's future safety, the Jews built high walls and strong towers around Jerusalem and stationed a garrison there to defend it. They took similar measures also at Bethzur on the borders of Idumaea to the south (I Macc. 4:60-61).

The Jews were now in a relatively secure position, and Judas carried out a series of successful campaigns against the Idumaeans in the South, the Baenites in Trans-Jordan, and the Ammonites northeast of the Dead Sea. With the help of his brothers Simon and Jonathan, he also engaged in a campaign in Galilee and Gilead, bringing many Jewish inhabitants back to Judea. Subsequently he captured Hebron and Ashdod and returned home with much plunder (I Macc. 5:1-8, 63-65).

Another great task remained: the Akra, still in the hands of the Syrians, had to be liberated. Judas attacked it in 163 B.C. Some Syrians managed to escape, making their way to Antioch to the king. Antiochus IV (Epiphanes) had died the previous year, about two months before the rededication of the Temple, and was succeeded by his eight-year-old son, Antiochus V (Eupator). Philip had been appointed guardian of the young king, but Lysias

(Antiochus' regent) saw his opportunity, marched toward Judea with a strong army, forced Judas to retreat, and besieged Jerusalem. The Jews were saved, however, when Lysias heard that Philip was going to take over the government in his absence. Generous terms were offered to Judas, who agreed to surrender the fortifications around the Temple. In return, he was granted a general amnesty, rescinding the orders of Antiochus IV made in 167 B.C., and so the religious freedom of the Jews was at last won (I Macc. 6:5-17, 28-62; II Macc. 9: 1-29).

The Maccabees now had a new goal—political freedom and independence. At this time the Seleucid throne was shaky, beset by a bitter and bloody struggle for power. The victor was Demetrius, the brother of Antiochus IV, who appointed a new High Priest in Jerusalem, Alcimus. Alcimus put to death sixty Jewish Hasidim, and a Syrian general, Bacchides, killed many Jews in a village not far from Gophna. This stirred Judas and the Maccabees to renewed action. They now used the same guerrilla tactics that they had used at the begining of the struggle. Soon the Syrians appealed to Demetrius for help, and he immediately dispatched a force, headed by Nicanor, to dispose of the Maccabees. Fighting with their original tactics, the Jews drove Nicanor back to Jerusalem to appeal for reinforcements. Nicanor tried once more, flushing some of the Maccabees out of the hills. Once again, the Maccabees attacked in guerrilla style, killing Nicanor and annihilating his army (I Macc. 7:26-50).

Judas, needing the support of a powerful ally in his quest for political freedom, appealed to Rome for support, sending two ambassadors to the Roman Senate to establish a treaty of friendship. The Romans accepted, agreeing to aid the Jews as allies in case of war and to warn Demetrius to cease oppressing the Jews. In return, the Jews agreed to fight for Rome in case of war and to withhold economic support from the enemy (I Macc. 8:17-31). But Rome did not help the Jews—Rome simply overlooked the conflict between the Seleucids and the Jews.

Demetrius ignored the warning from Rome, and in 161 B.C. his generals Bacchides and Alcimus again attacked the Jews of Judea. They marched toward Jerusalem with 22,000 men, slaughtering the Jews of Arbela on the way. Judas now had only 3,000 men, and desertions quickly reduced his army to 800. He attacked anyway, and succeeded in driving back the right flank of the army. While pursuing the Syrians' right flank, Judas' forces were pursued by their left and the Maccabees were sandwiched between the two. Many were killed on both sides, including Judas himself (I Macc. 9:1-22; Jos., *Ant.* xii. 11, 2). Bacchides tracked down the friends and followers of Judas and executed them. The remaining Maccabees fled to the wilderness where they built fortresses and fortified the area, trying to keep the Jews calm.

Jonathan was chosen leader in Judas' place. The Maccabees regrouped, and reverted to the tactics that they had used so successfully at the beginning of the revolt—guerrilla training and the use of underground contacts, messengers, spies, and recruits. Once again they confined the Seleucid troops in Jerusalem, and Judea soon came under Maccabean rule once again.

Bacchides was sent to defeat the Maccabees and to free the garrison in Jerusalem, but Jonathan launched a surprise attack, driving him back. Jonathan then made a treaty with the Syrian general, stipulating in it that all Jewish prisoners would be released and that peace would be established (I Macc. 9:58-73). This treaty marked the end of the war in Judea between the Seleucids and the Jews (c. 142 B.C.) The Maccabees were no longer outlaws. They had achieved a partial independence and were now free from Hellenistic domination.

In 150 B.C., Alexander Balas, claiming to be the son of Antiochus IV, and his rightful heir, took possession of Ptolemais and proclaimed himself king. He was backed by Rome, Egypt, Cappadocia and Pergamum. Demetrius was the ruling king at the time, but he was unpopular with his subjects because he was harsh and negligent, and he had no allies or support. Both king and claimant, recognizing that the Jewish rulers held the balance of power, sought to secure the active support of the Jews of Judea. The Jewish resistance to the Seleucid army had proved that the Jews were a potent factor in the affairs of Palestine. They courted the favor of the Jews with bounteous offers, appealing to Jonathan for his friendship and military help.

Demetrius acted first. He ordered that all Jewish hostages in the Citadel be returned to Jonathan and he conferred on Jonathan the title of "ally," giving him authority to raise and equip an army. Jonathan took advantage of this and established himself in Jerusalem. He refortified the Temple Mount and rebuilt the walls of Jerusalem. The Hellenistic party fled to Antioch. Only Beth-Zur (on the borders of Idumea in the south) and the Citadel remained refuge for Hellenists. Judea, now virturally free, though without formal independence, came under the operational control of Jonathan. Alexander then made *his* offer to Jonathan; he ordained him as High Priest of the Jews and sent him a purple robe and a gold crown (Jos., *Ant.* xiii. 4, 2f).

Demetrius, seeking to outbid Alexander, exempted Judea from a wide range of taxes, tributes, imposts, and levies, such as the tax on salt, one-third of the grain harvest, and one-half of the fruit harvest; restored to Judea three districts of Jewish population; evacuated the Citadel of Seleucid troops, assigning the city of Jerusalem to Jonathan; and granted 15,000 silver shekels annually for the cost of repair to the Temple, the wall of Jerusalem, and all Judean fortresses.

In the final battle between the two rivals, Demetrius was killed and Alexander became emperor. Alexander treated Jonathan with great respect, calling him a friend. Alexander appointed Jonathan, the High Priest, commander and governor of Judea.

After three years of peace, there was another struggle for the throne—this time between Alexander and Demetrius II (Nicator). In the ensuing battle, Macedonian mercenaries and refugee Hellenists again inhabited the Citadel in Jeruslem. Alexander was killed and Demetrius became king.

Jonathan laid siege to the Citadel, trying once more to rid the land of the Seleucid presence. Demetrius demanded that Jonathan lift the siege and summoned him to his presence. Jonathan bribed Demetrius with 300 talents of gold and in return received a full guarantee of the concessions that Demetrius I had granted Jonathan. These concessions set Judea free from all tribute and gave the Jews additional territory. Judea was now close to national independence.

The Seleucid kingdom was now split. Demetrius ruled one-half, and Antiochus VI the other, the latter giving Jonathan control and authority over the territory of Judea. The territory Jonathan now controlled was approximately the size of the original land of Israel. The Maccabees were reaching their goal. Simon was appointed military commander of the whole of Coele-Syria, and the two brothers made the most of their new powers. Simon captured the fortress of Beth-Zur and replaced the Seleucid garrison with his own men. Jonathan marched north through the entire country to Damascus and then toward Galilee, securing cooperation and friendship along the way. He sent an embassy to Rome and renewed the friendship established under Judea. His brother built fortresses in Judea, heightened the walls of Jerusalem, and erected a barrier separating the Citadel from the city.

Another fight for the throne followed between Antiochus and Trypho (Jos., *Ant.* xiii. 5). Trypho sought to remove Jonathan, who supported Antiochus, and persuaded Jonathan to visit him on the pretense of peace. When Jonathan came with 1,000 men, the city gates were shut, Jonathan was taken prisoner, and his men were slaughtered. Trypho eventually executed Jonathan.

Simon, the last surviving son of Mattathias, assumed command in Jonathan's place and became the High Priest. He conquered Jaffa, Gezer, and Jamnia. When Trypho dethroned Antiochus and became ruler of his half of the Seleucid empire, Simon transferred his support back to Demetrius, who once again granted Judea freedom from all taxation and tribute. This action in the year 142 B.C. was hailed by the Jews as marking the lifting of "the yoke of the heathen from Israel," and the people began to write on their contracts and agreements "In the first year of Simon the great high-priest captain and leader of the Jews"(I Macc. 13:41-42). This also marked the beginning of the Hasmonean dynasty (The name "Hasmonean" being derived from Hasmon, the great-great-grandfather of Mattathias).

After the imperial troops of the Citadel in Jerusalem had surrendered to Simon, he leveled the Citadel to the ground and later built the Hasmonean palace on its ruins.[12]

The whole of Jerusalem was at last under Maccabean control, and Judea was again an independent Jewish state. As Seleucid authority in the divided empire grew weaker, Simon continued to advance the strength, size and welfare of Judea. In addition to religious freedom the Macabees had now achieved political freedom and independence. Antiochus VII, heir to the throne of Demetrius, wrote to Simon:

> Now therefore I confirm all the tax remissions which my royal predecessors granted you, and all their other remission of tribute. I permit you to mint your own coinage as currency for your country. Jerusalem and the Temple shall be free. All the armies you have prepared, and the fortifications which you have built and now hold, shall remain yours. When we have reestablished our kingdom, we shall confer the highest honors upon you, your nation, and Temple, to make your country's greatness apparent to the whole world. (I Macc. 15:3-9).

No endorsement of Judean independence could have been more explicit.

In looking back, we can see that the Maccabean revolt had important effects upon the Jewish nation. Through it they were able to win their independence, religiously and politically. The work of the Maccabees thus also helped to set the scene for the time of Jesus.

One effect of their work was the cleansing and restoration of the Temple in Jerusalem, and the reestablishment of Temple worship and sacrifices. This led to the observance of Hanukkah, the Feast of Dedication, a festival instituted in the time of the Maccabees to commemorate the rededication of the Temple after it had been recovered and cleansed from the defiling hands of the Seleucids by Judas and the Maccabees. To this very day, the Jews have celebrated Hanuakkah eight days out of every year. All other great feasts celebrated by the Jews are prescribed by the Torah. Hanukkah alone has survived through the centuries without justification in the Bible.[13]

Josephus shows that from the time this festival was first instituted by the Maccabees until his own day (37 A.D.-100 A.D.) there had been no interruption in its annual observance.

> So much pleasure did they find in the renewal of their customs and in unexpectedly obtaining the right to have their own service after so long a time, that they made a law that their descendants should celebrate the restoration of the temple service for eight days. And from that time to the present we observe this festival, which we call the festival of Lights, giving this name to it, I think, from the fact that the right to worship appeared to us at a time when we hardly dared hope for it.[14] (Jos., *Ant.* xii. 7, 7).

The New Testament provides evidence that Hanukkah was observed by the Jews during the first century A.D. Unlike the other three Gospels, the fourth refers to journeys of Jesus to Jerusalem except the final one. On one occasion Jesus is spoken of as being in Jerusalem during the Feast of Dedication (John 10:22). Since there is no other festival with such name or description, this reference is undoubtedly to Hanukkah. The New Testament thus witnesses to the fact that the Jews observed Hanukkah, remembering, respecting and commemorating the valiant Maccabees. Jesus himself knew of them and what they did, and honored the festival. Even if one takes a doubtful, questioning view about the authenticity of the journey of Jesus to observe Hanukkah, we still must admit that the Feast of Dedication witnesses to the fact that He knew something about a Jewish festival called the Feast of Dedication. In fact, He must have known a good deal about a Jewish feast so named, for He places the feast in the correct season of the year.[14]

We have seen that the Maccabean revolt saved and preserved Judaism. The revolt established and strengthened the religious identity of the Jews and bound them together under a religious unity. The importance of this can be seen in the fact that Judaism, as is seen throughout the New Testament, was the foundation of Jesus' life and ministry and of Christianity itself.

The revolt, it will be recalled, was based on religious convictions, and the first goal was religious freedom. Before the revolt, the traditional Jews were separated—conforming to the Hellenists out of fear, some running and hiding, some simply avoiding and not participating in the Hellenistic culture, some standing against Hellenism and dying for their beliefs. After gaining religious freedom, the Jews were able to establish themselves and be known as Jews. United in religious identity, all could worship as Jews. They were no longer separated or divided among themselves, nor did they have to comply out of fear, or hide, or avoid being recognized as Jews, or be tortured and killed.

Thus, an important effect of the revolt was that the Jews gained and were guaranteed, in the form of a treaty, religious freedom to worship as Jews. They could once more follow the Laws of Moses and offer sacrifices. They could worship God in their own way. And they worship today the same way they did after the Maccabees gained religious freedom, except for the offering of sacrifices in the Temple. They observe the Torah, the Sabbath, festivals and holidays, and still refrain from eating swine's flesh.

The Maccabean revolt also established a national unity of the Jews. When political freedom was obtained and the Hasmonean state was established the Jews were united under an established nation. In the letter from Antiochus VII to Simon, he spoke of conferring high honors upon the nation, and making their country's greatness apparent to the whole world. The Jews were pulled together under three unifying factors. The first was the Torah. The intense zeal for the Torah was what started the revolt and kept it going until religious and political freedom were obtained. And it must be noted that the centrality of the Temple for Judaism was fixed in and by the Torah. The Torah is the set of rules, provisions, hopes, and promises of God that the Jews live by and die by. It is the very strength of their existence. The second unifying factor was the rededication and reestablishment of the Temple. Philo says that "above all other observances their zeal for their holy Temple is the most predominant, and vehement, and universal feeling throughout the whole nation." (Philo, *Legatio ad Gauim* 31, 211-12). The third factor was the establishment of Jonathan as their High Priest. The High Priest was the spiritual leader of the Jews and also exercised civic authority. The very quality of the Jewish way of life was governed by the spirit and ordinances of the Jewish religion, so that the High Priest was their guide in all things. So under Jonathan, the leader of the Maccabees, the Jews were united nationally.

The Maccabean revolt preserved the Judaism which existed in New Testament times. Jesus addressed people with these ideas, He argued with Jewish religious leaders, and threatened the religious-political system. Again, the Maccabean revolt was of vital significance for setting the scene for the time of Jesus.

Chapter III

THE JEWS UNDER THE ROMANS
63 B.C. - 4 B.C. (Circa)

Chapter III

THE JEWS UNDER THE ROMANS
63 B.C.—4 B.C. (Circa)

The Maccabean revolt brought political as well as religious freedom, which existed until the Herodian times when the Romans took over and Judea again became part of a larger Empire. This was the world into which Jesus was born. The history of the Jews had been long and tragic to the time of the Romans, but now there was to be even more bloodshed and oppression; it would not end until after the destruction of the Temple in 70 A.D.

Between 350 and 50 B.C. Rome, through a series of wars, grew from a small nation to become the ruler of the world. What once was the Empire of Greece became the Empire of Rome. Greece and Rome shared a peculiar relationship: Greece was beautiful, cultured, haughty and intellectual, while Rome was strong, rich, uncouth, and practical. The saying, "To the glory that was Greece and the grandeur that was Rome" implies their differences. Rome depended on Greece for its culture; thus, when Greece was separated from Rome, Rome collapsed for lack of the intellectual support of Greece. As a result, the Jews were not culturally affected by Rome, though they were greatly affected by the intellectual culture of Greece.[1]

Pompey's conquest of the Hasmonean Kingdom came about because, while contending for the throne of the Hasmonean Kingdom, Hyrcanus II and Aristobulus II (Hasmoneans) came before Pompey to settle their dispute. The people of Jerusalem, disliking both of them, sent their own delegation to Pompey, but Pompey ignored them all, marched on Jerusalem, and took the defended and fortified Temple. He entered the Holy of Holies, but was so struck with awe because there were no representations of a deity within that he left the sacred treasures alone and reinstated Hyrcanus II as both High Priest and the ruler of Judea.[2] Thus, the Hasmonean Kingdom became a Roman province. The area involved was the western part of the Seleucid Empire, which was of the utmost importance to Rome because it formed a line of defense against the continuous Parthian invasions from the east. This new province could be used to full advantage only if there was complete unity within it, and if it was controlled by a central government. So, administrative reforms took place: some areas of the Hasmoneans were liberated and given to the Governor of Syria—Samaria (the city and the land), and the Jordan Valley (the Decapolis of ten cities); while other areas were put under Jewish control—Judea, Galilee (N), Idumea (S), and Perea. The Jews were now no longer independent: They were a religious community with their center of worship in Jerusalem, but they were governed by the High Priest, Hyrcanus II, who was responsible to the Roman governor, and who levied annual tax upon the people.

Ostensibly, six years of peace followed; yet underneath, the people were resentful against Hyrcanus II because he was personally responsible to the Roman government to whom the people had to pay their annual tax. Revolt began to brew. Hyrcanus II was not entirely to blame for his actions against the Jews as he was influenced and supported by Antipater, his political advisor, a crafty, self-seeking Edomite, whose only thought was to further his own cause. Thus in 57 B.C. the pent-up emotions of the people erupted in Egypt with Alexander, son of Aristobulus, leading the revolt. He captured the fortresses Alexandreion, Hyrcania, and Machaerus. Gabinius, governor of Syria, requested Antipater's aid in trying to win the confidence of the Jews, but Antipater refused. Then Gabinius appealed to Mark Antony, who responded and helped to defeat Alexander near Jerusalem. Alexander was captured at Alexandreion, but was later freed. Political and territorial changes resulted from this revolt: Government control was tightened over the Jews, and as Antipater wished, the territory was divided into five independent districts. These districts were responsible to the provincial governor for government and taxation. But this caused further revolts and uprisings.[3]

In 54 B.C., Crassus replaced Gabinius as governor of Syria. He was even more severe with the Jews: He ransacked the Temple, taking the sacred treasures to finance his planned campaign against the Parthians. A year later he was killed by the Parthians near Carrhae.

Civil war broke out in 49 B.C. between Julius Caesar and Pompey, resulting in Caesar's becoming the master of Rome. Pompey withdrew eastward, leaving Antipater open to invaders. Antipater, seeking Caesar's friendship, aided Caesar's campaign, which was underway in Egypt. Hyrcanus II also supported Caesar, urging the Egyptian Jews to join his side. For this help, Antipater was made procurator of Judea, with all the rights of Roman citizenship, including exemption from taxes. Hyrcanus was also rewarded—he was made High Priest and the five districts were abolished and united under his leadership. In the meantime, Antigonus' plea for his right to inherit the high priesthood went unheeded. (cf. Jos., *Ant.*, xiv, 8, 1-5; xiv. 10,1-7; *Wars*, i, 9,1-10, 3.). This arrangement benefited not only Antipater and Hyrcanus personally, but also the Jews. No Roman troops were billeted in Judea during the winter and no money was exacted from the people for their maintenance. Permission was granted to rebuild the walls of Jerusalem, and the seaport of Joppa was restored, along with other sites. The Jews of the dispersion in Alexandria and Asia Minor also enjoyed these privileges, including possibly the best privilege of all—the freedom to worship in the place and manner that pleased them.[4] It is no wonder that the Jews so deeply mourned the death of Caesar a few years later.

In 47-46 B.C., Antipater appointed his eldest son, Phasael, governor of Jerusalem, over Judea and Perea, and his second son, Herod the Great, governor of Galilee. Soon afterward, Herod decided to take things into his own hands—he routed Ezekias and his men, who had been troubling Galilee with their crimes, and executed them. This enhanced Herod's reputation, causing Hyrcanus II to become jealous. He summoned Herod before the Sanhedrin, which so insulted Herod that for a while he planned vengeance on Jerusalem. Fortunately, his father, Antipater, persuaded him against the use of violence. Upon returning to Galilee, Herod was appointed governor of Coele-Syria and Samaria by Sextus Caesar.[5]

After the death of Julius Caesar in 44 B.C. Cassius became governor of Syria. He exacted large sums from the people for support of the army, an action that soon brought upon him the hatred of the Jews. This hatred was also aimed at Antipater and Herod, for they had again shifted their allegiance, offering to collect these sums from the Jews. For this, Herod was confirmed by the Romans as governor of Judea. Antipater was poisoned soon after (43 B.C.) by his rival, Malichus, whom Herod later put to death.

Not long after, Cassius joined Brutus. Violence involving Antigonus broke out in Judea and Galilee. Herod defeated Antigonus, banishing him and his followers, thus gaining favor in the eyes of Cassius and Brutus. Herod strengthened his favorable position even more by becoming engaged to Mariamne, the daughter of Antigonus' brother Alexander and Hyrcanus' daughter Alexandra, (Jos., *Ant.* xiv. 12,1).[6] But Cassius and Brutus were defeated at the Battle of Philippi by Mark Antony, who took over Syria upon the fall of Octavian. Herod changed sides once again, winning the approval of Antony despite the charges the Jews had brought against him; Antony appointed him and Phasael joint tetrarchs over Judea. ("A tetrarch literally

PALESTINE
UNDER
HEROD THE GREAT
(40-4 B.C.)

Sidon

Damascus

(SEA)

PHOENICIA

MT LIBANUS

Tyre

TRACHONITIS

Paneas

ULATHA

BATANAEA

GAULANITIS

AURANITIS

Ecdippa

GALILEE

Ptolemais

Tarichaea
Magdala
Arbela

Gamala?

Canatha

Sepphoris
Gaba

Hippo

Nazareth

MT CARMEL

Dora

MT TABOR

Gadara

Caesarea
Strato's Tower

Scythopolis
Pella

DECAPOLIS

SAMARIA

Sebaste
Samaria
MT. GERIZIM

Amathus

Apollonia

Antipatris

Alexandrium

Joppa

Phasaelis

PERAEA

Jamnia

Gazara

Jericho

Jordan River

Philadelphia

Azotus

Jerusalem

Essebon
Esbus

Ascalon

Bethlehem
Herodium

Hyrcania

JUDAEA

Marisa

Anthedon
Gaza

Adora

Hebron

(Dead

Callirhoe
Machaerus

Sea)

Raphia

Masada

IDUMAEA

(MEDITERRANEAN

N

A

B

A

T

A

E

A

Petra

SCALE OF MILES
0 5 10   20   30

KINGDOM OF
HEROD THE GREAT

DECAPOLIS

FREE CITY

CITIES AND TOWNS   ○

Map 4

60

means 'ruler of the fourth part,' but is loosely applied to any subordinate prince.'"[7]) Hyrcanus II again lost his power over Judea.

In 40 B.C., Antigonus (one of the last Hasmoneans) attempted to gain the throne. He bribed the Parthians to help him, and to their own astonishment they defeated Jerusalem's Roman overlords and took the capital (Jerusalem). Antigonus set himself up as High Priest and king. He captured and mutilated Hyrcanus II, making him unfit for the priesthood, also taking Phasael prisoner, who later committed suicide from despair. Antigonus reigned for three years (40-37 B.C.)[8]

Meanwhile, Herod had escaped from the revolt to Masada, a fortress near the Dead Sea. He left his family there and went to see Octavian and Antony (cf. Jos., *Ant.* xiv. 14,3-6). Josephus says that Herod met Octavian at Rhodes "dressed as a private person with the demeanour of a king."[9] He was so impressed by Herod that he and the Roman Senate unanimously elected Herod king of Judea (39 B.C.). Now the problem was to possess the throne, and Herod still lacked an army. He therefore went to Galilee to rid the land of robbers and insurrectionists, for which service Antony gave him the military support he needed. He made himself master of Galilee and the surrounding country, and with Antony's Roman force besieged Jerusalem. In 37 B.C. Herod and the Roman army prevailed, capturing Jerusalem; Antigonus and forty-five members of the Sanhedrin were put to death, and Herod married Mariamne. Thus, possessing the throne, he ended the Hasmonean dynasty. There is great irony here, as Dimont points out that the Idumeans, who had been forcibly converted to Judaism eighty years previously by John Hyrcanus, the son of the founder of the Hasmonean Dynasty, now ruled the people who had converted them.[10]

Herod was now king of the Jews. In religion he was a Jew, in race an Idumean, in cultural sympathies a Greek, in political allegiance a Roman. To his inferiors he was ruthless, to his own family sometimes cruel, though usually affectionate, and to his superiors he was an opportunist.[11] He "played along with" whatever ruler was in power at the time; he was constantly ready to change sides to further his own ambitions.[12] Emperor Augustus says of him, "I had sooner be Herod's swine that his son" (in reference to his sons' murders by Herod[13]). From most accounts of Herod, one pictures him as a hideous madman, almost inhumanly evil, but in Josephus' report he does not appear quite so terrible. While he was not virtuous, and was often ruthlessly cruel, in comparison to other rulers of his age (the Seleucids, Ptolemies, Romans and previous priest-kings) Herod did more good than harm. In his day harem intrigues, mutual jealousies between brothers, and the desire to find a suitable heir were common factors in the life of any Eastern monarch.[14]

THE HERODIAN FAMILY

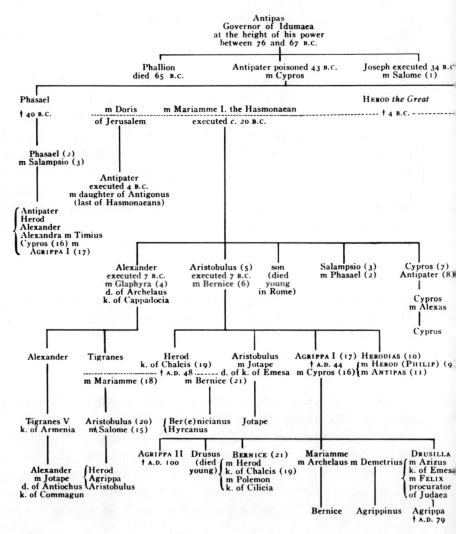

Illus. 4

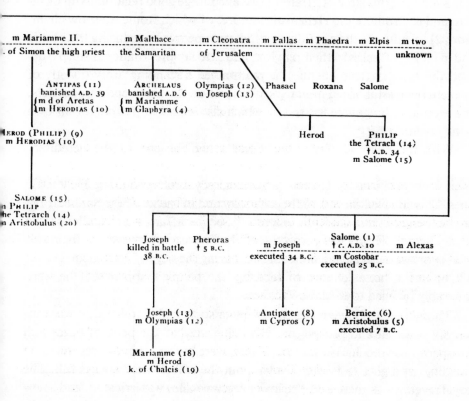

m Mariamme II.
. of Simon the high priest

ANTIPAS (11)
banished A.D. 39
{ m d of Aretas
{ m HERODIAS (10)

HEROD (PHILIP) (9)
m HERODIAS (10)

SALOME (15)
m PHILIP
the Tetrarch (14)
m Aristobulus (20)

m Malthace
the Samaritan

ARCHELAUS
banished A.D. 6
{ m Mariamme
{ m Glaphyra (4)

m Cleopatra
of Jerusalem

Olympias (12)
m Joseph (13)

m Pallas

Phasael

Herod

m Phaedra

Roxana

m Elpis

Salome

PHILIP
the Tetrarch (14)
† A.D. 34
m Salome (15)

m two

unknown

Joseph
killed in battle
38 B.C.

Pheroras
† 5 B.C.

m Joseph
executed 34 B.C.

Salome (1)
† c. A.D. 10
m Costobar
executed 25 B.C.

m Alexas

Joseph (13)
m Olympias (12)

Antipater (8)
m Cypros (7)

Bernice (6)
m Aristobulus (5)
executed 7 B.C.

Mariamme (18)
m Herod
k. of Chalcis (19)

Looking at Herod from this angle, he seems more to be pitied than scorned.

Herod was one of the most competent rulers of his day. During his reign he regained almost the entire area that had been the Hasmonean Kingdom. In 37 B.C. his kingdom consisted of Judea, Idumea, Perea, Galilee, the port of Joppa, and the villages of Jezreel. In 34 B.C. Octavian restored to him the coastal cities of Phoenicia and Philistia, which had been Cleopatra's; and when Cleopatra died in 30 B.C. he received the whole of Palestine minus Decapolis and north Caesarea. The fact that he kept this extensive kingdom until his death speaks well of his powers of diplomacy. He had three policies in maintaining this state of affairs: 1) To encourage good relations with Octavian and to promote the Hellenistic culture, of which Rome was now champion; 2) to cultivate the confidence of his own people by reducing their taxes and avoiding offenses to their religion; and 3) to suppress nationalism. To defend the country from enemies he maintained a standing army (mostly of mercenaries), established military settlements on the north and east borders, and erected impregnable fortresses, which also served as palaces for his own family members.[15]

With the reign of Herod the Great came the end of the hereditary aristocracy. There arose instead a new aristocracy of service—those who were given their positions by Herod—a bureaucracy structured along Hellenistic lines. This signaled the end of the authority and influence of the Sanhedrin in any but religious and academic matters.[16] Secular affairs were handled by the royal Council. Herod was protective of the Pharisees, however, as the result of a favor two of them had done for him during the siege of Jerusalem; Herod felt he had a better chance of securing the people's approval if he were favorably inclined toward the Pharisees.[17]

Though Herod's reign was one of inner strife and bloodshed, it was outwardly peaceful and prosperous. His reign marked the peak of peace and prosperity for the Jewish nation. There were lavish expenditures made on buildings and gifts to foreign leaders, but the coffers were always full. The royal revenue was increased, the lower Jordan valley was irrigated, and a new city and port were built on the site of Straton's Tower. This new harbor, called Caesarea, encouraged overseas trade with the western world.[18] Herod also began an extensive building program in the middle period of his reign: He erected fortresses, magnificent buildings, and cities in the Hellenistic style; he instituted quinquennial games (athletic and gladitorial contests) in honor of the Emperor, supported and managed the Olympic games, built hippodromes, gymnasiums, public baths, colonnaded streets and marketplaces with elegant statues and temples. In Jerusalem he erected a hippodrome, a theatre, and an amphitheatre; and in other cities he dedicated altars, shrines and temples to Octavian and to pagan deities. His most notable work was the reconstruction of the Temple at Jerusalem, begun in 20 B.C. It took eighteen months to complete the main edifice and eight years more to finish the outer courts and porches. It was built according to Jewish scruples: He was careful not to enter the Temple; he did not erect statues in the Temple area or stamp his image on the coins. He even had the workmen build silently, as the Old Testament had instructed (I Kings 6:7). But Herod did permit the Roman eagle to be placed over the great gate of the Temple, an act which later was to lead to violent reaction from the Pharisees. The Temple was not fully completed until A.D. 65, just before its destruction in A.D. 70.[19]

Despite all the seemingly good things Herod had done during his reign, the people disliked him: The Greeks did not like a Jew ruling them and the Jews did not accept an Idumean. Besides, everything Herod did showed his devotion to the Hellenistic culture: The classical architecture, the urban centers, the games—everything spoke of the Greek and Roman influence and of his utter neglect of the Jewish culture. The taxes were heavy (even if they were devoted to public works), Roman legionaries were always in Jerusalem, and Roman institutions prevailed. The old constitution of the country had been overruled, the Sanhedrin had lost its power except in religious affairs, and the High Priests were changed so frequently that it was impossible to establish a way of life as it had been before. The Jews even suspected Herod's reason for reconstructing the Temple. Foakes Jackson comments, "In demolishing the ancient Temple and entirely rebuilding it, Herod doubtless hoped to gain immortal fame and to conciliate his Jewish subjects."[20] The only reason the Jews even slightly accepted Herod was because his wife, Mariamne, was a Maccabean princess. They hoped that eventually one of her sons would inherit the throne and bring back the Maccabean lineage to Judea. But Herod grew suspicious of these sons and in 7 B.C. had them put to death. (cf. Jos., *Ant.* xvi. 11,1-7).

The peaceful and prosperous atmosphere created by Herod the Great was continued by his sons, Herod Antipas (tetrarch of Galilee) and Herod Agrippa (King of Judea). Into this setting Jesus was born and carried out His ministry. The suspicion and cruelty of the Herods also touched Jesus' life as seen in the killing of the children (Matt. 2:16), the beheading of John the Baptist by Herod Antipas (Matt. 14:1ff.), and the mockery at Jesus' trial (Luke 23:8ff.).

Herod's personal life flowed with blood. Josephus says that the evil influences behind Herod were his sister Salome and his son Antipater. Salome convinced him of his sons' (Mariamne's) supposed plot to take the throne, and of Mariamne's infidelity, and this led to their execution by Herod. Herod was driven by "unscrupulous ambition" and "fierce jealousy," (cf. Jos., *Ant.* xv. 7,1-6, for Salome's accusation against Mariamne), which led him to murder several other of his wives and children, other relatives, members of the Sanhedrin and other Jews.[21] Josephus lends a tragic note to the murders of Mariamne and her two sons. He tells of Herod's undying love for them, even when Mariamne was unfaithful. Only when he was persuaded of her infidelity did he order her death, and then he went almost mad with remorse (Jos., *Ant*. xv. 7,5-6).

After Herod had disposed of his two sons by Mariamne, he named Antipater as heir-apparent; but when Herod was dying of an excruciatingly painful disease, he was told of Antipater's part in a plot against him. He then condemned Antipater to death and unceremonial burial. Josephus says that although Herod's career had been otherwise successful, Herod put to death the wife he loved, and her two sons, as well as his first-born whom he had designated as heir to his vast dominions (Jos., *Ant*. xvii. 6-7). Again he altered his will, making Archelaus king of Judea, and Antipas tetrarch of Gaulonitis, Trachonitis, and Paneas. Five days later, in 4 B.C., Herod died and was buried with elaborate ceremony at the fortress of Herodium (Jos., *Ant*. xvii, 8,1-3).

Josephus tells of an event that shows us something of the man: Herod assembled the chief men of his kingdom and locked them in the hippodrome in Jericho, giving express orders to Salome that they were to be massacred as soon as he himself expired, so that the time of his death would be marked by national mourning (Jos., *Ant*. xvii. 6,5). But tradition holds that these "intended victims were released and the city of Jerusalem, which the tyrant had both beautified and cursed, was filled with rejoicing instead of lamentation."[22] (Jos., *Ant*. xvii. 8,2).

Thus, the thirty-four-year reign of Herod, called the Great, came to a close. In one sense he was a great ruler and a terrible one in another: He brought peace and prosperity to Judea, yet he was the most hated ruler of his day. He left behind him the greatest expansion of the kingdom, prosperity unknown since Solomon, freedom from the elements of disorder, an increasing population, an entirely Jewish Galilee of teeming villages, and a prosperous Jerusalem. These blessings came at the expense of liberty, but, in the true sense, what liberty had the Jews enjoyed since the Captivity? The main blot on Herod's reign was the lack of religious advancement; there was always an undercurrent of piety, but during his reign the Jewish religion had been somewhat diluted by the Hellenistic culture.

The contribution of the Romans to the scene of Jesus can be seen through the Herods: The atmosphere was peaceful and prosperous but also suspicious, cruel and politically tense. Such a situation enabled the growth of Christianity and heightened the longing of the coming of the Messiah.

The death of Herod the Great did not end the bloody history of the Jews. Worse was to follow: Jewish persecution by Vespasian and other Roman rulers, and the destruction of Jerusalem in 70 A.D. The study of their history makes one ask with Raskin:

"The Eternal Riddle"[23]

Hated and hunted,
Ever thou wand'rest,
Bearing a message:
God is but One!

Israel, my people,
God's greatest riddle
Will thy solution
Ever be told?

Chapter IV

THE PHARISEES AND THE SADDUCEES

Chapter IV

THE PHARISEES AND THE SADDUCEES

I. The Pharisees

The scene of Jesus' time is not complete without a study of the religious sects that so frequently appear in the New Testament, especially in opposition to Jesus.

We know about the Pharisees from several primary sources. Josephus writes in his *Antiquities* xviii. 1,2.:

> The Jews had for a great while three sects of philosophy peculiar to themselves; the sect of the Essens, and the sect of the Sadducees, and the third sort of opinions was that of those called Pharisees; of which sects, although I have already spoken in the second book of the Jewish War, yet will I a little touch upon them now.

He also mentions them in several other passages that we shall discuss later. The New Testament, of course, tells us some things about the Pharisees, but for the most part it discusses them with a negative bias; that is, they stood in opposition to Jesus and were thus viewed as the "bad guys." There were also the Rabbinic documents, but these are mostly of late composition so they do not shed much light on the early Pharisees.

The problem of the origin of the Pharisees is complicated. George F. Moore states the problem clearly when he says, "Of the origin and the antecedents of the Pharisees there is no record."[1] That is exactly the problem; even Josephus does not mention where they came from. It is commonly surmised among scholars, however, that they succeeded those who earlier called themselves Hasidim "to distinguish themselves as what we call religious men from their worldly and indifferent countrymen."[2]

D. S. Russell takes another view, that the Pharisees were *spiritual* descendants of the Hasidim, since it is uncertain that they can claim *literal* descent from them. "It is perhaps more accurate to say that their origin is to be traced to those lay scribes who, from the beginning of the Greek period, did so much to 'democratize' religion through their everyday life." The exact relation of the Pharisees to the Hasidim is unclear. I Maccabees 7:12ff. mentions "a company of scribes along with the Hasidim," so the two groups *may* be linked; but *how* they are linked cannot now be determined. The fact that two groups are mentioned may lead to Russell's conclusion: "If this is so, then the Pharisees, though sharing the Hasidim's zeal for the Torah of God, can hardly trace their origin back to this group of men."[3]

Another possibility of the origin of the Pharisees is set forth by Eduard Lohse. He suggests that they began during the Maccabean times, when it was necessary to defend the Jewish faith against Hellenistic influences. I Maccabees 2:42 characterizes them as, "A company of pious Jews, brave men from Israel, none but those who willingly submitted themselves to the law." Out of these "Chasidim" who supported the Maccabean revolt came the Pharisees.[4] When the Maccabees became more concerned with the political issue than the religious one, the Chasidim lost interest.[5]

Werner Foerster suggests yet another theory:

> Those of the Hasidim who did not follow the Teacher of Righteousness and did not make the break with the high priesthood and the temple constituted the sect of the Pharisees . . . The common origin which links them with the Essenes is still evident in the Habakkuk Commentary where, on Habakkuk 1:13b, it is said: "This refers to the 'house of Absalom' and their cronies who kept silent when charges were levelled against the teacher who was expounding the Law aright, and who did not come to his aid against the man of lies when the latter rejected the Torah in the midst of their entire congregation."[6]

Foerster explains that the "house of Absalom" and "their cronies" refers to the Pharisees. Other references to the Pharisees in the Qumran documents characterize the Pharisees as "those who seek after smooth things." Thus the Pharisees are reproached because, in relation to the Hasmoneans or to the Law, they had chosen the easier and smoother path.[7]

What, then, is the truth as to the origin of the Pharisees? We must conclude that it cannot definitively be known. We do know, however, that Josephus first mentions them by name at the time of John Hyrcanus (135-105 B.C.), when the Hasidim broke with the Hasmoneans (Jos., *Ant.* xiii. 10,5). They are mentioned as distinct from the Essenes in *Antiquities* xiii. 5,9: "At this time there were three sects among the Jews, who had different opinions concerning human actions; the one was called the sect of the Pharisees, another the sect of the Sadducees, and the other the sect of the Essens . . ."

F. F. Bruce suggests that the Hasidim who withdrew from the Hasmoneans were the Pharisees. They withdrew from them when the issue became political rather than religious.[8]

The derivation of the name "Pharisee" does not shed much more light on the problem. Lohse says it is derived from the Hebrew *peruschim* or the Aramaic *perischaya* meaning "the separated ones."

T. W. Manson suggests that the name "Pharisee" derives from the Aramaic word "Persian" and indicates innovators in theology, and that they were nicknamed thus because so many of their ideas were derived from Persian (Zoroastrian) sources. Later, it was linked with *paras*, "separate," and became more edifying. This appears to indicate the Pharisees' open attitude in regard to religious innovations, but Russell stresses that too much emphasis should not be put on the idea that life after death, as held by the Pharisees, could have Persian origin.[10]

Moore points out that a more important question is, what does the name "Pharisee" mean?

> The word Pharisee represents the name in its vernacular form, *Perīsha*. The derivation from the verb *pĕrash* (Hebrew *parash*) is plain; not so the significance and occasion of the name. The interpretation that first suggests itself is 'one who is separated, or is separate'; but from whom or from what—a complement which is necessary to give it meaning—the word contains no intimation; nor does either usage or tradition supply the deficiency.

> From the peculiar rules and customs of the Pharisees it is commonly inferred that they were so called because they religiously avoided everything that the law branded as unclean, and for fear of contamination kept aloof from persons who were suspected of negligence in such matters. Definitions in this general sense were current among the church fathers. In the 'Aryt' the name is defined: 'A Pharisee is one who separates himself from all uncleanness and from eating anything unclean,' in distinction from the mass of the common people, who were not so particular. In the Tannaite and Amoraic sources the name *Perushim* is used in contrast to 'Am ha-Ares, the ignorant and negligent *vulgus*.[11]

Russell explains that the Hebrew word for *Pharisee* (*Perusim*) in the passive form can mean "those who are separated" from the people of the land or from unclean things; thus these "separate ones" are given over to fulfilling the Law (cf. Jos., *Ant.* xviii. 1, 2-3); or "separate" may refer to their distinction from the Sadducean Sanhedrin, thus meaning "schismatics." The active form of the word *Parasim* originally meant "expounder" or "interpreter" (of the Law). The verb *paras* can mean "interpret" as well as "separate."[12]

In Rabbinic literature, the word means "to separate" and *Pharisee* usually means "one who has been separated." Bo Reicke stresses that it *does not* mean "dissident" or "separatist." He explains that in Rabbinic passages the Pharisees are an "expansive popular party with highly developed social relationships and structures," not an isolated group. In the context where the name is usually found, "puritan" is suggested, one who is a zealous proponent of ritual purity (see Mishna *Hag.* ii. 17; Talmud Yerushalmi *Ber.* ix. 146, 40; *Schwab* i. 169). This agrees with the characterization in both Josephus and the New Testament (Jos., *Ant.* xviii. 1,3; Matt. 15:2). Thus, Bo Reicke points out that *Pharisee* as "puritan" would also agree with the Old Testament idea of separation from the pollution of the peoples of the land (Ezra 6:21; 9:1; 10:11; Neh. 9:2 10:28) and "from the nations of the world with their abominations" (Mekilta *Exod.* 19. 6, 71a).[13]

The Pharisaic sect was composed of priests, laymen, craftsmen, farmers, merchants, those from the city and the country, Judea and Galilee. In other words, they were made up of the middle class. They came together for meals in order to maintain purity (Luke 7:36; 11:37-8), and there were at one time "more than 6,000 members in the Pharisee's fellowship" (Jos., *Ant.* xvii. 2,4 §42). The first Pharisees were law-observing Jews with no political aims. They were filled with zeal for the Law by which Israel led its life (I Macc. 7:l3).

Tcherikover points out that the Pharisees were skillful in politics:

> The slogan chosen by the Pharisees testifies to their great skill in political tactics. 'The royal crown is sufficient to you, leave the priestly diadem to the seed of Aaron!'—in these words the Talmud defines the Pharisean demands upon King Jannaeus. At first sight this demand did not detract from the power of the dynasty, for the Pharisees were ready to leave the royal crown—the army, foreign affairs, the court and the administration—in its hands; it was to concede only the Temple.[14]

The Pharisees can further be defined as, "A body of Jews who profess to be more righteous than the rest and to explain the laws more precisely." (*Bell. Jud.* 1, 8, 14 §162; cf. *Ant.* xvii. 2, 4 §41; xviii. 1, 3 §12)

The Jewish Talmud makes interesting distinctions among the Pharisees. It differentiates seven types:

1) The "wait-a-little"—puts off doing a good deed.
2) The "bruised" or "bleeding"—shuts eyes to not look at a woman, so stumbles against wall.
3) The "shoulder"—wears good deeds on shoulders for all to see.
4) The "hump-backed"—walks stooped in mock humility.
5) The "ever-reckoning"—continually counts up good deeds to balance his bad deeds.
6) The "God-fearing"—stands in awe and dread of God.
7) The "God-loving" or "born"—is a true son of Abraham and a genuine Pharisee.[15]

This particular study does not intend to give a detailed history of the development of the sect. However, a brief account will be given of its major development through the various periods preceding and succeeding the time of Christ.[16]

As was stated before, it is unknown exactly when the Pharisees originated or became known as a sect. We do see them emerge, however, around the time of the Maccabees (c. 175 B.C.). Their roots seem to lie in the Jews who were exiled in Babylon (in the sixth century B.C.) and in the reformers in Jerusalem.[17] Probably, when the Jews no longer could worship at the Temple (after being carried captive to Babylon), they formed groups to study the Law and the Scriptures in their own homes or in some public place. We see the seeds of these scholars in Ezra and Nehemiah when, as reformers, the Pharisees developed the ideal of Ezra and the Levites (e.g., Neh. 8:7-9,13; 10:29f.).

It is not until the Maccabean revolt (167 B.C.) that the Pharisees are actually mentioned by name as a party. The writer of I Maccabees states that a group of Hasidim, or pietists ("pious"), pledged to obey the Law and withstand Hellenistic influence (I Macc. 2:42). Of course, this assumes a certain origin of the Pharisees. In 161 B.C. some outstanding scribes were deceived by Alcimus, the Hellenistic high priest (I Macc. 7:12-18). This forced the Pharisees' association with the Maccabees themselves.[18]

In the Hasmonean times (142-37 B.C.), the Pharisees were led by learned scribes and had authority as lay members of the *Gerousia* or *Sanhedrin*. Their religious influence was great in the synagogues and schools in Jerusalem and throughout the Dispersion, where they interpreted and explained the Scriptures. They formed "brotherhoods" and had great influence on Judaism, although they were small in numbers.[19] They did missionary work among the Gentiles (Matt. 23:15).

When the Hasmonean cause became more political than religious, it appears that the Pharisees separtated from them. Under Alexander Jannaeus in particular, there arose a bloody conflict in which the high priest gained the upper hand by terror and execution of rebels.[20] At this point, the Pharisees began to change. They sought to prepare themselves by pious living, prayer, and fasting for the future change which God would bring about. This became their aim rather than seeking a political change by means of violence. Thus, they later refused to join the Zealots to bring in the Messianic age by force.[21]

According to Josephus, John Hyrcanus was a highly esteemed Pharisee until a personal grievance caused him to defect to the Sadducean party (Jos., *Ant.* xiii. 10. 5f.). This is attested by the Talmud of King Jannai and by another Baraita, which states, "Do not put confidence in yourself till the day of your death; for there was Johanan the high priest (Hyrcanus), he ministered for eighty years and became a Sadducee at the last."[22]

Hyrcanus, in retaliation, abrogated the ordinances which the Pharisees had established and punished those who disobeyed by observing them. Because of this, the common people hated him and his sons. (See *Bell. Jud.* i. 2, 8 §67, and *Ant. xiii. 10, 5* §288 (ultimately from the same source; cf. also *Ant.* xiii. 10, 7.)

The next we hear of the Pharisees is during the time of Herod, when they were described as "A body of Jews who profess to be more religious than the rest and to explain the laws more precisely." (*Bell. Jud.* 1. 8, 14 §162; cf. *Ant.* xvii. 2, 4 §41; xviii. 1, 3 §12).

We also have a wider knowledge of the Pharisaic party at this time because two famous Pharisees, Hillel and Shammai, were living then. Hillel was the liberalizing factor in Pharisaism while Shammai represented a stricter application of the Law. Thus, by this time there were conflicting differences within Pharisaism. In order to get a clearer idea of these differences, let us take a closer look at these opposing schools.

Hillel was known for his gentleness, humility and patience of character. He did not accept the rule of Herod, nor did he advocate Messianism and apocalyptic speculation. In fact these aspects were absent since they would lead to political conflict. He saw the future hope as present in the pursuit of peace and love of humanity. David Rhoads quotes him as saying, "He who has acquired for himself words of the Torah has acquired life in the coming world."[23]

In other words, the study of the Torah was the key to eternal life more than the acquisition of worldly things or information. A rule of Hillel was, "What is hateful to yourself, do not to your fellow. That is the whole Torah. All the rest is commentary. Now go forth and learn!"[24] Jacob Neusner says:

> Hillel taught a methodology of interpreting Scripture which in time revolutionized the intellectual life of Pharisaism. These principles, . . . included the following: 1. Inference *a minori ad majus*; 2. Inference by analogy; 3. Constructing a family on the basis of one passage (extending a specific regulation of one biblical passage to a number of passages); 4. The same rule as the preceding, constructing a family on the basis of two biblical passages; 5. The General and the Particular, the Particular and the General; 6. Exposition by means of another, similar passage; 7. Deduction from the context.[25]

Thus, Hillel made his interpretation as broad and as liberal as possible. He innovated many things for the good of the people. For instance, Bruce explains, "To Hillel is assigned a legal innovation which went far to modify, if not to nullify, the ancient law that debts owed by a fellow-Israelite were to be remitted every seventh year (Deut. 15:1-6)."[26] Thus, the Pharisees who followed Hillel could interpret a law so far as to actually change its original meaning. Hillel employed logical argument as the basis for the exposition of the text, and this helped to apply the Law to take account of the existing social conditions of the time.[27]

On the contrary, Shammai represents a much stricter interpretation of the Law. He was remembered mainly for his petulance, but these accounts are most likely prejudiced. Shammai left few sayings; those we do have were written by Hillel's disciples.[28] Bruce observes,

> It is probable that the Lawyers in the Gospel record, who 'load men with burdens hard to bear' but do not themselves lift a finger to ease their weight (Lu. 11:46), are Shammaites. But in the reconstruction of national life that followed the war of A.D. 66-73 it was the school of Hillel, under Yohanan ben Zakkai and his associates, that became dominant.[29]

There are 316 recorded controversies between these two schools, the Shammaites taking the stricter side and the Hillelites the milder. Most of the conflicts had to do with ritual and legal matters, although some were more fundamental. For instance, the two schools debated for two-and-one-half years over the question, "Was it good that man had been created?"[30]

An example of the differences is in regard to divorce. Shammai held that the only valid reason for divorce was adultery, whereas Hillel acknowledged the problem of incompatibility. (For more examples see Grant, p. 258.) In the early period, during Jesus' ministry (6-44 C.E.), Josephus tells that the Pharisees staged a passive sit-in before Pilate at Caesarea. Several of these acts of passive resistance evidently took place. One particular event occurred in a later period (44-66 C.E.) when irate Jews protested the burning of the Torah by a Roman soldier (Jos., *Wars* ii. 12,2; *Ant*. xx. 5,4).

During the Apostolic era, the Pharisees had great influence on the High Council and in government (Jos., *Ant*. xviii. 1,4). They were especially powerful under Agrippa I (41-44 A.D.), who sought to cultivate the Pharisees in order "to win additional popular support."[31] After A.D. 50, however, their popularity yielded somewhat to the Zealots. Throughout this era the Pharisees remained within the society in accordance with the words of Hillel, "Do not separate yourself from the community" (*Avot* 1.5).

There arose still other differences within Pharisaism. The Zealots among them sought to restore Israel through war, while the others centered on spiritual reform. Josephus wrote of the Pharisees,

> . . . on account of which doctrines they are able greatly to persuade the body of the people; and whatsoever they do about divine worship, prayers, and sacrifices, they perform them according to their direction; insomuch that the cities gave great attestations to them on account of their entire virtuous conduct, both in the actions of their lives and their discourses also. (Jos. *Ant*. xviii. 1,3).

Thus, the Pharisees fostered their opinions among the people.

At this time, the Pharisees seem to have been more favorable toward the new Christian community, as seen in several accounts in the New Testament,

1) Gamaliel I opposed the arrest of apostles (Acts 5:34).

2) His disciple, Paul, persecuted the Church (Acts 9:1f.; Phil. 3:5f.).

3) Pharisees joined the church (Acts 15:5).

4) Pharisaic Scribes spoke in Paul's behalf (Acts 23:9).[32]

Gamaliel I followed his father Hillel and his rival Shammai as head of the Pharisaic community.[33] Simeon ben Gamaliel and Yohanan ben Zakkai succeeded him, two decades before the revolt of 66-70 A.D. [34] Zakkai actually took the lead (*Avot* 2.9).

Since Zakkai was Hillel's disciple and student, we can see Hillel's teaching reflected in Zakkai's ideas; for example, in his concept of responsibility toward social problems and his devotion to the Torah.[35]

Although Zakkai represented the Pharisees in the disputes with the Sadducees, he attempted to unite the religion of Galilee and Jerusalem. Neusner comments that the two dynamics in religion were united in the experience of the Torah, which meant to the sages the act of continuing study and application of Scripture as at once a pneumatic and a disciplining spiritual experience.[36]

The book of Acts tells us that the Pharisees had influence in the Sanhedrin (5:34-40; 23:6-8). But when the revolt came, in A.D. 66-70, not even the Pharisees could prevent disaster. Some joined the revolt, others did not. Some survived the war and exerted influence after A.D. 70 on the Synagogue, both spiritually and intellectually.[37]

During the revolt, Zakkai preached passivism. When he saw that war was imminent, however, he escaped while it was still possible. All accounts agree that he met Vespasian and prophesied his imminent rise to power and was thus allowed to go to Yavneh, in Galilee, to take refuge.[38] Here, Zakkai established an Academy that insured the future of Pharisaism, while the other parties met disaster.

Why did the Pharisees survive, while the Sadducees and the Essenes did not? Why did the Romans permit the Pharisees to establish an Academy that preserved the seeds of the later revolt in 139 A.D.?

> The Pharisees . . . have by far the greatest influence with the people. Any government which secures their support is accepted; any government which alienates them has trouble. The Sadducees, it is true, have more following among the Aristocracy . . . But they have no popular following at all, and even in the old days when they were in power, they were forced by public opinion to follow the Pharisees' orders.[39]

Neusner adds two other reasons: 1) The other parties were ineligible for serious consideration by the Romans; Josephus presents them as follows: a) The Essenes as a "philosophical curiosity," b) The Zealots as anti-Roman, and c) The Sadducees as an aristocratic minority (see Jos., *Ant.* xviii. 1,3-6). "So any Roman government which wants peace in Palestine had better support, and secure the support of, the Pharisees." 2) The Pharisees actively advanced their own candidacy as Roman supporters; they possibly even negotiated for it.[40]

The worst problems that the Pharisees faced after A.D. 70 were liturgical. Yohanan and the Academy eventually claimed "that the academy held the authority formerly exerted by the Sanhedrin in Jerusalem. The Yavneh Academy was now *the* high court capable of issuing authoritative enactments."[41]

Zakkai's method was Hillel's—to issue decrees on specific legal problems. By A.D. 75, and again by A.D. 145, Jewish autonomous government was again functioning. The Judaism that survived was different from pre-war Judaism. "It was a Judaism shaped by men who shared a community of interest with Rome."[42]

Neusner says that "What survived in time became a force for peace, not subversion, and its central institutions consistently and, after the Bar Kokhba War, effectively worked to secure loyalty to Rome and tranquility in Palestine" (p. 171).

The answer to our question, then, as to why the Pharisees outlived the other religious parties can be stated as follows. When the social structure collapsed, the Pharisees survived because they continued to evolve their own ideas about the proper conduct of society according to the biblical imperative. In contrast to the Sadducees and the Essenes, they pursued their studies and tried to apply them to public life. Gamaliel represented Pharisees in the Sanhedrin.[43]

In their beliefs and practices, the Pharisees were separatists; that is, they separated themselves from those who did not know the Law. They were thus disassociated from such people as tax collectors, prostitutes, fallen men, and sinners (Mark 2:14-17; par. Luke 15:2). This separatism was largely for the purpose of maintaining purity. The Pharisees felt that the Old Testament commandments were necessary, not only for priestly purity but also for the purity of all Pharisees in everyday life. For instance, anyone who made contact with a dead corpse or an animal, or anyone who had a bodily discharge had lost his cultic purity. In order to gain it back, one must undergo a bath of purification and sometimes a period of time before he was regarded as clean. For this reason, the Pharisees washed their hands before every meal (Mark 7:3-4). The Pharisees paid attention not only to the purity of the person but also to the purity of the vessels that they used. For example, if a mouse ran across a plate or if a bone fell into a cup, the plate or cup was rendered unclean (Matt. 23:25-6; par Luke 11:39-40). The Pharisees felt that "God had revealed the norms of purity through holy scriptures, traditions and scribes; the Pharisees sought to develop this revelation and make it applicable to society, so that every Jew could realize the ideal of the covenant people" (Neh. 10:29-30).[44]

In order to preserve and develop this purity, the Pharisees analyzed and discussed the books of the Bible. This exegesis was called "midrash," meaning "investigation" (c. 20 B.C.). This material became revered almost above the Biblical material itself.

Beyond the Midrash other writings were developed:

hālakâ ("walking")—tradition of observances, based on the legal material of the Bible.

haggāda ("narration")—tradition of edification, based on narrative and parenetic (sic) material.

Talmud ("teaching")—literature of the systematic tradition comprising two collections:

1) Hebrew Mishna ("instruction") contains sixty-three tractates assembled c. 200 A.D. in Tiberias.
2) Aramaic Gemara ("supplement") contains thirty-six (or thirty-nine) tractates of the Mishna, being preserved in a Palestinian version dating c. 400 A.D. and a Babylonian version dating c. 500 A.D. Talmud Yerushalmi and Talmud Babli.

Tosefta ("addition")—like the Mishna but larger, edited c. 250 A.D.[45]

The Pharisees accepted the Prophets and Writings as authoritative sacred Scripture, and used them in their interpretation of the Torah. Russell comments on this aspect of Pharisaism, "In course of time they [Pharisees] declared that this 'tradition of the elders' was as authoritative and binding as the written Torah itself, and so gave it an honoured place alongside Scripture."[46]

Josephus comments on the situation that the Pharisees had passed on to the people certain regulations handed down by former generations and not recorded in the Laws of Moses, for which reason they are rejected by the Sadducaean group, who hold that only those regulations should be considered valid which were written down (in Scripture), and that those which had been handed down by former generations need not be observed. And concerning these matters the two parties came to have controversies and serious differences (Jos., *Ant.* xii. 10, 6; Russell, pp. 161-62).

Hence, the Pharisees accept as Law certain legal regulations which have been handed down by the fathers. Bruce explains the purpose of these "traditions of the elders": "The 'traditions of the elders' was largely designed to mitigate the rigours which a literal application of the written law would impose on people living under conditions widely different from those which were obtained when the law was first promulgated."[47]

On the other hand, the whole life of the Pharisee was to observe the Law exactly. Josephus sums it up by saying that "The Pharisees are a group of

Jews who have the reputation of excelling the rest of their nation in the observance of religion, and as exact exponents of the laws" (*Wars* i. 5,2).

Again in the *Wars*, Josephus calls the Pharisees the "leading sect" and the "most accurate interpreters of the Laws" (*Wars* ii. 8, 14).

The Pharisees also differed from the Sadducees in that they tried to adapt the written commands to the present and thus discover practicable regulations regarding everyday things; for example, the Sabbath rules.[48]

In fact, Rhoads goes so far as to say that the *essence* of Pharisaism was "the attempt to put the whole life under the control of the Law."[49]

It is interesting to note that even when Pharisaism split into the two schools of Hillel and Shammai, both groups held to the oral tradition, although Hillel had to learn to do so.[50]

The Pharisees believed in God's predetermination of Israel's destiny (*Heilsgeschichte*). They held that people must contribute to its sanctification and perfection through a precise fulfillment of the Law (Jos., *Bell* ii. 162ff.; *Ant.* xiii. 5,9; xviii. 1,3).

The Pharisees taught the resurrection of the dead, the survival of the soul (Acts 23:8; Jos., *Bell* ii. 163; *Ant.* xviii. 1,3), a last judgment (Jos. *ibid.*) and a world to come (*Pirke Aboth.* ii. 8; *Ant.* xviii. 1,1-3). They supported their belief in the resurrection of the dead by their interpretation of the entire Scriptures, since this had been expanded by oral tradition. (Also see Mark 6:16; Luke 9:9.) They developed this expectation of resurrection into a tightly formulated doctrine.

The Pharisees observed voluntary fasting twice a week to show penitence and to pray for Israel and its salvation.[51]

They also observed the commandment to give a tenth of the harvest and one's earnings so that the tribe of Levi could be supported and the sacrificial service in the Temple could be maintained (Lev. 27:30-33; Num. 18:21-4). The Pharisees not only tithed on the produce from their land but also on anything which they acquired by purchase (Matt. 23:23; par. Luke 11:42).

The Pharisees believed that when the people were prepared in purity and holiness their Messiah would appear as the Son of David, and would father the scattered tribes of Israel and reestablish the kingdom. The more the pious rejected the Hasmonean rule (142-37 B.C.) the greater was their expectation that the Anointed One from David's lineage would soon appear to cleanse Jerusalem of the heathen, overthrow the ungodly, and take over political rule.[52] This belief in a warrior-Messiah was based on the Psalms of Solomon, a Pharisaic work of the first century B.C. Although the Pharisees themselves were not particularly militant in this hope, the founder of the Zealot party was a Pharisee, as was the reknowned Rabbi Akiba, who was involved in the revolt of Bar Kochba (132 A.D.).[53]

The Pharisees so oriented their lives to the Messianic age and to the fulfillment of its righteousness that they exaggerated the Law in order not to commit any offense as an oversight. In other words, they "built a fence around the Law."[54]

Let us look briefly now at the relation of the Pharisees to the New Testament. For the purpose of this study, only a few points will be mentioned. For a more detailed study, see Everett F. Harrison, *A Short Life of Christ*, pp. 123ff., where he discusses at length the conflict between the Pharisees and Jesus.

It is interesting to note that the famous Pharisee Rabbi ben Zakkai lived in Galilee as a contemporary of Jesus for eighteen years, only a few miles from Jesus. The "silent years," the public ministry, the crucifixion, resurrection, and ascension of Jesus all took place during this period. Could it be that ben Zakkai met or heard Jesus? The encounter of Jesus with a Galilean schoolteacher named Zacchaeus is preserved in the *Gospel of Thomas*, and Neusner suggests that "Zacchaeus" could represent the Greek translation of "Ben Zakkai."[55]

Neusner also suggests that the story of Jesus disputing with the scholars at the age of twelve arose after A.D. 70 in order to liberate the Christian community from the authority of Ben Zakkai's Academy at Yavneh. "Those who held that the destruction of Jerusalem represented divine retribution for the rejection and crucifixion of Jesus could hardly acknowledge the continuity of Jewish religious authority and the legitimacy of Yohanan's institution at Yavneh."[56]

In relation to beliefs and practices Jesus stood near the Pharisaic position on several points; for instance, the resurrection of the dead and the call to repentance and conversion. Jesus broke with the Pharisees, however, by eating with tax collectors and sinners (Mark 2:15), thus breaking the Pharisees' law of purity (see above). Jesus was above the Sabbath rules (Mark 2:23-3:6) and was not bothered by the intricate rules of Pharisaic purity (Mark 7:1-5). Jesus, in fact, called them hypocrites for being so intent on observing the Law outwardly but being oblivious to the purity of the heart (Luke. 11:39-43). This was not the only point on which Jesus opposed the Pharisees. He criticized the power of the Pharisaic scribes (Matt. 23:2-31) and considered his own revelation as superior (Matt. 7:29, 12:23f.). He also criticized them because sometimes the Pharisees' interpretation of law was so stretched that it nullified or neutralized the force of a given commandment.[57]

Jesus actually expressed some Pharisaic principles such as the Sabbath being made for man, not man for the Sabbath (Mark 2:27) and that only a deliberate oath was to be binding (Matt. 23:16).

Even so, Jesus was on friendly terms with some Pharisees; for example, Simon (Luke 7:37), and some who warned him about Herod (Luke 13:31).

Most of the time, however, we see them plotting against his life (Mark 3:6; John 11:47-57). Jesus had criticized them because "The Pharisees, led by Yohanan ben Zakkai, were attempting not merely to rule the sanctuary but to *exclude* from the Temple all who did not accept their rulings . . . Whatever had not been done in the Pharisaic manner was thereby to be declared profane."[58] Do we not see these principles reflected in John, Chapter 9, where the blind man and the followers of Jesus are excommunicated from the Synagogue?[59]

Many other issues could be set forth for comparison or contrast but this study will not go into further detail.

Other New Testament references could be cited. We know that Paul studied with the famous Pharisee Gamaliel (also ben Zakkai's predecessor).[60] Thus, it is not surprising to see some likeness in the writing style of Paul and Gamaliel. (For a comparison of Paul's epistles with Gamaliel's letter, see Neusner, p. 67.)

Finally, we can see the extreme Shammaite position reflected in the theology of James (2:10, "Whoever keeps the whole law but fails in one point has become guilty of all of it.").

This differs, however, from the idea of Rabbi Aquiba (c. A.D. 100) that "the world is judged in mercy, and all is according to the amount of the work."[61]

II. *The Sadducees*

Josephus says of the Sadducees, "The Jews had for a great while three sects of philosophy peculiar to themselves; the sect of the Essens and the sect of the Sadducees . . ." He describes them more fully later, but here he categorizes them as one of the three major sects of the Jews (*Ant.* xviii. 1,2). Most of our information comes from Josephus, the *Antiquities* and the *Wars*, and though he gives a somewhat biased viewpoint, he describes them quite at length. As for other sources, the New Testament gives us some idea of the beliefs and practices of the Sadducees, but obviously it shows no sympathy for them; it shows them mainly in opposition to Jesus. In Talmudic literature (the Mishna and the Tosephta) we see them in conflict with other scholars on questions of religion and law.[62] We have at the present time no source that is acknowledged to have been written by a Sadducee since the sect disappeared after the destruction of Jerusalem in A.D. 70. Thus, no actual sources were preserved, and our picture of the Sadducees must be drawn largely from Josephus, the New Testament, and portions of Talmudic literature.

Most scholars attribute the origin of the Sadducees to the priesthood of Zadok, established by David.[63] Lohse agrees, but traces it rather to the time of Ezekiel,

> The label "Sadducees" certainly is to be connected with the name Zadok who, long ago under King Solomon, was installed as high priest (I Kings 2:35) and from whom, as their ancestor, the priests traced their lineage. In the sketch of the future of Israel, of the land, and of the sanctuary which is presented in Ezekiel 40-48, the priestly ministry is committed to the sons of Zadok (Ezek. 40:46; 43:19; 44:15; 48:11). Then in the construction of the postexilic community the Zadokites played a crucial role and as the legitimate priests in Jerusalem, took care of the temple service.[64]

Rhoads points out that during the Maccabean revolt several groups claimed to be "sons of Zadok"; for example, the Qumran group: a group that retained control of Jerusalem; and a group that cooperated with the Hasmoneans and eventually came to be called "Sadducees."[65]

Another theory regarding the origin of the name *Sadducee* is that rather than being connected with the high priest Zadok it comes from their association with the word *Saddikim*, "righteous ones" (cf. *Assumption of Moses*, 7:3). Russell, however, sees such a connection as etymologically impossible.[66]

T. W. Manson puts forth another theory. He says that the origin derives from the Greek *Syndics*, meaning "legal counsel".

> It is that the meaning of the name is to be found, not in the priestly connexions of the party, but rather in the realm of international politics. He finds its derivation in the Greek word *sundikoi* (Syndics) which can be traced back in Athenian history as far as the fourth century B.C. and is also mentioned in documents from Roman and Byzantine times.[67]

Bo Reicke, however, criticizes this on the basis that this derivation does not adequately explain the vowels of the words as found in the New Testament and Josephus and the consonants found in Rabbinic literature. He allows that "Manson has, however, emphasized some historically important facts".[68]

Still another theory is that the origin is a scholar named Zadok, who was active in the second century B.C. (*Abot, R. Nath.* 5). But Bo Reicke also criticizes this theory on the ground that since it is so similar to another passage about a certain Böethus who is an ancestor of the Böethus priests, the rivals of the Annas priests, " the passage is merely an etiological legend".[69]

Bruce combines Manson's theory with another theory. Like Manson, he says that it is "probable" that *Sadducee* is a Hebraization (*Sadduqim*) of the Greek word *syndikoi* (syndics), members of the Council; but unlike Manson he goes on to say, "and that it marks them out as the councillors of the Hasmomeans; although they themselves come to associate the word with the Hebrew *saddiq*, 'righteous'."[70]

In view of these many theories, it is next to impossible to conclude with any certainty just where the Sadducees originated. It is possible, though, that they began, not as a religious party but because of their close ties with the Temple and the priesthood; and because politics and religion could not easily be separated from one another they eventually took on a religious character.[71]

We can be certain of a few facts, however. Unlike the Pharisees, they were members of the aristocracy, and their membership included both laymen and priests, traders and high-ranking government officials (Jos., *Ant*. xiii. 10,6). They included a small group of influential and wealthy men who had considerable power in the civic and religious life of the nation of Israel. They basically represented the sophisticated, urban class of Jerusalem, including educated men in prominent positions (Jos., *Ant*. xviii. 1,2-3).

In later Talmudic literature, the Sadducees appear as men without religion or morality. Enoch presents them as pagans. If these sources are reliable, then the Sadducees were extreme Hellenists; this view appears in literature on the subject.[72] In regard to their behavior, Josephus remarks, "But the behaviour of the Sadducees one towards another is in some degrees wild; and their conversation with those that are of their own party is as barbarous as if they were strangers to them." (Jos., *Wars* ii. 8,14).

It is possible to trace briefly the history of the Sadducees from the time of the Seleucids (third and second centuries B.C.) to the time of their disappearance in A.D. 70. They were influenced by the Hellenization of the Jews during the time of the Seleucids. As their political authority grew, their religious devotion decreased. The writer of I Maccabees regards such leaders as renegades and traitors to the heritage of the fathers (I Macc. 1:15). During the time of the Romans and the Herods, the Sadducees were so politically prudent and skillful that they occupied high offices in Jerusalem. The high priests were always chosen from among the Sadducees.[73]

Rhoads comments,

From the time of Herod (37-4 B.C.E.) the high priests were appointed and deposed at will by the Roman representative in Palestine, either the Herodian king or the procurator. They quite naturally appointed people, usually from several leading families, who were sympathetic to the Roman presence in Palestine. This close association between high priests and Romans has led to the traditional characterization of the Sadducees as 'collaborators' with the Romans.[74]

By the time of the first century A.D. it is difficult to trace the Sadducees except through the high priesthood and, to some measure, the aristocracy.

The Sadducees opposed the revolt against Rome. Rhoads again explains, "Although the evidence for resistance to Rome is scant in the case of Joazar [a Sadducee] . . . the Sadducees played an important role in the national resistance against the Romans in subsequent years."[75] Although the Sadducees opposed the Zealots' active resistance and the Pharisees' rejection of Gentile authorities, the Sadducees' power and influence was limited. As Josephus says, "For whenever they gained office, they held firm — even though under compulsion and unwillingly — to what the Pharisees say, because otherwise the people would not tolerate them" (Jos., *Ant*. xviii. 14).

During Jesus' time the Sadducees were a small group with widespread influence in politics and religion. We do not see them as often in the New Testament as we do the Pharisees, but they did play a part in the ministry of Jesus.

The war of A.D. 70 had a great effect on the Sadducees. Neusner comments that "The Sadducees, many of whom were upperclass priests and landowners in the Judean region, furthermore lost considerable wealth in the war and concomitant social upheavals."[76]

Thus, with the fall of Jerusalem and the Temple, the Sadducees met their fate — they disappeared. The Pharisees of course did not preserve the Sadducean documents or writings, so even their views no longer exist. We can get glimpses of their beliefs, however, from Josephus.

The Sadducees were actually conservative in regard to the Law. They rejected the oral tradition of the Pharisees and did not admit legal or doctrinal deductions from the Prophets (Jos., *Ant*. xiii. 10,6; xviii. 1,4). To them, the Torah alone was authoritative, Russell, however, feels that it is not likely that they denied the sacredness of the Prophets and Writings as some Church Fathers suggest. They merely rejected any doctrines which could not be justified by the Torah.[77] In practice also the Sadducees were more strict than the Pharisees; for instance, they saw no way to avoid or "get around" the Sabbath commands. Also, they always prescribed penalties exactly according to the Law; that is, the death penalty was always stoning.

The Sadducees denied the belief in angels and demons (Acts 23:8). They also rejected the idea of the immortality of the soul. Josephus says, "They also take away the belief of the immortal duration of the soul, and the punishments and rewards in Hades." (Jos., *Wars* ii. 8,14). Hence, it also follows that in the view of the Sadducee there was no resurrection of the dead.

The Sadducees believed in man's free will, that man is responsible for his actions (Jos., *Bell*. ii. 164; *Ant*. xiii. 5,9). They held that man must make good his transgressions on earth since there is no life after death (Acts 23:8; Jos., *Bell*. ii. 165; *Ant*. xviii. 1,4). In their doctrine of free will, they "do away with Fate altogether" and "remove God beyond the sight of will." (Jos., *Wars* ii. 8,14).

The Sadducees, since they had no belief in apocalyptic intervention or Fate, embraced a "this-worldly eschatology" in which they hoped to set the nation of Israel free, as it was under David's rule.[78] Rhoads states that "In practice, however, the Sadducees sought to bring about their eschatological vision of an independent temple-state by trying to achieve as much autonomy as possible within the Roman Empire by use of the realistic political and diplomatic means at their disposal."[79]

The lack of a doctrine of retribution or recompense in the world to come was possibly one of the reasons that the Sadducees could not cope with the disaster of A.D. 70. After their central sacrificial system was gone, they were left without anything to compensate for it.[80]

In regard to political views, the Sadducees are usually seen as sympathizers with the Hellenists of the Maccabean times, who subverted the pure Jewish faith. Russell points out, however, that the high priestly house lent support to the Hellenizers, but after the Maccabees sympathy for Hellenistic culture is not a feature that distinguishes the Sadducees from the other sects.[81]

They did hold political offices and positions, however, which committed them to practical action and to a realistic view of their situation. Thus, they adjusted to the existing politics. Lohse comments, "As the Sadducees had always been concerned with linking their beliefs with an attitude of receptiveness to the world at large, they recognized the existing government and strove to moderate the hostility toward the Romans which was increasing among the people."[82] Rhoads suggests that the Sadducees had more freedom in their life style than the Pharisees because decisions about matters not in the written law were left up to the individual.[83] Thus, the Sadducees had greater possibilities than the Pharisees of adapting to the Roman and Hellenistic cultures, but "most . . . maintained a basic commitment to the Jewish institutions of the Law, the Temple, and the state."[84]

Russell points out that "As conservatives in politics they [the Sadducees] stood for the Israelite ideal of a theocratic state under the leadership of the High Priest."[85] Thus, any suspicion of a popular Messianic faith and hope for the future would be seen as a direct threat to the existing social and political order. Jesus' teaching was in fact a direct threat to their wealth and their social and political positions.

According to Mark 12:18-27, the Sadducees agreed against the resurrection of the dead on the grounds given in Deuteronomy 25:5-6. By their example of the woman with seven husbands, the Sadducees hoped to show Jesus that the belief in the resurrection of the dead was absurd. Instead, Jesus showed their position to be absurd—he merely said that after the resurrection there would be no marriage; relationships would be different from those on earth.

The High Priest Annas and his colleagues were closely associated with the Sadducees, so the Luke equates the supporters of the high priest with the Sadducees (Acts 5:17). As mentioned above, the Sadducees opposed every popular movement that threatened the power of the imperial officials and high priests. Accordingly they attacked Jesus in conjunction with the

Pharisees (Matt. 16:1, etc.).[86]

Tcherikover sums up the conflict between the Pharisees and the Sadducees very well,

> The sources describe the conflict between them in various ways. Josephus on one occasion speaks of them as philosophical schools preoccupied with questions of religion and ethics; on another as political-social parties struggling for power. In Talmudic literature (the Mishnah and Tosephta) the conflict assumes the character of differences of opinion between scholars on various questions of religion and law.
>
> These accounts do not in fact contradict one another: for this sectarian strife lasted more than two hundred years and quite naturally took various forms at various periods. Under the Hasmoneans the quarrel between the Pharisees and Sadducees was mainly political, and two strong parties, each supported by certain social strata, fought for power in the state. Herod put an end to the independent political life of the Jewish community, and henceforward anyone desiring to engage in politics was forced to tread the path of revolution. This road was taken by the "left" wing of the Pharisees, the Zealots, who under Herod split off from the former and founded an independent sect, while the Pharisees themselves gave up interfering in affairs of state and restricted themselves to activity within the walls of the schools. The Sadducees also, whose political power had been broken under the last Hasmoneans by Rome and Herod, now turned their attention to questions of religion and law. The parties appeared again as political forces for the last time during the Jewish war with Rome (66-70 C.E.).[87]

In summary, the Pharisees and the Sadducees held diametrically opposed views on key theological issues.[88] They represent the opposing religious faction in Jesus' ministry and thus play a key role in the scene of the New Testament.

PHARISEES	SADDUCEES
Foreordination	Free will of man
Immortality of Soul Resurrection of Dean Rewards in Future Life	Rejected
Belief in Angels and Demons	Rejected
Recognized Torah and Oral Tradition	Recognized only the Torah

Chapter V

THE SAMARITANS

Chapter V

THE SAMARITANS

". . . for Jews have no dealings with Samaritans" (John 4:9). Why? Who were these mysterious people who were looked down upon as idolaters by the Pharisees, but made an object of Christ's ministry of reconciliation and healing and evangelized by the early Jewish Christians? What were their origins, beliefs, religious practices and Messianic expectations that distinguished them from the Jews of Jesus' day? This chapter identifies some of the problems that must be faced in attempting to answer these questions, discussing the Samaritans from both the traditional Jewish and the Samaritan perspectives. The Samaritans were regarded by Jesus as part of the "lost sheep of the House of Israel" and closer adherents to the Law, in some ways, than were the Jews themselves.

The Jewish people identify the Samaritans as a schismatic sect claiming to be a remnant of the House of Israel, and surviving as a small community in Nablus, site of ancient Shechem, in Samaria, Palestine.[1] Members of this "schismatic sect" are thought to be descendants of the colonists that King Shalmaneser of Assyria brought back from Cutha, Babylon, Hammath, and other places after he had conquered Samaria, and deported the native population in 722 B.C.[2]

The story begins with the first "settlers" bringing their own gods into Samaria and worshiping them according to their own customs. Josephus says:

> . . . they provoked Almighty God to be angry and displeased at them, for a plague seized upon them, by which they were destroyed; and when they found no cure for their miseries, they learned by the oracle that they ought to worship Almighty God as the method for their deliverance. So they sent ambassadors to the king of Assyria, and desired him to send them some of those priests of the Israelites whom he had taken captive. And when he thereupon sent them, and the people were by them taught the laws and the holy worship of God, they worshipped Him in a respectful manner, and the plague ceased immediately; and indeed they continue to make use of the very same customs to this very time . . .

And when they [the Samaritans] see the Jews in prosperity, they pretend that they are changed, and allied to them, and call them kinsmen, as though they were derived from Joseph, and had by that means an original alliance with them: but when they see them falling into a low condition, they say they are in no way related to them, and that Jews have no right to expect any kindness or marks of kindred from them, but they declare that they are sojourners that came from other countries.[3]

The Samaritans, therefore, were regarded by the Jews as a "mixed stock." They were even dubbed *Kuthim*, or men of *Cuthah*, in order to stigmatize them as non-Israelite.[4] John Bright, a leading Old Testament scholar, supports this view as he says, "These foreigners brought their native customs and religion with them and, together with others brought in still later, mingled with the surviving Israelite population. We shall meet their descendants later as the Samaritans."[5]

The Samaritans of today disagree with the preceding view and dismiss it as Jewish folklore. They say that the deportation in 722 B.C. of the native population was neither total nor final, but that the exiles returned to Samaria after fifty-five years. It is the descendants of these native Israelites that they claim to be.

The origin of this people is of the tribe of our lord Joseph (upon whom be peace), who are the descendants of Ephraim and Manasseh. Their priests are of the house of Levi, the descendants of Aaron (upon whom be peace). Once there followed this people some of the other tribes, though now there is none among them who is not from the tribe of our lord Joseph (upon whom be peace), excepting the family of the priesthood, which is of the tribe of Levi, as we have already stated. (Priest Amram Ishak, *The History and Religion of the Samaritans*, A Modern Samaritan Document, p. 5)

According to the Samaritan version the breach with the Judeans goes back to the time of Eli, who took it upon himself to set up an apostate sanctuary to Yahweh at Shiloh, whereas the true "chosen place" prescribed in the law of Moses was Mount Gerizim.

Gerizim the Original Holy Place—Now the causes of their separation from the remnant of the tribes of Israel and the causes of their attachment to the faith which they now have and which differs in many points from the faith of the Jews are many. The principal cause happened during the life of Eli, the priest, who lived in the year 280 of the entrance of the children of Israel into the land of Canaan. For when the children of Israel (according to the chronicles with the Samaritan people) entered the holy land, their high priest was the wise Eliazar the son of Aaron (upon whom be peace). His place of dwelling was in Gerizim, where he served in the tabernacle, which was built in the wilderness, according to the commandments of the Truth (may He be extolled), and according to the plan of our lord Moses (upon whom be peace), as it was given him from Him (may He be extolled). Those who made its vessels were the wise men Bezaleel and Eliab, and other skilled men who joined in with them, as it is narrated in the Holy Torah. (*Hist. and Rel. of Samaritans*, pp. 5-6)

This misinformation regarding the place of worship was later reinforced by the "accursed Ezra," who falsified the sacred text and thereby seduced the people on their return from the Babylonian exile to erect the second temple beside the Judean capital.[6]

The Inventions of Ezra—When Ezra and his people became settled in that land, and had found the people of Joseph were in the best condition so far as fulfilling their religious duties is concerned, many of his people were convinced to turn from their foolish way and to return to their true religion. The Jews had no book in their possession, and they could not read the Torah and they only had the name Israelite, but the majority of them were in ignorance and negligence like illiterate people, for the Torah was lost from among them during the reign of Sorday the king.

And Ezra, seeing these things, began to gather books from the legends and from some chronicles and narratives. He invented things which never occurred, and he wrote them in the Assyrian writing, which is still found in the books of the Jews. He began to gather into books as he thought best, and he gathered narratives of the Israelites, and began to alter according to his judgment. Then he mentioned the people of Samaria whose origin is from the tribe of Joseph and descendants of the tribe of Phinehas, and he called them Samaritans. He said that they were Gotin (Gentiles?). It is recorded in the book of Kings, the seventeenth chapter, and he filled it with many phrases which are refuted by us and which have no truth in them. All of this was because of his hatred of the aforesaid people, whom he called Samaritans. (*Hist. and Rel. of Samaritans*, p. 34)

Landman says that the Samaritans do believe that pagan colonists were brought in by the Assyrian monarchs but feel that they, the true natives, Israelites, should not be confused with them. Along with this view the Samaritans prefer to call themselves *Shamerim*, which means the "observant" rather than *Shomeronim*, meaning "the inhabitants of Samaria."[7]

One of the most recent views is propounded by Coggins, who rejects the earlier assumption that Samaritan origins date to the eighth century B.C. and that the later Samaritans were descendants of the foreigners who were settled in the land by the Assyrian conquerors. He also maintains that "there is nothing in the references to those who remained in the land which would connect them with the Samaritans by way of religious practice or even geography."[8] Coggins argues furthermore against the idea of a sudden event that divided the Jews and Samaritans. He concludes that,

All the evidence suggests that the decisive formative period for Samaritanism was the epoch from the third century B.C. to the beginning of the Christian era; and that it emerged from the matrix of Judaism during this time, with some measure of communication continuing well into the Christian era between Samaritans and various Jewish groups.[9]

If the solution to finding the correct view were a simple matter the Samaritans and Jews would not have continued arguing over their identity throughout the years, and books would not have been written pro and con. There is truth within each view, as well as folklore and plain untruth, but it seems that the ultimate truth lies between the extremes.

Following the fall of Samaria in 722 B.C. the biblical story is confirmed by Assyrian records. These documents show that Sargon, Shalmaneser's successor, completed the siege that effected the exchange of the races in question. These documents also show that the colonization mentioned in II Kings 17:24 really took place over several years and of course under different rulers. The Hamathites were probably brought to Samaria only after Sargon had stopped a revolt in that city in 721 B.C., in which the Samaritans had openly participated and which they had supported. The Assyrian documents also show that the introduction of Babylonians and Cutheans is assigned to Ashurbanipal rather than to Shalmaneser, for it could have been an act of retribution by Ashurbanipal for their share in the civil war raised by his rival Shamashsumukim.[10]

The fact that the biblical account is confirmed by the documents does not prove that the Jews are right in regarding the Samaritans as merely offspring of the colonists rather than as true descendants of Israel. The Samaritans have much to support their claim.

To begin with, Sargon himself says that he deported only 27,290 persons, and a count based on a contemporary record in II Kings 15:19 shows that wealthy land owners alone numbered 60,000 at that time.[11] In II Chronicles 34:9 we read of a "remnant of Israel" still residing in Ephraim and Manasseh in the days of Josiah, about one century later. II Kings 24:14 reads: "And he carried away all Jerusalem, and all the princes, and all the mighty men of valour, even 10,000 captives, and all the craftsmen and smiths: none remained, save the poorest sort of the people of the land." Through this we can see that all the influential citizens were driven into exile while the lowliest of the lot were left. We must realize that there is nothing in the Samaritan doctrine that shows any indebtedness to Assyrian ideas, and that the attitude of the Samaritans toward the Jews is a fully visible continuance of the immense hostility between Israel and Judah.[12]

The conclusion seems to be that after the fall of Samaria in 722 B.C., the local population consisted of two distinct peoples living side by side: a) the remnant of the native Israelites, and b) the foreign colonists. For obvious reasons, however, the Jewish version ignores the former and the Samaritan version, the latter.[13]

We now look at some of the beliefs of the Samaritans. Their Creed states, "We believe only in God and in Moses, the son of Amram, His servant, and in His sacred laws, and in the Mount Gerizim and in the day of punishment and reward."[14]

The main tenets of the Samaritans can be seen in six separate concepts. They are as follows:

a) Belief in God

b) Moses, as the supreme apostle of God

c) The Torah, as the only authentic law of God

d) Mount Gerizim, as the chosen place of God

e) The day of Punishments and Rewards

f) The Taheb

A) God exists beyond time and space and transcends a physical body. He is in all things and yet cannot be localized (שותף). He cannot be described; His being is epitomized by the phrase: "I am who I am" (אשר אהיה אהיה) (Exod. 3:14). He created all things and sustains all things. The esteem and respect of the Samaritans is so intense that they avoid using the name of God (Tetragrammaton) and substitute it with Shēma, which means "the Name."[15] The Samaritans express their belief of God in this way.

> God did not bear, and was not born; He has no second, no companion, and is incomparable. He is alone, separate, pristine, eternal, by Himself. God dwells in an isolated state, has no form; there is none like Him; He is matchless, incomparable. He has no place, no bound. Apart in Oneness, having none second to Him in His divine state . . .[16]

B) Moses is considered as "the exalted prophet" (הרם הנבי), "the seal of the prophets" (חותם הנביים), "the apostle" (שליח), and "the choicest of creatures" (הבוראים דמע). He is "the light of the world" and existed before creation, which in fact was created for him (Marqeh 67b). He intercedes for the people and is the prophet foretold in Deuteronomy 18:18.[17] Apparently the Samaritans revere Moses as Christians do Jesus Christ.

C) The Samaritans recognize the Torah as sacred Scripture but reject the Prophets and the Writings. The Samaritans' Torah, however, is different (it was mentioned before that Ezra "invented" parts of the Text). They consider that the Torah was given by God to Moses on Sinai, along with the Ten Commandments which are as follows:

THE TEN COMMANDMENTS—

Samaritans cling faithfully to the Ten Commandments addressed to Moses by God and mentioned in the Torah in Exodus (20th chapter, 1)(Deuteronomy 5th):

1) Recognition of the monotheism of God.

2) Making no false oaths by God.

3) Taking into consideration the importance of the days of the Sabbath in its blessing and holiness.

4) The necessity of avoiding stealing.

5) Respect and homage of the parents.

6) The necessity of avoiding murder.

7) The necessity of avoiding committing adultery.

8) The necessity of avoiding false testimony.

9) The necessity of avoiding having a lust to other's woman.

10) Faith in Gerizim mountain.

(Hasanein Wasef Kahen, *The Samaritans*, A Modern Samaritan Document, p. 14).

They observe the Sabbath and circumcision.

THE SABBATH (SATURDAY)

Every Samaritan prepares to the approach of the Sabbath by executing three essential duties (Lev. 23:3).

1) Performance of bathing.

2) Performance of wearing new and clean clothes.

3) Performance of the prayers required. The prayers are done at that day seven times during Friday's night and Saturday's morning and noon. It is made up of mentioning words of gratifying, exalting, naming, extolling and thanking.

4) Performance of all kinds of worshipment.

ALSO THERE ARE SOME RESTRICTIONS

1) Talking about business and outdoor works is forbidden.

2) Voyaging by sea is forbidden.

3) Strolling and going out in the streets of the town is forbidden.

Samaritans are inspired to have every Saturday off with the fact that God (may He be extolled) went off to full rest in the beginning of the 7th day after He had covered the creation of heavens and earth.

CIRCUMCISION

The Samaritan child is circumcised on the 8th of his birthday, otherwise he should be sentenced to death because his scripture is very strict if even the 8th day happens to fall on Saturday or even for him to be cured from his illness (Gen. 17th chapter, verse 12).

It is permissible for a Muslim to circumcise the Samaritan as long as he is circumcised. (*The Samaritans,* pp. 7,8,19)

In regard to such aspects of the Law, Rabbi Simon Gamaliel comments, "Every command the Samaritans keep, they are more scrupulous in observing than Israel."[18]

D) Mount Gerizim is the special place where God abides on earth; it is the Mount of Blessing. Buttrick says that the Patriarchs are said to be buried upon it, and regular pilgrimages are made to their graves. It was also the scene of Jacob's dream, Noah's altar, and is believed to be the navel of the earth. An addition to the Ten Commandments in Deuteronomy ordains its sanctity.[19]

E) The "day of punishments and rewards" is taken from the Samaritan text of Deuteronomy 32:34,35 which reads: "Is it not stored and sealed up in my treasures, against the day of vengeance and reward?" At that time the deeds of men will be weighed on the scales and angels will prosecute and defend. The text (v. 39) continues, saying that God will cry out, "See now that it is I, even I?" The earth will split open, graves will open and the dead will rise. The righteous will be dressed in clean robes while the wicked are seen in tatters. Following judgment, the former will enter Eden while the wicked will be sent to the fire (Marqeh 189b-191a).

F) The Samaritans believe in the Messiah, who is called the Taheb or "Restorer." He will appear on earth to initiate the new dispensation and to restore the Temple on Gerizim, where he will reinstate the sacrifices. He is expected to live 110 years. Although the exact date of his coming is uncertain, they hold the idea that the earth will dissolve after 6,000 years. The Taheb will announce this event.[20]

Another point of interest is the Samaritan interpretation of historical figures which differs from that of the Jews; for example, Samuel (a Jewish prophet of God) is called by the Samaritans "a sorcerer."

Samuel the Sorcerer—Immediately after that event took place, there came to Shiloh a man from Sophin of the children of Levi by the name Elkanah, from the family of Pahat, of the children of Abisoph, the son of Korah, the son of Ishar, who rebelled against Moses (upon whom be peace), and coveted from him the great highpriesthood to take the place of our lord Aaron (upon whom be peace), and whom, that is Korah, the earth swallowed. This man Elkanah was of his seed, and he was the father of Ishmael, whom the Jews called Samuel. His father brought him to Eli to the tabernacle, and the ancestors of Samuel the son of Elkanah, the son of Nor, the son of Azariah, the son of Haphnia, the son of Tahat, the son of Abiso, the son of Korah, who has been mentioned before. There is a clearer narrative concerning them given in the book of history, but we mention it briefly.

When the aforesaid Samuel grew and became a man Eli took him and taught him whatever he knew, and brought him up according to his plan. And he followed Eli in his ways; because his children know what their fathers knew, for the ways which he trod were very clear to them, and their rebellious conduct became known among the people. And some of his people left him on account of his evil doings, and the doings of his children, who have been already mentioned. Therefore, he was compelled to take this young child in their stead, in order that he might succeed him, because he adopted him as his son. And this Samuel was obedient to Eli, and he was a sorcerer and knew things well, and was of a bright intellect; and he learned science and astrology through Abrahmich, the greatest philosopher of those days. His origin was from the land of the Greeks. And the cause of the presence of this sorcerer in this land was that when he heard that a separation had taken place between the tribes of Israel, he took advantage of this, and befriended Eli and Samuel.

And this man Abrahmich began to corrupt and to mislead the children of Israel. He tried to instigate quarrels among them. He did well to some of the children of Israel in order that they might worship his gods. He taught them witchcraft and the production of phenomena. The heart of Eli was indeed stubborn to turn aside from his plan, and behold the result. They learned from him witchcraft and the production of phenomena. Even Samuel claimed prophecy, and they believed his claim. Thus Samuel knew well the purpose of Eli, his master. Therefore, he remained in his service, and obeyed him, and both of them directed their people after their own directions. (*Hist. and Rel. of Samaritans*, pp. 14-16)

In summary, it can be said that the Samaritans believed in monotheism, holding the concept of a unique and powerful God; Moses was an almost Christ-like figure; the Torah alone was considered sacred; Mount Gerizim was the special abode of God on earth; there were rewards and punishments at the end of judgment, and finally the Taheb, or Messiah, will announce the new dispensation.

The Samaritans are seen in the New Testament in contact with Jesus and also in illustration of his teachings. For example, in the parable of the Good Samaritan (Luke 10:25-37) Jesus uses the Samaritan character in contrast to the Jewish characters, as the one who reflected the true attitude of the Law, love for one's neighbor regardless of circumstances. This shows the manner in which Jesus regarded the Samaritans, those hated by his own people.

The account of the healing of the ten lepers, in which the Samaritan alone returned to give thanks to Jesus, shows that they were included in his ministry and treated himn with reverence and respect even to a greater degree than did the Jews.

The account of Jesus and the Samaritan woman (John 4:7-26) is the most detailed story of Jesus' interaction with the Samaritans. The conflict between the Jews and Samaritans is reflected in verse 9, where John comments, "for Jews have no dealings with Samaritans." Certain beliefs are also seen in the woman's words; for example, "our father Jacob" (v. 12) and "the place of worship" (v. 20), and in her belief that the Messiah was coming (v 25). The story concludes with the Samaritans' reception of Jesus as Saviour (v. 42).

In the early church the Samaritans again appear. Jesus includes them in the plan for evangelization: "Ye shall be my witnesses both in Jerusalem, and in all Judea and Samaria, even to the remotest part of the earth." Acts, chapter 8, tells of the ministry of Philip, Peter and John in Samaria and later Luke speaks of the churches there enjoying peace (Acts 9:31). Therefore, though the conflict between the Jews and Samaritans is reflected in the New Testament, these people do appear in a positive light in the ministries of Jesus and the apostles.

Chapter VI

THE ESSENES

Chapter VI

THE ESSENES

The Essenes were another religious sect of Judaism at the time of Jesus. Though they are not mentioned in the New Testament, they are important to an understanding of the religious atmosphere in Jesus' time.

There are four major ancient sources for our knowledge of the Essenes. The most extensive is Flavius Josephus who describes them at some length after having actually spent some time with them. The fullest description of them is in Josephus' *Jewish Wars* (written a few years after 70 A.D.), but they are also mentioned more briefly in the *Antiquities* book xiii. (written about 20-30 years after the *Wars*). F. F. Bruce points out, however, that Josephus must be read with some reserve and "as his 'close familiarity' with the Essenes was wedged in along with his other experiences between his sixteenth and nineteenth years (c. A.D.53-56) it does not appear to have been very extended."[1] Also, it must be remembered that Josephus was writing for a Gentile audience, and so it appears that he describes the sects as Greek philosophical schools. For the most part, though, Josephus' account is "factual and reliable."[2]

Another quite lengthy account of the Essenes is found in Philo's *Every Good Man is Free*, and a shorter account in his *Hypothetica* (an apology for the Jews). Since both accounts were written between 20 B.C.-50 A.D. these are some of the earliest records existing.

Pliny has left us a valuable paragraph about the Essenes in his *Natural History* (v. 73) written about 73 (the year that Masada fell) and 79 (Pliny's death) in the eruption of Vesuvius. Pliny's account is especially significant because it gives us some indication of where the Essenes lived and is important for the debate about whether the Essenes were the sect which lived at Khirbet Qumran. Although Pliny tends to exaggerate (he writes for instance, that the Essenes have existed for "thousands of generations"), his locations of the cities, etc. seem to be quite accurate.

The fourth source which exists is Hippolytus, *Refutation of All Heresies,* book 9 (written in the early years of the third century). Although he presents the Essenes as an heretical sect he does make some contributions to our knowledge of them not paralleled in his predecessors."[3] His account follows Josephus quite closely, but his additions are quite significant.

Until recently, scholars have depended on these ancient writers from outside the sect itself for descriptions. Now, a body of Essene literature has been found so that the Essenes can be seen from within. These are the Dead Sea Scrolls. The only problem is that there is no *absolute* evidence to substantiate whether the Qumran sect was the Essenes. Yadin, in his *Message of the Scrolls*, p. 185, does make the conclusion: "Either the sect of the Scrolls is none other than the Essenes themselves, or it was a sect which resembled the Essenes in almost every respect, its dwelling places, its organization, its customs."

The Essenes were an ascetic sect whose origins can be traced to the early decades of the second century, B.C. They continued in existence until the Jewish war of 66-70 A.D.[4] Their history is uncertain. Philo says that Moses started the order and Josephus states that they existed "ever since the ancient time of the fathers." As mentioned above, Pliny says that their history covers "thousands of generations." Although this is probably an exaggeration, it agrees with the other accounts that the Essenes had existed for a long time. We are certain that they existed since the second century B.C. and lived among Jewish communities. They later settled at Qumran and at scattered communities in Palestine and Syria.[5] The Scrolls indicate that the Essenes have their historical basis in Judaism. Bo Reicke points out that there are some analogies to Persian and Greek dualism, but since these analogies do not extend to terminology or organization, they "should therefore be considered more as formal convergences."[6]

The first documentary evidence for the name "Essene" refers to the time about 144 B.C. Josephus mentions the Sadducees, Pharisees and Essenes in connection with negotiations carried out by the High Council with Rome and Sparta (*Ant.* xiii. 171-73). Bruce suggests that there is a thorny case for the derivation of "Essene" from the Aramaic 'āsyā (healer). This is interesting in view of the fact that it is similar to the "Therapeutai," a pious community of Jews in Egypt mentioned by Philo (*De uita contemplatiua*, 2ff.) as he points to the Essenes to confirm his thesis that "every good man is free."[7] Russell suggests that the word could be derived from the Greek form of the Aramaic word, which is the equivalent of the Hebrew Ḥasidhim.[8] Thus, the origin of the name "Essene" is uncertain.

It is generally agreed, however, that the ancestry of the Essenes is found in the "pious ones" of the Maccabean and pre-Maccabean era which resisted Hellenism and showed a zeal for the Torah.[9] The Scrolls further indicate that

Illus. 5   Flavius Josephus

the sect was associated with the Hasidim of the period around 167 B.C. (see *IQS* i.8). In fact, they may have participated in the Maccabean struggle against Hellenism (*IQM*). However the Essenes began, by the first century B.C. they had become a monastic order of priests and laymen, dedicated to the ritual and fulfillment of the Torah and to an interpretation different from that of the Sadducees and Pharisees.[10]

The best description of the Essenes comes from Josephus (*Wars* ii. 8).

For there are three philosophical sects among the Jews. The followers of the first of whom are the Pharisees; of the second the Sadducees; and the third sect, who pretends to a severer discipline, are called Essens. These last are Jews by birth, and seem to have a greater affection for one another than the other sects have. These Essens reject pleasures as an evil, but esteem continence, and the conquest over our passions, to be virtue. They neglect wedlock, but choose out other persons' children, while they are pliable, and fit for learning; and esteem them to be of their kindred, and form them according to their own manners. They do not absolutely deny the fitness of marriage, and the succession of mankind thereby continued; but they guard against the lascivious behaviour of women, and are persuaded that none of them preserve their fidelity to one man.

These men are despisers of riches, and so very communicative as raises our admiration. Nor is there anyone to be found among them who had more than another; for it is a law among them, that those who come to them must let what they have be common to the whole order—insomuch, that among them all there is no appearance of poverty or excess of riches, but every one's possessions are inter-mingled with every other's possessions; and so there is, as it were, one patrimony among all the brethren. They think that oil is a defilement; and if one of them be anointed without his own approbation, it is wiped off his body; for they think to be sweaty is a good thing, as they do also to be clothed in white garments. They also have stewards appointed to take care of their common affairs, who every one of them have no separate business for any, but what is for the use of them all.

They have no certain city, but many of them dwell in every city; and if any of their sect come from other places, what they have lies open for them, just as if it were their own; and they go into such as they never knew before, as if they had been ever so long acquainted with them. For which reason they carry nothing with them when they travel into remote parts, though still they take their weapons with them, for fear of thieves. Accordingly there is, in every city where they live, one appointed particularly to take care of strangers, and provide garments and other necessaries for them. But the habit and management of their bodies are such as children use who are in fear of their masters. Nor do they allow of the change of garments, or of shoes, till they be first entirely torn to pieces, or worn out by time. Nor do they either buy or sell anything to one another; but every one of them gives what he hath to him that wanteth it, and receives from him again in lieu of it what may be convenient for himself; and although there be no requital made, they are fully allowed to take what they want of whomsoever they please.

And as for their piety towards God, it is very extraordinary; for before sunrising they speak not a word about profane matters, but put up certain prayers which they have received from their forefathers, as if they made a supplication for its rising. After this every one of them are sent away by their curators, to exercise some of those arts wherein they are skilled, in which they labour with great diligence till the fifth hour. After which they assemble themselves together again into one place; and when they have clothed themselves in white veils, they then bathe their bodies in cold water. And after this purification is over, they every one meet together in an apartment of their own, into which it is not permitted to any of another sect to enter; while they go, after a pure manner, into the dining-room, as into a certain holy temple, and quietly set themselves down; upon which the baker lays them loaves in order; the cook also brings a single plate of one sort of food, and sets it before every one for them; but a priest says grace before meat; and it is unlawful for any one to taste of the food before grace be said. The same priest when he hath dined, says grace again after meat; and when they begin and when they end, they praise God, as he that bestows their food upon them; after which they lay aside their [white] garments, and betake themselves to their labours again till the evening; then they return home to supper, after the same manner; and if there be any strangers there, they sit down with them. Nor is there ever any clamour or disturbance to pollute their house, but they give every one leave to speak in their turn; which silence thus kept in their house appears to foreigners like some tremendous mystery; the cause of which is that perpetual sobriety they exercise, and some settled measure of meat and drink that is allotted to them, and that such as is abundantly sufficient for them.

And truly, as for other things, they do nothing but according to the injunctions of their curators; only these two things are done among them at every one's own free will, which are, to assist those that want it, and to shew mercy; for they are permitted of their own accord to afford succour to such as deserve it, when they stand in need of it, and to bestow food on those that are in distress; but they cannot give anything to their kindred without the curators. They dispense their anger after a just manner, and restrain their passion. They are eminent for fidelity, and are the ministers of peace; whatsoever they say also is firmer than an oath; but swearing is avoided by them, and they esteem it worse than perjury; for they say that he who cannot be believed without [swearing by] God, is already condemned. They also take great pains in studying the writings of the ancients, and choose out of them what is most for the advantage of their soul and body; and they inquire after such roots and medicinal stones as may cure their distempers.

But now, if any hath a mind to come over to their sect, he is not immediately admitted, but he is prescribed the same method of living which they use, for a year, while he continues excluded; and they give him a small hatchet, and the forementioned girdle, and the white garment. And when he hath given evidence, during that time, that he can observe their continence, he approaches nearer to their way of living, and is made a partaker of the waters of purification; yet is he not even now admitted to live with them; for after this demonstration of his fortitude, his temper is tried two more years, and if he appear to be worthy, they then admit him into their society. And before he is allowed to touch their common food, he is obliged to take tremendous oaths; that, in the first place, he will exercise piety towards God; and then, that he will observe justice towards all men; and that he will do no harm to any one, either of his own accord, or by the command of others; that he will always hate the wicked, and be assistant to the righteous; that he will ever shew fidelity to all men, and especially to those in authority, he will at no time whatever abuse his authority, nor endeavour to outshine his subjects, either in his garments, or any other finery; that he will be perpetually a lover of truth, and propose to himself to reprove those that tell lies; that he will keep his hands clear from thefts, and his soul from unlawful gains; and that he will neither conceal anything from those of his own sect, nor discover any of their doctrines to others, no, not though any one should compel him so to do at the hazard of his life. Moreover, he swears to communicate their doctrines to no one any otherwise than as he received them himself; that he will abstain from robbery, and will equally preserve the books belonging to their sect, and the names of the angels [or messengers]. These are the oaths by which they secure their proselytes to themselves.

But for those that are caught in any heinous sins, they cast them out of their society; and he who is thus separated from them does often die after a miserable manner; for as he is bound by the oath he has taken, and by the customs he hath been engaged in, he is not at liberty to partake of that food that he meets with elsewhere, but is forced to eat grass, and to famish his body with hunger till he perish; for which reason they receive many of them again when they are at their last gasp, out of compassion to them, as thinking the miseries they have endured till they come to the very brink of death to be a sufficient punishment for the sins they have been guilty of.

But in the judgments they exercise they are most accurate and just; nor do they pass sentence by the votes of a court that is fewer than a hundred. And as to what is once determined by that number, it is unalterable. What they most of all honour, after God himself, is the name of their legislator [Moses]; whom, if any one blaspheme, he is punished capitally. They also think it a good thing to obey their elders, and the major part. Accordingly, if ten of them be sitting together, no one of them will speak while the other nine are against it. They also avoid spitting in the midst of them, or on the right side. Moreover, they are stricter than any other of the Jews in resting from their labours on the seventh day; for they not only get their food ready the day before, that they may not be obliged to kindle a fire on that day, but they will not remove any vessel out of its place, nor go to stool thereon. Nay, on the other days they dig a small pit, a foot deep, with a paddle (which kind of hatchet is given them when they are first admitted among them); and covering themselves round with their garment, that they may not affront the divine rays of light, they ease themselves into that pit, after which they put the earth that was dug out again into the pit; and even this they do only in the more lonely places, which they choose out for this purpose; and although this easement of the body be natural, yet it is a rule with them to wash themselves after it, as if it were a defilement to them.

Now after the time of their preparatory trial is over, they are parted into four classes; and so far are the juniors inferior to the seniors, that if the seniors should be touched by the juniors, they must wash themselves, as if they had intermixed themselves with the company of a foreigner. They are long-lived also; insomuch that many of them live above a hundred years, by means of the simplicity of their diet; nay, as I think, by means of the regular course of life they observe also. They contemn the miseries of life, and are above pain, by the generosity of their mind. And as for death, if it will be for the glory, they esteem it better than living always; and indeed our war with the Romans gave abundant evidences what great souls they had in their trials, wherein, although they were tortured and distorted, burnt and torn to pieces, and went through all kinds of instruments of torment, that they might be forced either to blaspheme their legislator or to eat what was forbidden them, yet could they not be made to do either of them, no, nor once to flatter their tormentors, nor to shed a tear; but they smiled in their very pains, and laughed those to scorn who inflicted the torments upon them, and resigned up their souls with great alacrity, as expecting to receive them again.

For their doctrine is this: — That bodies are corruptible, and that the matter they are made of is not permanent; but that the souls are immortal, and continue for ever; and that they come out of the most subtile air, and are united to their bodies as in prisons, into which they are drawn by a certain natural enticement; but when they are set free from the bonds of the flesh, they then, as released from a long bondage, rejoice and mount upward. And this is like the opinion of the Greeks, that good souls have their habitations beyond the ocean, in a region that is neither oppressed with storms of rain or snow, nor with intense heat, but that this place is such as is refreshed by the gentle breathing of the west wind, that is perpetually blowing from the ocean; while they allot to bad souls a dark and tempestuous den, full of never-ceasing punishments. And indeed the Greeks seem to me to have followed the same notion, when they allot the islands of the blessed to their brave men, whom they call heroes and demi-gods; and to the souls of the wicked, the region of the ungodly, in Hades, where their fables relate that certain persons, such as Sisyphus, and Tantalus, and Ixion, and Tityus, are punished; which is built first on this supposition, that souls are immortal; and thence are those exhortations to virtue, and dehortations from wickedness collected; whereby good men are bettered in the conduct of their life, by the hope they have of reward after death, and whereby the vehement inclinations of bad men to vice are restrained, by the fear and expectation they are in, that although they should lie concealed in this life, they should suffer immortal punishment after death. These are the divine doctrines of the Essens about the soul, which lay an unavoidable bait for such as have once had a taste for their philosophy.

There are also among them who undertake to foretell things to come, by reading the holy books, and using several sorts of purifications, and being perpetually conversant in the discourses of the prophets; and it is but seldom that they miss in their predictions.

Moreover, there is another order of Essens, who agree with the rest as to their way of living, and customs, and laws, but differ from them in the point of marriage, as thinking that by not marrying they cut off the principal part of human life, which is the prospect of succession; nay rather, that if all men should be of the same opinion, the whole race of mankind would fail. However, they try their spouses for three years; and if they find that they have their natural purgations thrice, as trials that they are likely to be fruitful, they then actually marry them. But they do not use to accompany with their wives when they are with child, as a demonstration that they do not marry out of regard to pleasure, but for the sake of posterity. Now the women go into the baths with some of their garments on, as the men do with somewhat girded about them. And these are the customs of this order of Essens.

But then as to the two other orders at first mentioned; the Pharisees are those who are esteemed most skilful in the exact explication of their laws, and introduce the first sect. These ascribe all to fate [or providence] and to God, and yet allow, that to act what is right, or the contrary, is principally in the power of men, although fate does co-operate in every action. They say that all souls are incorruptible; but that the souls of good men are only removed into other bodies — but that the souls of bad men are subject to eternal punishment. But the Sadducees are those that compose the second order, and take away fate entirely, and suppose that God is not concerned in our doing or not doing what is evil; and they say, that to act what is good, or what is evil, is at men's own choice, and that the one or the other belongs to everyone, that they may act as they please. They also take away the belief of the immortal duration of the soul, and the punishments and rewards in Hades. Moreover, the Pharisees are friendly to one another, and are for the exercise of concord and regard for the public. But the behaviour of the Sadducees one towards another is in some degrees wild; and their conversation with those that are of their own party is as barbarous as if they were strangers to them. And this is what I had to say concerning the philosophic sects among the Jews. (Jos., *Wars,* ii. 8).

For differences between the accounts of Philo, Pliny and Hippolytus, (see chart) Hippolytus mentions their intolerance toward Gentiles, especially toward those who spoke of God but were not circumcised. In fact, Hippolytus relates that if a group of Essenes came upon a Gentile speaking of God, they would surround him and force him to be circumcised or be killed. (Hipp. *Ref.* ix. 21). This attitude toward Gentiles caused the Essenes to be sometimes confused with the Zealots or *sicarii*. The Essenes themselves were never called Zealots; their attitude simply caused the confusion.[11] The Essenes were definitely not pacifists, though. This is "further indicated by the appearance of an Essene named John as an energetic commander of the insurgent Jewish forces in the war against Rome."[12]

Most of the practices of the Essenes are clearly described in the above passage from Josephus, but there are a few clarifications which should be made. In reference to Josephus' comment that the Essenes were sun worshipers, the Essenes did not actually worship the sun, itself, as is clear from Philo and Hippolytus. Their worship began at sunrise so that it only appeared that they worshiped the sun as it rose.

Hippolytus gives several examples which illustrate the Essenes' strictness in regard to the Sabbath and the Law. Some Essenes would not handle coins with the Emperor's image because this was against the second commandment (idolatry) (Hipp., *Ref.* ix. 21). The Essenes abstain from *all* work on the Sabbath; some are so strict that they do not even get out of bed on the Sabbath (*Ref.* ix. 25). The *Damascus Document* says that it is unlawful to lift an animal out of a pit on the Sabbath. This was considered extreme even by the Pharisees (cf. Matt. 12:11).

From our sources, it is clear that the Essenes were competent in farming, herding and other occupations. They took no role in politics.[13]

Evidently there were varieties of Essenes; for instance, there were some which forbade marriage and others who allowed it for the sake of childbearing (Jos., *Wars* ii. 8,13). All the groups seem to be characterized by an "ascetic ideal which sought separation from the ritual impurities of the world around them."[14] That there was more than one settlement is clear, for we are told that members of the sect were welcome in any of the Essene colonies. In fact, they went out of their way to help the traveling Essene even to providing clothes as well as provisions (Jos., *Wars* ii. 8,4; Hipp., *Ref.* ix. 20).

The Essenes considered only the Scriptures of Judaism as authoritative. They studied them diligently and often. They were devoted more esoterically to apocalypticism and to a future spiritual deliverance than were the Pharisees or Sadducees. Several apocalyptic books such as Daniel and I Enoch were found in their library. Josephus also regards apocalyptic teaching as typical of the Essenes (Jos., *Bell* ii. 159).

There is some contradiction between Josephus and Hippolytus on the Essenes' doctrine of resurrection. Josephus states "that bodies are corruptible and that the matter they are made of is not permanent; but that the souls are immortal and continue forever'' (Jos., *Wars* ii. 8,11). Hippolytus, on the other hand, states, ''For they confess that the flesh rises again and will be immortal, which soul, when it departs from the body, abides in an airy and well lighted place until judgment'' (Hipp., *Ref.* ix. 27). Bruce suggests that the contradiction may be resolved in the following way. Both Josephus and Hippolytus attest to the Essenes' belief in the immortality of the soul (which is not characteristic of Judaism), but Josephus makes a further concession to Greek thought by implying that the Essenes did not expect a bodily resurrection (it will be remembered that the Greeks did not accept a bodily resurrection). (Jos., *B.J.* ii. 154 ff.).[15] Thus, there is really no contradiction, rather the different purpose and audience is reflected.

In regard to angels, the Essenes (in the Scrolls) believed that ''the 'prince of light' battles against the 'angel of darkness' for control of the universe, and the 'spirit of truth' struggles with the 'spirit of error' for control of the heart of man.''[16] The Essenes were vehemently opposed to idolatry and believed in a life after death (cf. Josephus). It is debatable what the Essenes believed in regard to the Messianic hope. Different versions appear in the Scrolls (see Russell, p. 173). ''But the sect of the Essens affirm that fate governs all things, and that nothing befalls men but what is according to its determination'' (Jos., *Ant.* xiii. 5,9).

The Essenes rejected the temple cultus so revered by the Pharisees and Sadducees. They claimed to represent spiritually the priesthood of Zadok, spoken of by Ezekiel and the Chronicles (Ezek. 40:46; I Chron. 24:6). They saw themselves as an exiled community (under Onias III in 174 B.C.) led by the true Zadokite priests.[17] To become comrades of the true sons of Zadok, the members had to pledge themselves to asceticism, that is, strict obedience to the Law and self-control. These vows and tests were more difficult than those of the Pharisees (Jos. *Wars,* ii., 8,7; IQS. v. 7-24; vi. 13-23; Jos., *Bell* ii. 137-42).

The Essenes were organized like the Pharisees with Scribes in authority; they also lived in previously determined associations. They differed from the Pharisees in that they remained apart from society and sought to realize socially the cultic holiness of the priesthood. Thus, they wore white robes and had their own priesthood.[18] Members formed communities under the supervision of these priests and all goods and property were in common (Jos., *Wars,* ii. 8,3; Philo, *Hypothetica*; Hipp., *Ref.* ix).

Josephus describes several individual Essenes who were significant in history for one reason or another.

The first one mentioned by Josephus is Jonathan (160-143 B.C.) (*Ant.* xiii. 171f.) who lived during the reign of Aristobulus I; he was renowned for his ability to predict the future. It is said that he correctly predicted the day and place of the death of Antigonus, one of the King's brothers (Jos., *B.J.* i. 78ff.).

Simon was also an Essene prophet. He was remembered with others before Archelaus (in 6 A.D.) to interpret a dream. He interpreted it correctly about Archilaus' downfall. Five days later, Archelaus was summoned before Augustus in Rome and banished to Gaul (Jos. *B.J.* ii. 2J; *Ant.* xvii. 346f.).

Manahem was an unusual Essene. This is Josephus' account of his early meeting with Herod:

> Now there was one of these Essens, whose name was Manahem, who had this testimony, that he not only conducted his life after an excellent manner, but had the foreknowledge of future events given him by God also. This man once saw Herod when he was a child, and going to school, and saluted him as king of the Jews; but he, thinking that either he did not know him, or that he was in jest, put him in mind that he was but a private man; but Manahem smiled to himself, and clapped him on his backside with his hand, and said, "However that be, thou wilt be king, and wilt begin thy reign happily, for God finds thee worthy of it; and do thou remember the blows that Manahem hath given thee, as being a signal of the change of thy fortune; and truly this will be the best reasoning for thee, that thou love justice [towards men], and piety towards God, and clemency towards thy citizens; yet do I know how thy whole conduct will be, that thou wilt not be such a one, for thou wilt excell all men in happiness, and obtain an everlasting reputation, but wilt forget piety and righteousness; and these crimes will not be concealed from God at the conclusion of thy life, when thou wilt find that he will be mindful of them and punish thee for them." Now at that time Herod did not at all attend to what Manahem said, as having no hopes of such advancement; but a little afterward, when he was so fortunate as to be advanced to the dignity of king, and was in the height of his dominion, he sent for Manahem, and asked him how long he should reign. Manahem did not tell him the full length of his reign; wherefore, upon that silence of his he asked him further, whether he should reign ten years or not? He replied, "Yes, twenty, nay, thirty years;" but did not assign the just determinate limit of his reign. Herod was satisfied with these replies, and gave Manahem his hand, and dismissed him, and from that time he continued to honour all the Essens. We have thought it proper to relate these facts to our readers, how strange soever they may be, and to declare what hath happened among us, because many of these Essenes have, by their excellent virtue, been thought worthy of his knowledge of divine revelations. (Jos., *Ant.* xv. 10,5).

Now that we have briefly looked at the ancient sources which describe the sect of the Essenes, let us ask the question: What relation does this sect have to the group which lived at the recently discovered Khirbet Qumran?

To answer this question, we must look at Pliny's paragraph which raises the question whether these headquarters may not be identified with Khirbet Qumran—the more so since Pére de Vaux and other archaeologists assure us that there is no other installation west of the Dead Sea which could satisfy Pliny's description.[19]

The Scrolls themselves (especially the Qumran Manual, found at the Qumran Library) show "clear points of agreement with the statements of

Philo and Josephus about the Essenes, and there is no doubt that Qumran and Essenism represent the same movement in different stages of development."[20]

In order to clearly see the relation between the Essenes and the Qumran sect, the following is a summary of Yigael Yadin's description of the sect of the Scrolls. Since we have already looked at Josephus' description of the Essenes, we can easily compare.

> The sect is opposed to the unification of the priesthood and the kingship in one person. It believes that the lay leader should be a descendant of the House of David, and the religious head a descendant of the Sons of Zadok of the House of Aaron.
>
> The sect, following its particular interpretation of the first chapter of Genesis, kept a three hundred and sixty-four day calendar, based on the solar months of thirty days, with an additional four inter-calary days, one after every three months. They could thus obviously not follow the calendar in use in Jerusalem, which was a lunar calendar. As a result their festivals occurred on different days. They could therefore not partake in the holy service in the Temple, where the official calendar was observed.
>
> The deeds and thoughts of the sect were guided by the Law of Moses. They are the most orthodox in adhering to the rules of the Torah, and their interpretation of its laws is far more strict than was customary in Jerusalem at the time. Part of their daily life is devoted to studying the Pentateuch. The sect does not oppose the marriage of its members, but it is quite clear from its writings that their rules of personal status were extremely rigid and the Manual of Discipline even indicates that within the sect itself there were groups of members who refrained from marrying.
>
> Members of the sect attached particular importance to cleanliness of soul and body. This is evidenced in all their writings. They believe that everything has been pre-ordained, and that all creatures are divided into the Lot of Light and the Lot of Darkness . . . The sect, accordingly, had considerably developed beliefs about angels and their part in battle, which may account for the fact that the names of the angels were inscribed on their battle shields.
>
> They place great emphasis on knowledge and wisdom, with whose help they study the phenomena of the world and learn the secrets of creation. The words 'truth,' 'justice' and 'judgment,' which appear often on their standards, represent their principal beliefs.
>
> The sect rejects city life and its members live out of bounds. As far as concerns the members of the Dead Sea area, we know from their writings that they were organized in military fashion, and led a communal life devoid of individual possessions; newcomers swore to give the *Yahad,* or community, their 'wealth, wisdom and strength.' They are divided into groups in order of seniority, and the younger must obey the older. Severe punishments are inflicted on transgressors of all kinds, whether against religious belief or against daily behaviour.
>
> They have special rules for promotion and demotion in seniority. They eat together and follow a ceremonial pattern reminiscent of the ceremonies of sacrifices and offerings, with the priest officiating and uttering a special blessing. They have special functionaries such as supervisors and judges, whose duties are clearly laid down and who must be obeyed . . . They lead a life of modesty and fanatical orthodoxy, and spend their days studying the Bible and interpreting it. They prepare codes and rules for their way of life in the future, and wait patiently for the day of vengeance against all enemies of the Sons of Light. (Yadin, *The Message of the Scrolls,* pp. 173-76)

This description shows clearly the similarity between the Essenes and the sect of the Scrolls. With regard to the discrepancies between the Qumran sect and Philo's account of the Essenes, these differences do not discount their identification since these are also the same discrepancies between Josephus' and Philo's accounts of the Essenes.[21]

Pliny gives us a most significant passage which directly links the Essenes with the Scroll sect:

> On the west side of the Dead Sea but out of range of the noxious exhalations of the coast, is the solitary tribe of the Essenes, which is remarkable beyond all the other tribes in the whole world, as it has no women and has renounced all sexual desire, has no money, and has only palm-trees for company. Day by day the throng of refugees is recruited to an equal number by numerous accessions of persons tired of life and driven thither by the waves of fortune to adopt their manners. Thus through thousands of ages (incredible to relate) a race in which no one is born lives on forever; so prolific for their advantage is other men's weariness of life.
>
> Lying below the Essenes was formerly the town of Engedi, second only to Jerusalem in the fertility of its land and in its groves of palm-trees, but now like Jerusalem a heap of ashes. Next comes Masada, a fortress on a rock, itself also not far from the Dead Sea. This is the limit of Judaea. (Yadin, *The Message of the Scrolls,* p. 185)

This passage is significant for two reasons: 1) Pliny specifies that the Essenes lived on the western shore of the Dead Sea, and 2) his description of Engedi probably refers to the town lying south of the Essene settlement, and then Masada: so Pliny is mentioning the places from north to south.[22]

Yadin concludes that there are two alternatives: "Either the sect of the Scrolls is none other than the Essenes themselves; or it was a sect which resembled the Essenes in almost every respect, its dwelling place, its organization, its customs."[23]

We can now ask the question, what relation do the Essenes have to the New Testament? Because the Essenes are not actually mentioned in the New Testament, some have said that Jesus himself was an Essene in sympathy if not in origin. Renan called Christianity "an Essenism which succeeded on a broad scale," quoted by Pfeiffer, p. 118).[24] E. Schure went so far as to say that Jesus had been initiated into the secret doctrines of the Essenes.[25]

These theories do not hold up in light of Jesus' own teaching and practice. In fact, Jesus was diametrically opposed to the legalism and ascetism of the Essenes. For example, the Essenes considered contact with even their own members defiling; Jesus ate and drank with publicans and sinners (Matt. 11:19, Luke 7:34). The Essenes kept the Sabbath rigorously while Jesus continued to heal and to do good on the Sabbath, declaring that the Sabbath was made for man, not man for the Sabbath (Matt. 12:1-2; Mark 2:23-28; Luke 6:6-11; 14:1-6). The Essenes considered that matter was evil; Jesus said that evil emerges from within a man. The Essenes repudiated Temple worship and sacrifice; Jesus came to the feasts; his disciples, Peter and John, did likewise (Acts 3:1). The Essenes were a monastic, ascetic order which departed from society; Jesus came to the "common people" who "heard him gladly" (Mark 12:37). He was called "wine-bibber," "friend of publicans and sinners" (Luke 7:34).

John the Baptist is closer to the Essenes than is Jesus. He grew up in the desert of Judah and baptized near Qumran. His eschatological preaching was similar to the Essenes in that he emphasized spiritual purity (*IQS.* iii. 4-9; Jos., *Ant.,* xviii. 17). Both John and the Essenes used the passage from Isaiah, "Prepare ye the way of the Lord" (Isa. 40:3; Matt. 3:3, pars; *IQS*, viii. 14). Also baptism was a central feature of Essenism as well as John's ministry. There are several notable differences between John the Baptist and the Essenes. First, they were more isolated than John. John spoke to the crowds (see Mark 1:5: "And all the country of Judea was going out to him, and all the people of Jerusalem..."(NAS); also Matt. 3:5). Secondly, John's baptism was not merely a ritual cleansing as that of the Essenes appears to have been. John's baptism was clearly for the forgiveness of sins and for repentance (Mark 1:4; Matt. 3:6; Luke 3:3, John 1:23).

Menahem, the Essene who met Herod, may be mentioned in the New Testament. Luke mentions a Manaen (Greek spelling of Menahem) among the leaders of the church at Syrian Antioch. He says that this Manaen had been *syntrophos* (foster-brother, classmate or courtier) of Herod the tetrarch (Acts 13:1). "It has been suggested that one of the ways in which the elder Herod honoured the prophet Menahem was by selecting a grandson and namesake of his to be brought up at court as companion to his own son, Antipas, the future tetrarch of Galilee and Peraea."[26] Therefore, we see reflections in Essenism in the New Testament, particularly in the Gospels. They shed light on the religious thought and practices of other groups within Judaism at the time of Jesus.

JOSEPHUS	PHILO
(Wars, ii. viii.)	(Hypothetica)
Jews by birth	persuasion not based on birth
affection for one another	promote brotherly love
reject pleasures as evil	
esteem continence and conquest over passion as virtue	zeal for virtue
neglect wedlock	do not marry
adopt children, form them to their own manners	
guard against lascivious behaviour of women	
despise riches	do not hoard gold or silver
property in common	no private property
regard oil as defilement	
to be clothed in white garments is good	
stewards appointed to take care of common business afairs	
no certain city; dwell in every city	live in many cities of Judea
each place open to traveling members	
take nothing with them except weapons	
one appointed in every city to care for strangers, in regard to clothes, etc.	
do not buy or sell, give to one another	common clothing
piety towards God--very extraordinary	extraordinarily holy
speak nothing before sunrise but certain prayers from forefathers	begin at sunrise
after, they practice particular skill till 5th hour	various occupations
assemble together, clothed in white veils, bathe in cold water	
then they meet together in one apartment	
assemble for dining: loaves,	common meals
priest says grace before and after meal	
they then praise God, take of white clothes and work until evening	end work at sunset
they return to dine again;	
if any strangers, include them.	
everything is done according to injunctions of curators	
2 things are done at everyone's will: 1) to assist those that want it; 2) to show mercy.	

Illus. 6

114

ments on the Essenes by four different authors.

HIPPOLYTUS	PLINY
affection for one another	
observe continence	renounce sexual desire
renounce marriage	
adopt children, bring up in own custom	
distrust women altogether	no women
despise wealth	no money
share with one another common property	
regard oil as pollution	
wear white garments always	
stewards appointed to care for common property	
not a certain city, many dwell in every city; guests and travelers, or members accepted and cared for	
take nothing but arms	
do not buy or sell anything	
always pray at dawn; do not speak before praising God	
work till 5th hour	
assemble together	
bathe in cold water	
common meal	
priest blesses before the eating	
praise God after the meal.	
return to work till afternoon; supper	

JOSEPHUS	PHILO
(Wars, ii. viii.)	(Hypothetica)
they dispense anger and restrain passion eminent for fidelity ministers of peace swearing avoided, but word is as oath study the writings of the ancients inquire after roots and medicinal stones for distempers	not led by passion study diligently
new members are not accepted immediately prescribed same method for one year gradually partakes of rituals finally takes oaths	
those caught in heinous sins cast out of society -these often die in a miserable manner -sometimes taken back before death	

accurate and just in judgments
pass sentence by votes of no less than 100
after God, they honor Moses, their
  legislator
obey their elders
stricter than any other Jews on Sabbath
  resting
	* 3 defining standards: love of God
	  love of virtue, love of man
	
	* abstain from all work on Sabbath

parted into 4 classes seniors cannot be touched by juniors long lives--many over 100 years are above pain do not fear death	

doctrine: bodies are corruptible
souls are immortal, imprisoned in body
soul and body united in air
souls rejoice when set free, go upward
good souls have habitations beyond the
  ocean, gentle breezes,
bad souls go to dark and tempestuous
  den of punishments.	

HIPPOLYTUS	PLINY
abstain from anger and rage	
avoid oaths diligent in the Law and Prophets	
if any transgress, are cast out of the order -perish in fearful fate -sometimes group takes pity	
careful and just in judgment assemble not less than 100 to judge	
abstain from work on Sabbath	
divided into four parts	
long lives--over 100 years endure torture and death before denying beliefs.	
flesh rises again soul is immortal soul abides in airy state	
good souls go to Island of Blessed	
bad souls are punished	

JOSEPHUS	PHILO
(Wars, ii. viii.)	(Hypothetica)
some foretell things to come by	
reading holy books	
purification	
conversant in prophets	
seldom miss in their predictions	
another order of Essenes	
similar to others in customs and laws	
differ on marriage	
marry to carry on human race	
(Antiquities, xviii. ii. 5)	
do not offer sacrifices in the Temple	
excluded from court of Temple	
offer sacrifices themselves.	
course of life better than other men	
addict themselves to husbandry	sowing, planting, herding
4000 men in group	*more than 4000
do not keep servants	*no slaves
(Antiquities, xviii. ii. 9)	
fate governs all things	
	full grown, not
	common care in sickness, etc.
	*avoid the city because of iniquity
	*do not make weapons
	*Every Good Man is Free

HIPPOLYTUS	PLINY
rophecy and foretelling are practiced	

another order of Essenes
  same customs and way of life
  do not reject marriage	

Chapter VII

THE DISCOVERY OF THE DEAD SEA SCROLLS

Chapter VII

THE DISCOVERY OF THE DEAD SEA SCROLLS

In 1947, seven antique rolls of leather were found by two Bedouin shepherds in the Judean wilderness near the northwest shore of the Dead Sea. Several years went by and the scrolls came in contact with many people before their full significance was realized. Their discovery set off further discoveries of manuscripts, most of which occurred in the caves of Wadi Qumran, a gorge through the cliffs bordering the Dead Sea, seven or eight miles south of Jericho. The caves of Wadi Murabba'ât, twelve miles southwest of Qumran, have also produced a number of manuscripts and manuscript fragments. Besides these caves, a place to the south along the Dead Sea known only to the Bedouin, and the ruins of Khirbet Mird (Ancient Hyrcanus), lying inland from Qumran in the west side of the Judean Buqê, have yielded manuscripts and information concerning ancient generations. In the eleven caves of Qumran more than five hundred manuscripts have been found and placed in the museums of Israel. Some are well preserved while others are only mutilated fragments. The largest single cache of manuscripts was found in Cave IV (1952), which yielded tens of thousands of fragments belonging to over 380 manuscripts.[1] Many years lie ahead before the knowledge from these finds will have been assimilated and related to relevant biblical and auxiliary disciplines.[3]

The discovery of these caves captured the attention of the public, and thus many books have been written trying to shed light on the circumstances surrounding the first discovery. The story has been so obscured by time and legend that perhaps the complete truth will never be known, but certain facts have been established through interviews with the Bedouing and the middlemen in the discoveries and the events that followed.

In this chapter our purpose is to sketch the events as they are though to have occurred from the Bedouin discovery of Cave I, through the sale of the first scrolls, to their institution in the Shrine of the Book in Israel. We include the conflicting accounts of these events since so much controversy has arisen concerning them, although the points of conflict will probably never be

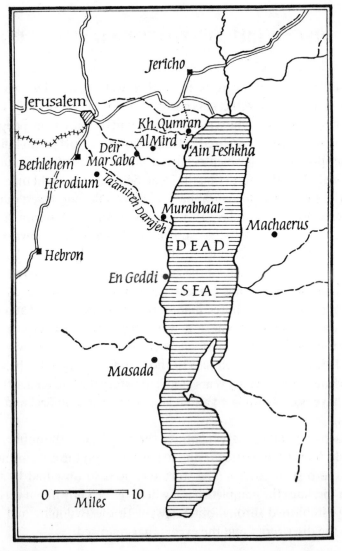

Map 5   The Dead Sea Geographical Area.

Important Dead Sea Scroll Discovery Sites

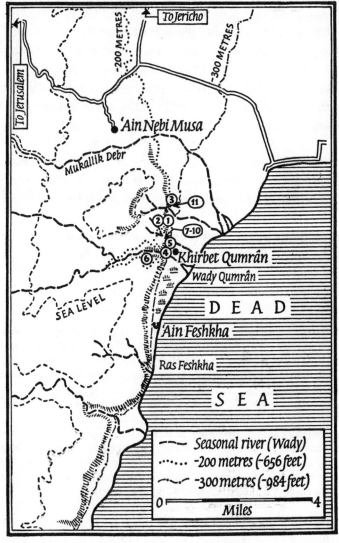

Map 6

resolved. We also mention the further discoveries of Caves II through XI, the ruins of Khirbet Mird, and the finds of the unknown care — our intention here being to present a clear outline of the discovery of the Dead Sea Scrolls.

An ancient discovery of scrolls near the Dead Sea was recorded by Origen (c. A.D.185-254), who mentions that Greek and Hebrew manuscripts were found stored in jars near Jericho. Eusebius quotes him: "The sixth edition, which was found together with other Hebrew and Greek books in a jar near Jericho in the reign of Antonius the son of Severus ... (A.D. 198-217).[3] Also, in about A.D. 800 Timotheus I (the Nestorian Patriarch) wrote to Sergius (the Metropolitan of Elam) describing a discovery of Hebrew manuscripts in a cave near Jericho. It is interesting to note the similarity in the account of this early discovery to the 1947 discovery in Cave I of Qumran; when a Bedouin was searching for his lost dog he entered a cave and found a library containing Biblical and secular books. Possibly these books influ- the theology of the Karaites (a medieval Jewish group who rejected the rab- binical interpretation of the Scriptures). The Jewish writer Kirkisani in a history written in A.D. 937 speaks of a sect of Jews, the al-Maghariya—the "Cave people"—so called because their books had been found in a cave. The Moslem writer Shahrastani dates these people around the middle of the first century B.C.[4] Thus, it is possible that the Dead Sea Scrolls were available to these people.

The following is a description of the Qumran area by J. T. Milik:

A cliff 1,100 feet high towers above the northwestern corner of the Dead Sea; its up- per edge is level with the Mediterranean and marks off the eastern limit of the plateau called the Wilderness of Judea. Its impressive reddish limestone face is honeycombed with countless natural caves, and, at its foot, a terrace of marl spreads out and falls away toward the Dead Sea, 1,292 feet below sea level. Long ages ago, the entire bed of the Jordan valley was covered with water, and the salt deposited at that time makes the soil barren even now. In the spring, however, a little vegetation appears and then the semi-nomad Ta'âmireh tribe brings its sheep and goats down into the valley. They can water the flocks at 'Ain Feshka, a strongly flowing but brackish spring lying to the south of the area. Towards its centre, this area is divided by the course of a seasonal torrent, the Wadi Qumran: a group of ruins on the terrace of marl to its left is called analogously Hirbet Qumran (the word 'hirbeh' means 'ruin').[5]

Dupont-Sommer describes Cave I as follows: "The cave opens onto a nar- row gully; there are two openings; the one, fairly high, acts as a window; the other, almost level with the ground, can only be entered on hands and knees."[6]

It was in this cave, in the spring or summer of 1947, that two Bedouin shepherds of the Ta'âmireh tribe, Mohammed edh Dhib and Ahmed Moham- med, found the first scrolls of the Qumran area. They had been grazing their sheep and goats along the cliffs of the Dead Sea near Qumran when one of the animals strayed. While trying to find it, Mohammed edh Dhib threw a stone into one of the small openings in the cliff face. A shattering sound came from the cave. The boys ran away but later returned, hoping to find buried treasure. In the cave they found eight large jars intact, five on one side and three on the other side of the cave. Some were covered with bowl-like dishes.[7]

G. Lankester Harding in *The Times* (August 9, 1949) describes this find: "Instead, however, of the expected golden treasure they drew forth a number of leather rolls covered in, to them, an unknown writing—had they but known it a treasure far greater than any gold."[8] Seven of the eight jars were empty, and there are varying accounts as to how many scrolls were found on the first visit. Barthelemy and Milik say that only one jar contained scrolls—one large scroll and two small ones.[9]

A variant account of the discovery was given by one of the Bedouin in Arabic to R. S. Khoury of Bethlehem, and it appeared in the *Journal of Near Eastern Studies* in October of 1957.[10] In 1945, this Bedouin entered the cave alone and found the jars. He broke nine of them but they contained only reddish seeds. The tenth jar was sealed with a substance like red clay and contained an inscribed roll of leather. This roll he took with hopes of making sandal-straps. He even gave some pieces of the scroll to his two companions for this purpose. When he arrived home, he put the scroll in a bag and it hung in his room for two years, after which time his uncle took it to an antiquities dealer in Bethlehem to find out its value. This version of the discovery, though agreeing in some points with the other account, is most likely an exaggeration, since Bedouin are noted for their stretched stories. However, the precise details will probably never be known.

The fact has been established, though, that the Bedouin realized the Scrolls' value as curios and took them to Bethlehem, where they tried to sell them to a Muslim antiquities dealer for twenty pounds. When the dealer said the price was too high,[11] the shepherds went to another dealer. This dealer, a member of the Syrian Orthodox Church, thought the documents might be Syriac manuscripts, so he contacted the Syrian Metropolitan of Jerusalem, Mar Athanasius Yeshue Samuel. The Metropolitan recognized the writing as Hebrew and the material as leather or parchment, but he did not know the significance of the Scrolls. He decided to buy them, but he was away when the dealer and the Bedouin came to his house. The Monk who answered the door saw the men with the "dirty rolls" written in Hebrew and, not realizing the situation, sent them away. The Metropolitan eventually contacted the dealer again and, after negotiations, bought four scrolls. He also dispatched monks to explore the cave but they returned empty-handed.[12]

The Metropolitan then began to search for expert opinion on the antiquity and value of the scrolls with the result that an official of the Mandatory

Government Antiquities Department, a member of the École Biblique, the Syrian Patriarch of Antioch, and two officials of the Hebrew University and the Jewish National Library—all failed to recognize the significance of the Scrolls.[13] The Dutch professor, Father J. P. M. van der Ploeg, visited the monastery and examined the Scrolls, but when he returned to the École Biblique, others convinced him it was unreasonable that such ancient manuscripts would still be in existence. Thus, he was persuaded that they were spurious in nature and abandoned any further consideration of them. The Metropolitan also tried to arrange an interview with G. L. Harding, but with no success. He did not give up, however; he continued searching for expert opinion and, with his limited knowledge of the subject, investigated the scrolls for himself. With the help of Jewish journalist Tovia-Wechsler, the Metropolitan identified the large scroll as an Isaiah text with slight divergences from the Masoretic version.[14]

In the meanwhile, Professor E. L. Sukenik, senior archaeologist of the Hebrew University, had returned from the United States (1947). On November 23rd a friend of his, an Armenian antiquities dealer, telephoned Sukenik and told him about an exciting "find" he had to show him. They met at the gateway to Military Zone B in Jerusalem and discussed the matter through the barbed wire separating the two divided parts of Jerusalem. The antiquities dealer told Sukenik about some scrolls that the Bedouin were trying to sell to an Arab dealer in Bethlehem. He said they were found in a cave near Jericho, and the Arab wanted to know if they were genuine. If they were genuine the Armenian friend wanted Sukenik to buy them for the Museum of Jewish Antiquities of the Hebrew University. To Sukenik, the letters of the script resembled those of the period before the Roman destruction in A.D. 70 and he felt that they were not a forgery, but actually genuine. He almost immediately decided to buy the scrolls, but he asked first to be able to see and examine them more thoroughly.[15]

On November 29th, the Armenian dealer took Sukenik to Bethlehem to see the scrolls and to negotiate with the Arab dealer. At this time Israel was in the midst of war between the Jews and Arabs; there was great risk involved for a Jew to go to Arab Bethlehem, but Sukenik did not wait for a more peaceful time. The Arab dealer told his version of the scrolls' discovery, which coincides with the story previously related—that the scrolls were found by a Bedouin looking for his goat. This account states, however, that only a few weeks had elapsed between the discovery and the sale in Bethlehem. As Sukenik examined the scrolls, his excitement mounted; he thought that perhaps the cave had been a "genizah," or book morgue. He later wrote, "It was written in beautiful Hebrew . . . suddenly I had the feeling that I was privileged by destiny to gaze upon a Hebrew scroll which had not been read for more than 2000 years."[16] Sukenik took the scrolls for further investigation, and two days later he was convinced of the originality of the text and of the scrolls' importance for biblical study, so he sent word that he would buy them. On December 1, 1947, he wrote in his diary: "I'm afraid of going too far in thinking about them. It may be that this is one of the greatest finds ever made in Palestine."[17]

A few days later Sukenik told a friend, an official at the Hebrew University, about the scrolls he had purchased. The friend was astonished and told Sukenik that Dr. Magnes had written to the University Library and asked for two officials to come and look at some manuscripts in the Syrian Monastery of St. Mark, in the Old City, that were owned by the Metropolitan Samuel. The officials went and were told by the Metropolitan that the Scrolls had been in one of the monastery libraries near the Dead Sea, and he wanted an opinion on their age and content. He also wanted to know if the University Library was interested in buying them. The official thought the scrolls were not very old and that the texts were in Samaritan. They recommended that a specialist be called in. They called the Monastery later to find out what the Metropolitan had decided, but he was away and could not be reached. Thus, nothing came of the visit.[18]

Until this time, Sukenik had been unaware of the five scrolls that the Metropolitan had purchased for the Syrian Monastery. Now he realized that the Scrolls his friend was telling him about must be from the same group as the ones he himself had purchased, and that they must have been found in the caves, as his had been. Sukenik then went to Dr. Magnes and received authority to visit the Syrian Monastery. In the meantime, he urged the Armenian dealer to get more scrolls from the Bedouin.

At the end of January, 1948, Sukenik received a letter from Jerusalem, saying that he (a member of the Syrian Church) had the Hebrew scrolls for Sukenik to see. Upon seeing the scrolls Sukenik thought one of the manuscripts looked very much like the Book of Isaiah, and he was told that the Metropolitan had bought them from the same Bethlehem dealer from whom his scrolls had been purchased. The dealer had bought them from a Bedouin of the same Ta'âmira tribe. Sukenik then told the Metropolitan he was willing to buy the five scrolls for the Hebrew University, and he took them home for further investigation. He read the scrolls, showed them to Dr. Magnes and his other colleagues and made copies of some of the texts. He could not decide on the price to offer; he wanted to offer 2000 pounds cash but there was no place to secure a loan because of the tension of the war.

On February 6th, 1948, Sukenik returned the Scrolls to the Monastery,

Map 7

A map showing the general area of the discovery of the Dead Sea Scrolls.

planning to meet the following week to decide the price. In the meanwhile, Sukenik had talked to the Bialik Foundation, and Ben-Gurion and the Jewish Agency leaders were so impressed by the fragments from the scroll that they put at Sukenik's disposal any sum that would be necessary. Sukenik anxiously waited for the Syrian letter naming the meeting place and time, but it never came. Later, a letter came saying they had changed their minds—they wanted to wait for peace to find out the market value of the scrolls before they would sell. Sukenik found out later that one of the Syrians, Father Sowmy, had gone to the American School of Oriental Research and had let the Americans photograph the Scrolls. They had assured the priest of far higher prices for the Scrolls after their publication in the United States. Sukenik wrote in his diary: "Thus the Jewish people have lost a precious heritage."[19] He died in 1953 with this belief. Yigael Yadin says in his book (p. 29):

"He (Sukenik) was not to know that the Scrolls were to be restored to the Jewish people and permanently housed in Jerusalem, and that I, his son (Yadin), in the strangest possible way, would have something to do with their acquisition." However, Sukenik did see the first three scrolls that he had acquired published in Jerusalem. They were a compilation of thanksgiving psalms or hymns, an imperfect copy of Isaiah, and "The War of the Sons of Light Against the Sons of Darkness."[20]

The above is the account of the events as seen from Sukenik's point of view. What follows is the view of the American School representing a different side of the problem.

At the time the Metropolitan was searching for an expert opinion on his scrolls, Dr. Burrows, the Director of the American School, had gone to Baghdad and left Dr. Trever and Dr. Brownlee in charge.[21] On February 18, 1948, Father Sowmy telephoned the American School and told Dr. Trever that "while working in the library of the Convent, cataloging the books, he had come upon five scrolls in ancient Hebrew about which their catalogue contained no information."[22] Father Sowmy asked if Dr. Trever would look at the Scrolls. Since the Orthodox Christian garb of the Syrian priests made it safe for them to move around Jerusalem, Father Sowmy and his brother, Ibrahim, brought the Scrolls to the American School. When they arrived, they told Dr. Trever that the former Metropolitan had purchased these documents for the Monastery forty years earlier from Bedouin who had found them in a cave near Ain Feshka, on the northwest shore of the Dead Sea.[23]

Trever describes his first impression of the Scrolls: The first scroll "a very brittle, tightly rolled scroll of cream-colored leather, less than two inches in diameter . . . written in a clear, square Hebrew script, not at all like Archaic Hebrew." The second scroll was 10½" long and 6" in diameter, a thinner, softer leather, more pliable, the same color as the first except with a darkened

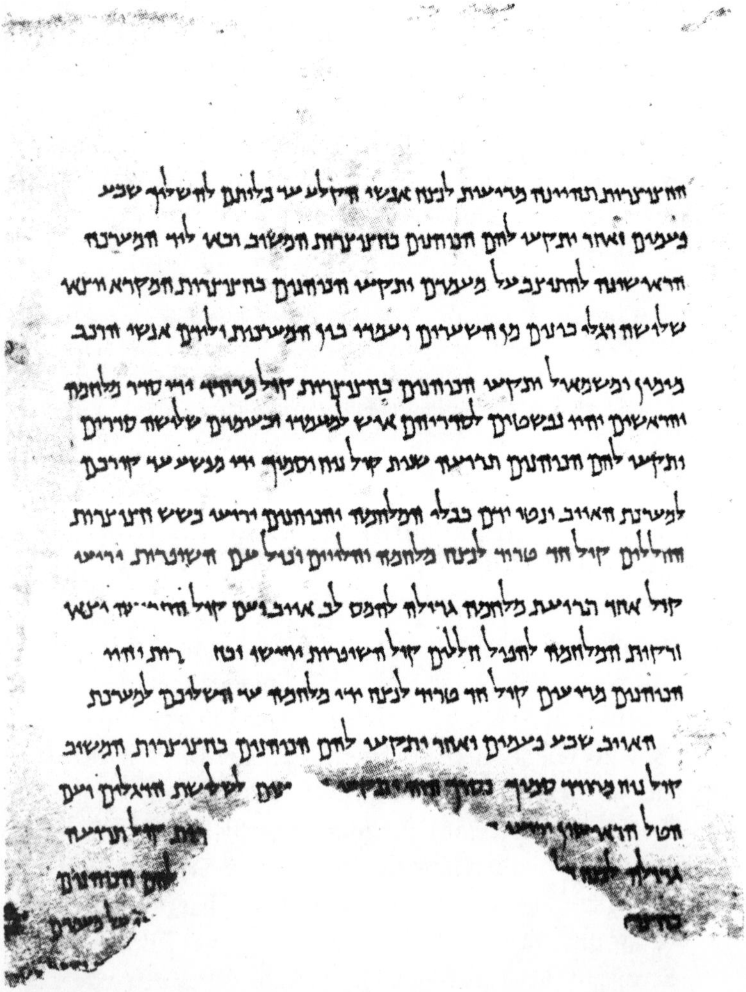

Illus. 7 Scroll of the *Rule of Battle for the Sons of Light:* col. VII
(after Sukenik, *Megolȯth Genûzȯth*, I, plate VIII.

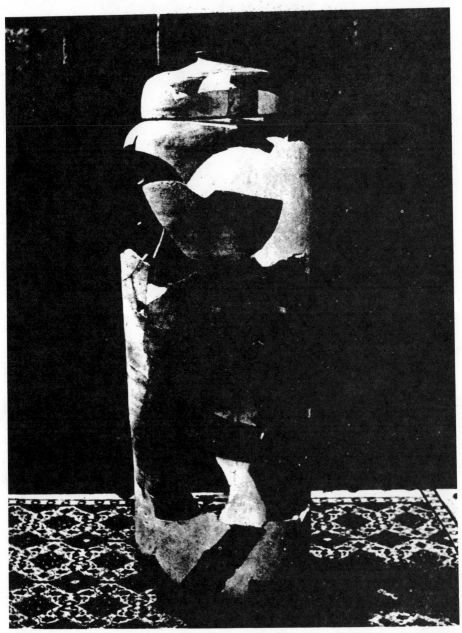

Illus. 8

Scroll Jar from Cave I. Fragments discovered in Cave I were reconstructed at the Palestine Archaeological Museum. Such jars were used for the storage of manuscripts belonging to the Qumran Community. (Courtesy, Zion Research Library.)

133

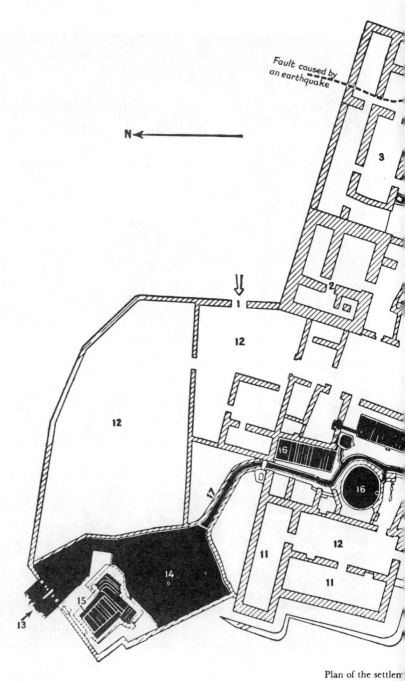

Plan of the settlem

Illus. 9

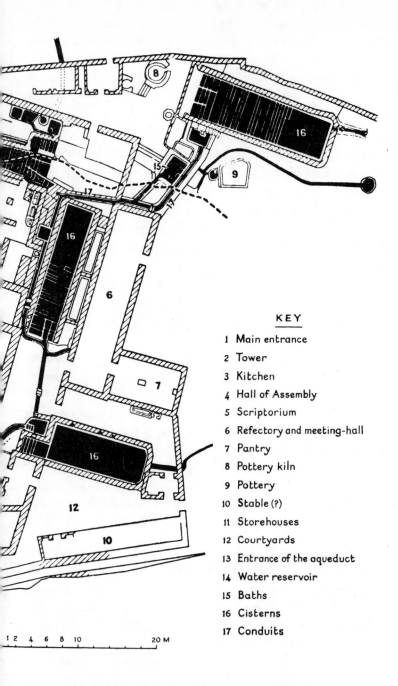

KEY

1 Main entrance
2 Tower
3 Kitchen
4 Hall of Assembly
5 Scriptorium
6 Refectory and meeting-hall
7 Pantry
8 Pottery kiln
9 Pottery
10 Stable (?)
11 Storehouses
12 Courtyards
13 Entrance of the aqueduct
14 Water reservoir
15 Baths
16 Cisterns
17 Conduits

bet Qumran (Essene period).

center. Of the three other scrolls, one was the same size, texture and color as the first; one was narrower, on dark brown leather and inscribed with large clear characters with its lower edge disintegrated; and the third was too brittle to open and in an advanced state of decay. But the script of all of them was extremely puzzling.[24]

As Dr. Trever looked at the scrolls the words of Dr. Burrows came to his mind: "Let your evidence lead you where it will." Dr. Trever was sure it would take time to decipher the evidence before he could pass judgment on the antiquity and value of the scrolls, so he copied a few lines to compare with other ancient manuscripts. That night Dr. Trever found that the copy's words matched Isaiah 65:1 word for word, almost letter for letter: "I am sought of them that asked not for me; I am found of them that sought me not . . ." (Isa. 65:1). Brownlee, in his account, remarks: "But to me, in retrospect, the scroll has said something different: 'I was ready to be sought by those who did not ask for me; I was ready to be found by those who did not seek me.' (RSV) The Scroll had been seeking me, but I had successfully escaped it."[25]

That night Dr. Trever also found that the script was very similar to that of Nash Papyrus, the oldest known existing Hebrew manuscript. The Nash was from the second half of the second century B.C., so Dr. Trever and Dr. Brownlee estimated the Isaiah Scroll to be around the same age or older.[26]

Dr. Trever was now convinced that the Scrolls should be published so they could be studied and debated by scholars. The Metropolitan agreed to let Trever photograph them, and gradually Trever won the confidence of the Syrians so that they left the Scrolls to be photographed at the American School. Trever examined the Isaiah Scroll again and found the evidence of authenticity that he had been looking for—corrections in the margins with a different script and ink. There had also been rips repaired with pieces of leather. He now realized that this scroll was the whole Book of Isaiah.

After photographing the scrolls, Trever sent negatives to Professor W. F. Albright, one of the leading authorities on the subject, and wrote: ". . . it has some indications to show it may be earlier than the Nash Papyrus . . ." And to a friend-colleague, Edgar J. Goodspeed, he wrote: "If Dr. Albright is correct in dating the Nash Papyrus in the second century B.C., then this is as old or older! . . ."[27] At the same time, Trever sent a set of photographs to the Metropolitan. Here there is an unresolved conflict as to what really happened. The Metropolitan says that after he received the photographs, Kiraz asked permission to show the Scrolls to Sukenik (Kiraz was the one who met Sukenik to show him the Scrolls). The Metropolitan suggested that Kiraz take the photographs instead of the Scrolls themselves, but Kiraz said they were not large enough. This disagrees with Sukenik's account that "after copying some of the Isaiah manuscript, he returned the Scrolls to Kiraz on the sixth of February, three weeks before Trever's photographs were finished." This conflict seemingly cannot be resolved.[28]

Dr. Trever also took the photographs and showed them to R. W. Hamilton, Director of Antiquities of the Department of Antiquities, and asked for help in securing more adequate film for more photographs of the manuscripts, but besides giving a few suggestions, Mr. Hamilton was of little help.[29]

Dr. Burrows returned and Dr. Trever told him about the Scrolls, but being a cautious scholar he would not be convinced of their authenticity until he could see more evidence. Dr. Burrows then visited the Monastery and after seeing the fourth scroll, he exclaimed, "This is Aramaic!" The full significance of this realization did not show up until later. Now that Dr. Burrows was becoming convinced of the Scrolls' value, he joined Dr. Trever in trying to persuade the Syrians to let them photograph the Scrolls again. Eventually the Syrians agreed and they told Dr. Trever the true story of the discovery. "We have been keeping something from you, Dr. John [Trever], until we were certain we could trust you. The scrolls have not been in our Monastery for forty years, as I told you. They were purchased last August from some Bedouin who live near Bethlehem."[30]

As mentioned near the beginning of this chapter, several monks had visited the cave but found only fragments of broken jars and piles of fragments and cloth wrappings. Naturally, Drs. Burrow and Trever were shocked to hear this.

Now the subject of an expedition arose, and with it came many problems: To make the expedition, the friendship of the Syrians was necessary, but the Syrians did not want to work in cooperation with the Department of Antiquities. Moreover, the permission of this Department was needed to excavate. Dr. Trever therefore went to Mr. Hamilton and received permission, 1) to go to the cave with the Syrians and photograph everything in sight without disturbing anything; 2) to take any potsherds or other objects on the surface back to the school; and 3) to report back to the Department of Antiquities.[31] But when Trever approached the Metropolitan about the expedition, he was told that the situation in the area was much too dangerous at that time. This shows that the Department of Antiquities was not uninformed about the Scrolls. Actually, Stephan H. Stephan (of the Department) was one of the first to examine the Scrolls, and he appeared skeptical, so he did not report the matter to the Director of the Department. Mr. Wechsler, who was with him, also saw the Scrolls, but was misled by the marginal corrections in one of the manuscripts—the ink was so black that he felt it could not be very ancient. He said, "If that table were a box and you filled it full of pound notes, you couldn't even then measure the value of these scrolls if they are two thousand years old as you say!"[32] He did not realize that he was speaking the truth. Thus, the Department of Antiquities did know about the Scrolls; they just did not realize their significance. This denies the charge made by Mr. Harding that the Metropolitan, Dr. Trever, and others involved simply ignored the Department of Antiquities when they knew that the Scrolls rightfully came under the Department's jurisdiction.[33]

On March 15, Dr. Trever received a letter from Dr. Albright, exclaiming:

> My heartiest congratulations on the greatest manuscript discovery of modern times! There is no doubt in my mind that the script is more archaic than that of the Nash Papyrus . . . I should prefer a date around 100 B.C. . . . What an absolutely incredible find! And there can happily not be the slightest doubt in the world about the genuineness of the manuscript . . .[34]

Dr. Trever felt that the Syrians should now be told about the antiquity and value of the Scrolls and should be urged to let them be taken to a safer place than Jerusalem. At this time, the Metropolitan told Dr. Trever that Dr. Magnes, President of the Hebrew University, wanted to see the Scrolls, and that Dr. Sukenik wanted to buy them. Trever, who did not know the whole background, urged the Metropolitan to tell Dr. Magnes that the Scrolls were already being handled by the American School. This was the reason that Sukenik received the letter saying the Scrolls were no longer for sale. Dr. Trever was, however, able to impress the Metropolitan with the urgency of the Scrolls' need to be taken to a safer place, and soon afterward Father Sowmy left Palestine with them.[35]

On April 11, 1948, the news of the discovery of the Scrolls was released to the American press. Dr. Burrows had written, "The Scrolls were acquired by the Syrian Orthodox Monastery of St. Mark." The press, however, said the Scrolls had been "preserved for many centuries in the library of the Syrian Orthodox Monastery of St. Mark in Jerusalem." No one knows who was responsible for the error.[36]

The announcement of the discovery set off many reactions besides those of joy. Until the article in *Biblical Archaelologists* about the Scrolls came out in May, G. L. Harding had known nothing about the discovery. He had been placed in charge of the explorations in Arab Palestine and Transjordan and was responsible for everything found there. Under Jordanian Law, the Scrolls belonged to the government. Thus, when Sowmy and the Metropolitan exported the Scrolls they broke the law and put Harding in a very bad situation.[37] Harding describes the Metropolitan's decision to take the Scrolls to the United States: "Later he smuggled out of the country the Isaiah Scroll, the *Manual of Discipline,* the *Habakkuk Commentary,* the *Lamech Apocalypse,* some large fragments of Daniel, and eventually took them to the USA with him."[38]

Harding's attitude is understandable, since now the original site could not be located and examined with proper supervision.[39] Yadin smooths over the situation by saying that it was hard for scholars to keep in touch because of the tensions arising from the state of the Palestinian war.[40] But it was not that simple: the government of Jordan threatened to punish the Metropolitan unless he returned the Scrolls. In response the Metropolitan answered that when the Scrolls were exported the British Mandate had expired, and therefore there was no established legal body to regulate and enforce procedures. The Metropolitan also told the Jordanian government that the money from the sale of his Scrolls would go for "the expansion of religious and educational facilities in the Syrian Orthodox Church."[41]

In January, 1949, three of the four Scrolls were edited by Burrows and published by the American School. The fourth Scroll could not be unrolled. The Scrolls' publication did not increase their monetary value as Trever had thought. On the contrary, their value decreased and none of the American institutions would buy the Scrolls because of the legal problems involved.[42] Finally, in desperation, the Metropolitan advertised the Scrolls in the *Wall Street Journal* under "Miscellaneous Items." Dr. Yigael Yadin, in the United States on a lecture tour, saw the ad and after complicated negotiations with the Metropolitan bought the four scrolls for Israel for $250,000.[43] On February 13, 1955, Premier Sharett announced that the Dead Sea Scrolls were now owned by the State of Israel and the Government planned to erect a special museum for these and the other manuscripts that Professor Sukenik had given to the Hebrew University in 1947.[44] This special house, called the Shrine of the Book, is in the shape of a huge scroll and can be lowered into the ground to preserve the manuscripts in time of war. Eight years had passed, and finally, the Dead Sea Scrolls were under one roof.

Yigael Yadin says,

> Thus ended the adventures of the seven Dead Sea Scrolls, from the moment of their chance discovery by the Bedouin on the shores of the Dead Sea until their return to their home in Jerusalem. There, in the Shrine of the Book which is about to be built, they will be the most prized exhibits in what is intended as a centre for Biblical and scroll research for scholars all over the world.[45]

Discoveries did not end with these Scrolls. Already, Captain Lippens of the Belgian Army had taken a great interest in the cave in which the Scrolls were supposedly found, and with an Arab legion of soldiers had searched for three days in the Qumran area for it. This set off a series of systematic excavations in the area: On February 15, 1949, Harding and Père de Vaux led an expedition, but several non-professional excavators also began "some barbaric and illegal digging."[46] When Harding and Père de Vaux began investigating Cave I, they found what these illegal excavations had left behind—shards, cloth, and leather. The cave was filled with fine powdery grey dust and stones for a depth of about fifty centimeters, and the work had to be done with tools such as penknives, brushes, tweezers and fingers because of the "delicacy of the fragments." Harding relates that each day the excavators would put the new found fragments under glass for observation.[47] Harding also found linen wrappings and broken jars corresponding to those that had housed the original Scrolls, but the tribesmen had already removed many of the manuscripts or fragments. Dupont-Sommer says that altogether there were fifty jars found in Cave I, and four to five scrolls could have been in each jar, so there must have been 200-250 scrolls in this library at one time.[48] Harding says, however, that this idea is "no longer tenable" because similar pottery not housing scrolls had been found in the settlement at Qumran. The number of different books represented by the fragments is the only evidence for the possible quantity of scrolls. About seventy-five books are represented. The cause of the scrolls' removal from the jars, or the reason for their damage is unknown.[49]

The locations and contents of Cave I linked it to the ruins of Khirbet Qumran, the ancient community center of a monastic order whose identity is still controversial. These ruins, located nine miles southeast of Jericho, were identified in the nineteenth century as the site of biblical Gomorrah, but this idea was corrected in the twentieth century by Dalman, who identified them as signs of Roman existence.[50] E. de Saulcy says that the name Qumran, as pronounced by the Bedouin, sounds something like Gomorrah, and thus some European explorers identified it with Gomorrah. This is impossible, however, since Gomorrah was not located in this vicinity.[51]

From 1951-1956, these monastic ruins were systematically investigated by a team of archaeologists. In Byzantine writings, this monastery was called Castellion or Marda, both of which are Aramaic terms and mean "fortress"; it was built over the site of the ancient Hasmonean fortress, Hyrcanian.[52] In its underground chamber, the archaeologists found a library of manuscripts—Arabic, Greek, Christian, and Palestinian-Aramaic, dating from the end of the Byzantine period to the beginning of the Arab period.[53] They also found there a jar similar to the ones at the Qumran cave that definitely links the people who inhabited the Qumran settlement to those who owned the scrolls found in the Qumran caves.[54] Evidence was also found establishing the fact that the material must have been put in the caves in the first century A.D.[55]

Although many of the archaeologists digging in the Qumran area held the view that Cave I was the only one of its kind, the tribesmen continued searching. In November, 1951, some documents turned up for sale at École BibliqueBiblique—the Bedouin had been successful.[56] This cave was eleven miles south of Cave I, in Wadi Murabba'at. Closer investigation revealed three more caves near the summit. Three months later an official party visited these caves and found thirty-four Bedouin engaged in clandestine excavation.

Some of the tribesmen were hired by the archaeologists, and the excavation continued.[57] There were hazards involved in these caves: erosion had caused great crevices in the floors, the dust created added inconvenience, and the roofs were quite insecure because of a partial rock fall.[58] The investigation yielded several important discoveries of pottery, coins, and papyrus, including one of the earliest papyri in Hebrew (from the seventh century B.C.), Greek, Aramaic and Hebrew documents from a cache belonging to Bar-Kokba (late first and early second centuries A.D.), and a scroll of the minor prophets (second century A.D.).[59] Evidence of five distinct periods of human occupation was revealed: 1) Chalcolithic period (c. 4500-3000 B.C.), 2) Middle Bronze Age (c. 1700-1550 B.C.), 3) Iron Age (eighth-seventh century B.C.), 4) Roman period, and 5) the Arab occupation.[60]

In the meantime, while scientists explored the caves of Wadi Murabba'ât, the Bedouin began searching in the area of the original discovery, and they were not disappointed. In a cave near Cave I they found some fragments (1952). The archaeologists came running, and very soon many archaeological schools mounted expeditions to explore all of the caves north and south of Khirbet, an area of five miles.[61] Dr. W. L. Reed and Père de Vaux led an expedition in the vicinity of Wadi Qumran and located Cave II south of Cave I, and Cave III, north of Cave I.[62] These finds were not made without difficulties—the team had made two hundred unsuccessful soundings amongst the crevices and areas from Hajar el-'Asba' to Ras Feshka, a distance of six miles. In forty locations, they found pottery, fragments, lamps, utensils, jars, and two tiny fragments. The manuscript fragments from Cave II had already been sold by the Bedouin, and Cave III was in a bad state since its roof had collapsed. However, Cave III housed the two copper scrolls,[63] which contained directions for finding the buried treasure of the Essene Monastery.

By the end of March (they had begun in February), the heat, malaria, and fatigue brought the expedition to a halt. The archaeologists had explored the caves of the limestone cliffs, but had ignored the artificial caves and clefts in the marl terrace at the foot of the cliffs. When the expedition ended, the Bedouin carried on in the marl terrace around Khirbet Qumran.[64] One evening in September, 1952, the Bedouin were discussing their recent finds. One of the older men told a story of chasing a partridge into a hole near the ruins of Khirbet Qumran. He found the partridge in a cave, and while he was there he collected a terra-cotta lamp and some potsherds. The young Bedouin took careful note of the topographical details of the old man's tale, took a bag of flour, ropes, and primitive lamps, and went to Qumran. They found the cave, investigated, and found thousands of manuscript fragments.[65] Later they took them to various archaeological schools, giving false clues as to where they were found. Eventually, the archaeologists found the cave—Cave IV, the "main lode," which was almost as important as Cave I.[66] Harding and de

Vaux explored carefully and found fragments of more than one hundred manuscripts, some matted and decayed beneath the floor. During the excavation, Cave V was found by scientists in the marl north of Cave IV, and Cave VI was found near the waterfall of Wadi Qumran by the Bedouin. Both caves held minor but significant finds.[67]

In the summer of 1952 a series of manuscript discoveries in the wilderness remote from Qumran took place. The most significant of these were found by the Bedouin in an unknown site south of Murabba'ât in one of the wadis emptying into the Dead Sea. These documents appeared in Jerusalem in 1952. Most of them are from the era of the Jewish revolts against Rome; the most important item is the Greek minor prophets representing a lost recension of the Septuagint, from the third to the second century B.C. This find was most helpful to textual critics.[68]

Quiet settled on the Qumran area for about three years, except for the excavations at Khirbet Qumran. Then in 1955, during a "campaign" at Qumran, four more caves were discovered, Caves VII, VIII, IX, and X, in the marl. However, they had collapsed from erosion and produced only a handful of fragments. The others must have been washed away by the torrents that rushed down the gorge.[69] A little later, Cave XI, located near Cave III, north of Cave I, was found and excavated by the Bedouin. It contained several scrolls, excellently preserved: 1) the Psalter, 2) two copies of Daniel, and 3) part of Leviticus.[70] Cross mentions that not since the discovery of Cave I had the Bedouin broken pieces off the manuscripts; rather, they realized and appreciated the value of this material and worked patiently, skillfully, and gently with the documents.[71]

These scrolls of Caves I-XI have had a most suspenseful and exciting discovery, and are of priceless value to biblical and archaeological scholars. One of the main questions remaining is, who were the people who put these scrolls into these caves, and why did they put them there? It is doubtful that we will ever know the answers with certainty, but there are several theories based on existing evidence found in the caves. After excavating Khirbet Qumran, Professor Pfeiffer says it is evident that the people who lived in these caves and whose activities went on in the community center were those who hid the scrolls when they saw their community about to be destroyed by the Roman legion. (There is evidence in Khirbet Qumran of Roman occupation after A.D. 68.)[72] Harding agrees with this and adds that the charred ruins of Khirbet Qumran prove its destruction by violent means, after which it was never rebuilt.[73]

These discoveries shed light on the scene of the New Testament: Its people, their beliefs, and reactions to the political and religious situation. So discoveries continue, and translations and publications are increasingly produced, casting more light on the ancient past.[74]There is no way of knowing what information may still be buried in the remote wilderness of Judea.

Chapter VIII

MESSIANIC EXPECTATIONS

Chapter VIII

MESSIANIC EXPECTATIONS

The political and religious tensions before the time of Jesus created the longing for a Messiah figure. Several types of Messianic expectations existed in Judea, including the political figure and the prophet figure. These expectations were a part of the scene into which the true Messiah was born.

The Political Messiah

The Greek word χριστος (from χριω, to anoint), is a translation of the Hebrew *Mashiah,* in Aramaic, *Meshiha,* from which the Greek form *Messias* is derived). In the Talmud, it appears sometimes without the article as a proper name (Aramaic מְשִׁיחַ), sometimes with the article (Aramaic מְשִׁיחָא). Besides its use in Rabbinic literature, this word is used in Baruch 29:3; 30:1; II Esdras 12:32 (lat. Syr. Armen. Text); Enoch 7:28; Ar. 2: Slavonic Josephus *B.J.* 1 364. "Messiah" means "anointed" (with oil).[1] Anointing with oil had a special significance—it was thought to symbolize the transition of the person or object to a sanctified status. In the Old Testament, kings (foreign and Israelite) and high priests are described by this word. "The Anointed" denoted a special relationship with God.[2] Saul, the King of Israel, is called "the Lord's anointed." (I Sam. 24:7; Heb. 24:6-Eng.).

The title or name "Messiah" in later Judaism denoted an eschatological figure. As a king of the final age, the founder of a glorious kingdom, "Messiah" does not occur in the Old Testament; it first appears in the literature of later Judaism. It does occur, however, in the Old Testament as the religious title for the reigning king in Israel. Thus, the historical association of ideas indicates that the eschatological messiah has political significance: He will restore Israel, conquer other nations, rule over Israel as king.[3]

MOSAIC AND DAVIDIC INFLUENCES

"The political part of the belief in the Messiah took place in ancient times during periods of trouble and distress precisely because it proclaimed . . .comfort and hope that political freedom would return to the Jewish people."[4] "The people of Israel did not have a *glorious past*, hence it was forced to direct its gaze toward a *glorious future*. It longed for a . . . redeemer and savior."[5]

Klausner traces the idea as beginning with Moses, who not only redeemed Israel from her material troubles and political servitude, but also from her ignorance and spiritual bondage. He became the symbol of the redeemer.[6] A quote from the authors of the Talmud and Midrash show how closely the future Messiah is to compare with Moses:

> ...just as Moses brought redemption to his people, so also will Messiah bring redemption; just as Moses was brought up in the house of Pharaoh among the enemies of his people, so also will Messiah dwell in the city of Rome, among the destroyers of his land; just as Moses, after revealing himself to his brethren in Egypt and announcing to them that deliverance was near, was forced to go into hiding for a time, so also will Messiah be forced to hide himself after the first revelations; just as Moses crossed from Midian to Egypt riding on an ass (Exod. 4:20), so also will Messiah come riding on an ass; just as Moses caused manna to rain from the sky, so will Messiah bring forth different kinds of food in a miraculous way; and just as Moses gave to the children of Israel wells and springs of water in the wilderness, so also will Messiah make streams of water flow in the desert.[7]

The Mosiac concept of the Messiah was just one aspect of the expected redeemer. Israel also developed a King-Messiah ideal, although this concept was modified by Israel's own beliefs. The official Israelite conception of the king was that he was a superhuman, divine being; an "elohim," a powerful, superhuman being; a god.[8]

It was believed that when the king was anointed he was endowed with the divine Spirit and filled with superhuman power and wisdom. The anointing signified Yahweh's "choice" of him to be king over the people.[9] This sacramental act, which more than anything else linked the king with Yahweh, was probably practiced by the Canaanites, and also among the Egyptians and Babylonians.[10]

> When, in Ps. 2:7 Yahweh says to the king on the day of his anointing and installation, "You are My Son; *I* have begotten you today", He is using the ordinary formula of adoption, indicating that the sonship rests on Yahweh's adoption of the king. The act of adoption is identical with the anointing and installation.[11]

> The true king judges Yahweh's people with justice, relieves the oppressed, the helpless, and the unprotected, gives justice to the widow and the fatherless, protects them from the oppression of the wicked, and avenges them when their rights have been violated and their blood shed. . . .The righteous king also conveys good fortune.[12]

David was thought to have been such a king. It is emphasized that it was a "warrior chosen from among the people" that Yahweh exalted when he made David king (Ps. 89:20). He was considered the true "prototype" of the Messiah. His political prowess in unifying all the tribes of Israel, his courage in battle, his defeat of Israel's enemies, made him the "greatest political savior" in the eyes of Israel. Also, in spite of accounts of his human weakness, he was considered spiritually ideal.[13] The Messiah came to be known as "Son of David," and was expected to set up an earthly kingdom which would even exceed that of David.[14] Thus these two great "saviors" of Israel, Moses and David, influenced the people's concept of a future deliverer.

THE MESSIAH IN THE QUMRAN LITERATURE

The Qumran sect expected two types of Messiah:

1. The Priestly Messiah, the Teacher of Righteousness, Interpreter of the Law: These names were also used to refer to their own priestly founder, thus the idea originated that they are one and the same.[15]

2. The Qumran sect also expected an Anointed One, a prince of the line of David. In the *Manual of Discipline* both the Messiah of Israel and the High Priest are mentioned. This Davidic Messiah is a war leader, and a judge.[16] In the *Manual of Discipline*, he is described:

> He will renew for Him the Covenant of the Community (charging him) to establish the kingdom of His people for[ever, to judge the poor justly, and] to reprove with e[quity the hum]ble of the land, to walk before him in perfection, and in the ways of [. . .] and to restore his[hol] alliance [in] the time of distress with all those who seek [Him. May] the Lord li[ft th]ee up to an everlasting height like a fortified tower on a high wall, that thou [mightest smite the peoples] with the might of thy [mouth], with thy sceptre devastate the land, and with the breath of thy lips kill the wick[ed, armed with the spirit of coun]sel and everlasting might, the spirit of knowledge, and the fear of God. And righteousness shall be the girdle [f thy loins, and fai]th the belt of thy reins. [And] may he make thy horns of iron and thy hooves of brass to gore like a young bu[ll . . . and tread down the peop]les like the mire of the streets. For God has established thee as a sceptre over rulers. Bef[ore thee shall they come and do obeisance, and all the na]tions will serve thee, and by His holy name He will strengthen thee. And thou shalt be like a l[ion . . .] prey with none to resto[re], and thy [mess]engers will spread over the face of the earth . . .[17]

The study of the Messianic expectation in Qumran is not without problems. There is a great debate over whether there are one, two or three messiahs.[18] In the *Manual of Discipline,* two messiahs are expected, "*The Messiahs of Aaron and Israel*" (*IQS* 9:11). The *Testament of the Twelve Patriarchs* and the *Role of the Congregation* also refer to two messiahs.[19] *The Damascus Document*, however, in three places refers to one Messiah rather than two, "The Messiah of Aaron and Israel" (CD 19:11; 20:1; 12:21). A later finding of *The Damascus Document* in Cave IV which also had the singular reading confirmed the problem.[20] Should a slight emendation be made which would make the singular plural, or should the phrase "The Messiah of Aaron and Israel" be understood in the sense of "The Messiah of Aaron and the Messiah of Israel," or should the plural be understood in the light of the singular reference? It is not within the scope of this study to even survey the many varied solutions to the problem.[21] Some scholars see references to three messiahs: messianic king, messianic priest, and messianic prophet.[22]

There is also the question of whether the Messiah is eschatological or whether the word *messiah* is simply a common noun for "anointed one." LaSor has looked at all the references in Qumran literature and located the word *masiah* or some modification of it in the *Manual of Discipline (IQS)* and in *The Damascus Document* (CD), and in two fragments from Cave IV. (CD 2:12; 6:1; 7:21; 20:1; 13:21; *IQS* 9:11; IQ28[a]; 2:12, 14, 20; IQ30 1:2).[23] His conclusions from this study were that "anointed one/ones" (CD 2:12; 6:1; *IQS 9:11)*

> . . . may refer to the prophets or other persons of the present or past, and therefore need not necessarily refer to a future (whether imminent or remote) eschatological figure.[24]

> On the other hand, the references in CD 9:10; 20:1 and 12:23,24 seem quite definitely to be related to an eschatological figure.[25]

Thus from this evidence, LaSor concludes that the word "messiah" in the Qumran writings "partakes more of the nature of a common noun ("anointed one"). There is no clear evidence that any specific personage was known as "the Messiah."[26]

From this brief discussion of the Qumran literature, it is evident that opinions are varied regarding the presentation of the messianic expectation whether there are one, two, or three messiahs; whether or not the messiah is an eschatological figure or simply a common noun for "anointed one." It is clear, however, that it was thought that the messiah either included two aspects—priest and king—or that two separate persons would come, priest and king. Both, however, have significance for the restoration of Israel as a nation.

THE CONCEPT AT THE TIME OF JESUS

There were two concepts of the Messiah which were not consciously distinguished. "One was the national, political, this-worldly [concept], with particularistic tendencies, though universalistic at its best. The other was a super-terrestrial, other-worldly [concept] rich in religious content and mythological concepts, universalistic, numinous, at home in the sphere of 'Holy' and the 'wholly other'."[27]

The expectation of an earthly kingship developed more fully during the Babylonian exile when the throne of David no longer existed, and the Jews were forced to postpone the promise to a distant future. It became more active under the rule of Greece as Jewish nationalism developed, and the expectation of a political warrior emerged.[28] This concept of Messiah (political, national warrior) prevailed at the time of Jesus.

The older, nationalistic future hope prevailed among the masses because it appealed to the economic, social and political pressures, whereas the other-worldly concept was current in certain literary circles, among the learned, religious sects.[29] That the Messiah was regarded as an earthly figure is evident by the accounts of several people being proclaimed as such. For example, Zerubbabel was proclaimed king of the restoration by Zechariah and Haggai; Simon, during the Hasmonean rule, was considered the Messiah (I Macc. 14: 4ff.); the false messiahs, mentioned by Josephus, were called brigands, rioters, and saboteurs.[30] Hezekiah, the "robber-chief," so called by Josephus, was called "messiah" by R. Hillel. Other messiahs mentioned by Josephus are Hezekiah's son Judas the Galilean from Gamala, and his brother, Menahem ben Hezekiah, the unnamed Jew who appeared during the rule of Festus and took his followers into the wilderness where they were massacred by the Romans (Jos., *Ant.* xvii. 271; *B.J.* ii. 118, 433ff.; *Ant.* xx. 97f.; Acts 5,36; *Ant.* xxi. 38; Jos., *Ant.* xx. 169ff., 188; *B.J.* ii. 266ff.), and Simon bar Kochba, "Son of a Star" who claimed to be the "star out of Jacob." Rabbi Akiba called him Messiah.[31] This king or Messiah also appeared among the Samaritans (Jos., *Ant.* xviii. 85f.). From the above, it is evident that the people generally expected an earthly, political man.

Work of the Messiah—At the time of Jesus, the mission of the Messiah was the salvation of Israel, i.e., to restore Israel as a people to her former glory, to a leading position among all nations; to free her from enemies and destroy the world powers. This concept was influenced by the growing intolerance of everything foreign as a result of the Maccabean revolt and Roman rule. The future hope concentrated more and more on deliverance. The Messiah would be primarily a royal deliverer, enemy of Rome, a zealot.[32] His qualities and deeds would surpass ordinary standards, but had also been done by others, i.e., miracles by Elijah. "Only as a mighty ruler and an exalted and unequaled moral personality would the Messiah be superior to all the rest of the saints and prophets of Israel. His Kingdom was still *of this world.*"[33]

Suffering Messiah Concept—"In the Tannaitic period there was still no conception of a 'suffering Messiah'."[34] Mowinckel says the idea existed of a mortal messiah who would suffer or die in battle, but this had nothing to do with atonement; "Judaism knows nothing of a suffering, dying and rising messiah."[35] (See Mark 8:31; 9:31).

Eternal Being of Messiah—The concept of the messiah being an eternal Being is due to its association with the Son of Man concept. As he became unique and eternal, significant for salvation, he also became pre-existent.[36]

Appearing of the Messiah—

The day when the Messiah appears and accomplishes his Messianic work of salvation is the day when he "is revealed" as what he is destined to be, as the Messiah. These ex-

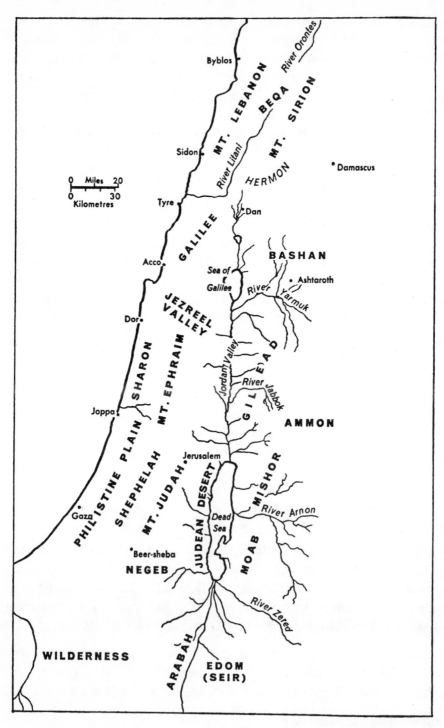

The Geographical Regions of Palestine.

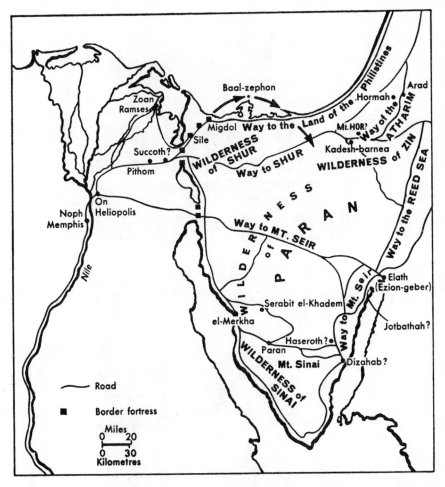

Map 8   The Exodus and the Desert Routes.

Illus. 10   Jerusalem, from the East

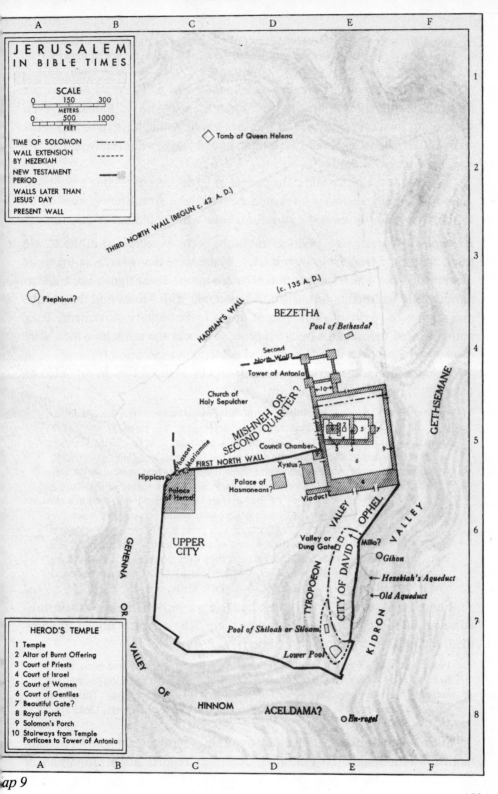

JERUSALEM
IN BIBLE TIMES

SCALE

0   150   300
METERS
0   500   1000
FEET

TIME OF SOLOMON
WALL EXTENSION
BY HEZEKIAH
NEW TESTAMENT
PERIOD
WALLS LATER THAN
JESUS' DAY
PRESENT WALL

◇ Tomb of Queen Helena

⬡ Psephinus?

THIRD NORTH WALL (BEGUN c. 42 A.D.)

HADRIAN'S WALL   (c. 135 A.D.)

BEZETHA
Pool of Bethesda?

Second
North Wall?
Tower of Antonia

Church of
Holy Sepulcher

MISHNEH OR
SECOND QUARTER?

—10—

Council Chamber

Phasael
Mariamme
FIRST NORTH WALL

Hippicus

Palace
of Herod?

Xystus?

Palace of
Hasmoneans?

Viaduct

VALLEY

OPHEL

Valley or
Dung Gate

Millo?

○ Gihon

UPPER
CITY

GEHENNA

OR

VALLEY

TYROPOEON

CITY OF DAVID

KIDRON

VALLEY

GETHSEMANE

← Hezekiah's Aqueduct
← Old Aqueduct

Pool of Shiloah or Siloam?

Lower Pool

OF

HINNOM   ACELDAMA?

○ En-rogel

HEROD'S TEMPLE

1 Temple
2 Altar of Burnt Offering
3 Court of Priests
4 Court of Israel
5 Court of Women
6 Court of Gentiles
7 Beautiful Gate?
8 Royal Porch
9 Solomon's Porch
10 Stairways from Temple
   Porticoes to Tower of Antonia

Map 9

pressions imply that it is this Messianic work which makes him the Messiah. He cannot be known and acknowledged as such until these actions have revealed his identity. By performing Messianic works he "reveals his glory" (his dignity as Messiah)...[37]

If it is the Messiah's work which makes him and reveals him as the Messiah, there may be a time in his human life when he is "hidden"—even without his own consciousness. It was thought he would have to be announced by Elijah who would make the human one of David's line renowned in performing Messianic deeds.[38]

In summary, at Jesus' time the people of Israel were expecting a political, national type of messiah who would deliver them from the oppression of Rome. They did not have the concept of one who would suffer and die.

Examples of Messiahs—Political messiahs were expected to authenticate their claims and leadership by miracles. There were many such claimants at the time of Jesus which are mentioned by Josephus. These figures appealed to nationalistic sentiments of liberation associated with Moses and the exodus and attempted to organize the people into a revolutionary movement. They authenticated their claims by attempting to repeat the miracles which were thought to have been done by the first wilderness generation.[39]

A Samaritan, during the procuratorship of Pilate (c. 26-36 A.D.) led an armed group towards Mt. Gerizim:

> Neither was the Samaritan nation exempt from disturbance. For a man, who had little concern about lying and manipulated everything according to the whim of the crowds, rallied them with the command to accompany him to Mount Gerizim, which is regarded by them to be the most sacred of mountains. He vigorously insisted that when they arrived he would show them the sacred vessels which were buried there where Moses had deposited them. Since they regarded the story as credible, they armed themselves ($'\epsilon\nu$ $'o\pi\lambda o\iota s$) and established themselves in a certain village called Tirathana, taking in others who could be collected since they planned to make the ascent to the mountain as a great multitude. Pilate appeared and blocked their ascent with a detachment of cavalry and armed infantry, who killed those whom they engaged in a battle as they were gathered in the village and took prisoner many of those who fled, of whom Pilate killed the leaders and those who were most influential. (Jos., *Ant.* xviii. 85-7; Tiede, p. 198).

Festus, who succeeded Felix, also had to cope with claimants who promised salvation if the people would follow them. These figures hoped to document their claims by signs in the desert.

> Festus also sent a force of cavalry and infantry against those who had been misled ($\alpha\pi\alpha\tau\alpha\nu$) by a certain fraud ($\alpha\nu\theta\rho\omega\pi os$ $\gamma o\eta s$) who promised salvation ($\sigma\omega\tau\eta\rho\iota\alpha$) and rest from troubles, if they would follow him into the desert ($\epsilon\rho\eta\mu\iota\alpha$). Those who were sent killed both the deceiver ($'\alpha\pi\alpha\tau\alpha\nu$) himself and the followers. (Jos., *Ant.* xx. 188; Tiede p. 201).

Such revolutionary activity did not cease with the fall of Jerusalem; neither was it limited to Palestine. Josephus reports about Jonathan of

Cyrene (c. 73 A.D.), a wilderness miracle-worker who was from North Africa.

> The madness of the Sicarii even touched the cities around Cyrene like a disease. Jonathan, a most evil man and a weaver by trade who had taken refuge there, convinced many of those without resources to listen to him and he led them into the desert ($\epsilon\varrho\eta\mu\iota\alpha$), promising to show them signs and apparitions ($\sigma\eta\mu\epsilon\iota\alpha$ $\varkappa\alpha\iota$ $\phi\alpha\sigma\mu\alpha\tau\alpha$). His knavish activity was not noticed by others, but the Jews who were in high positions in Cyrene reported his exodus ('$\epsilon\xi o\delta o\nu$) and preparations to Catullus, the governor of the Libyan Pentapolis. He sent his cavalry and infantry which quickly overcame the unarmed, most of whom were killed in the encounter, and some of whom were taken prisoner and brought to Catullus. At that time, Jonathan the leader of the plot escaped, but was caught after a long and weary meticulous search of the country. (Jos., *B.J.* vii. 437-41; Tiede pp. 201-202).

In observing these figures mentioned by Josephus, several pointes seem clear. Josephus links (lohtes) with Messianic movements to secure Israel's freedom.

> It would accordingly appear that Zealotism was closely linked with Messsianic expectation, and that the accepted evidence of Messianic leadership was the ability to work miracles or the claim to be able to work them at some crucial moment.[40]

Thus, the connection between revolutionary activity and miracles as authentication of claims to leadership is apparent. The people followed these claimants into the desert usually under assumption that signs and wonders would authenticate their claims that God would aid in deliverance. The motif of the wilderness also stands out as a significant feature of these revolutionary activities: The villains at the time of Felix persuaded the masses to follow them into the desert (Jos., *B.J.* ii. 258-63; *Ant.* xx. 167-172). A "certain fraud" at the time of Festus also promised salvation to those who would follow him to the desert (Jos., *Ant.* xx. 188). Jonathan likewise led people into the wilderness promising signs and wonders (Jos., *B.J.*vii. 437-41). These references to the wilderness probably have symbolic associations with the first wilderness generation (Moses, Joshua, etc.) where the nation gathered for the conquest of the land.[41] Thus, the Messianic figures attempted to demonstrate, by working signs and wonders in the desert, that God was with them in their attempt to conquer the enemies of Israel.

The Prophet Figure as Messiah

Another type of Messianic expectation was the prophet figure which was based on the belief that one of the great prophets of the Old Testament would return. These were known as eschatological prophets. The most popular were Elijah and Moses, although any of the prophets could fill this role.

Elijah is generally viewed as an eschatological prophet. In both the Old Testament and Intertestamental periods the belief existed that a prophet would return at the endtime. This general expectation of a returning prophet took several forms: Some expected a prophet to appear at the endtime, one who would fulfill all earlier prophecy. The idea also existed that since all prophets proclaimed basically the same truth, the same prophet had been successfully incarnated in different prophets, and would appear again at the endtime.[42] This idea is found in the Pseudo-Clementine writings and in the Gospel of the Hebrews.[43] Pseudo-Clement writes that the "true prophet" has appeared repeatedly in different forms and names since Adam, and in the endtime will come as Son of Man (Pseudo-Clement, *Hom.* III. 20,2; *Recogn.* II. 22).

That the expectation of a returning prophet was widespread is attested to by the religious groups outside of Judaism, e.g., the Samaritans and the Qumran sect. The Samaritans, on the basis of Deuteronomy 18:15ff., expect *Ta'eb*, whom they identify as Moses *redivivus*: He works miracles, restores the law and true worship, and brings knowledge to other nations.[44] The concept of a returning prophet was important for the Jewish sect, which is known through the *Damascus Document* (discovered in Cairo in 1896) as the "Community of the New Covenant."[45] In the *Manual of Discipline* a prophet as well as two messiahs are expected. The precedent for this expectation is found in Deuteronomy 18:18 where a prophet like Moses is promised: Apparently the sectarians still expected him, accompanied by an anointed priest and an anointed king. This is the clearest reference to the expected prophet by the Qumran literature.[46] The *Commentary on Habakkuk* also gives valuable information about the founder of this sect—the Teacher of Righteousness. This title is one of honor and was bestowed on Elijah in later Jewish literature.[47] Philo (*de spec. leg.* i. 65) also believed in the coming of a prophet on the basis of Deuteronomy 18. He saw the function of this prophet as bearing salvation and beginning the new era. According to Gaster, *Samaritan Esch.* 247, the Sadducees expected a liberator or prophet from the house of Levi. Josephus speaks of a leader of the people, a prophet who will bring salvation.[48] Thus, there existed the expectation of the return of prophecy in the form of a prophet who would arise to bring salvation and to announce the new era, the Kingdom of God. There were several variations of this hope as far as who the prophet(s) would be. The most popular opinions were Moses, Elijah, Enoch, or one of the more famous ancient prophets.

The belief that Elijah would return to earth in the endtime has its origin in the biblical text (II Kings 2:11) which relates how Elijah did not die but ascended to heaven in a chariot. This unique honor not only caused him to appear superior in the view of the Jews, but the fact that he was still alive would make a return to earth possible. The vividness of the historical account caught the popular imagination: Who was more fitting to announce the Kingdom of God than the great miracle-worker and anointer of prophets and kings—Elijah?[49] Another reason for the prominence of the belief in Elijah's return was the passage in Malachi 4:5,6:

Behold, I will send you Elijah the prophet before the coming of the great and dreadful day of the Lord.

And he shall turn the heart of the fathers to the children, and the heart of the children to their fathers, lest I come and smite the earth with a curse.

This prediction of the return of an individual is unique in the Old Testament. In order to find a parallel one must go to II Esdras 2:18: "For thy help I will send my servants Isaiah and Jeremiah."[50]

The Elijah tradition has developed by various interpretations and legends, most of which originated from the interpretation of the Malachi passage. The following is a brief sketch of the development of the tradition.

The interpretation based on the Massoretic text in Malachi 4:4,6 is simply that "To turn the heart of the fathers to the children" refers to repentance: Elijah will bring about reconciliation between families. Throughout the development of the tradition this continued to be considered one of the main reasons for Elijah's return.[51]

The first step of development appears in the LXX: "The heart of the children to their fathers" has become "the heart of a man to his neighbor," the plural of "father" has been replaced by the singular, and most important, the translation of the *Hiph'il* of שׁוּב has changed from 'επιστρεψι to 'αποκαρταστησψι (from "repent" to "restore"). Thus, Elijah is now expected to bring restoration as well as repentance (cf. Sirach 48:10: Ecclus. 18:10).

Ben-Sira marks the next step of development. In the section 48:1-12 (on Elijah), verse 10 reads as follows: "Who art ready for the time as it is written, to still wrath before the fierce anger of God, to turn the heart of the fathers unto the children, and to restore the tribes of Israel." Here, the idea of restoration is firmly established (see discussion in Scott, pp. 491-92; see also Ecclus. 48:10f. where the returned Elijah has the task of restoring the tribes of Israel).

The third step in the development of the Elijah tradition is revealed in the rabbinic writings where "Elijah redivivus" has become connected with the idea of the resurrection of the dead. This transition was probably due to the account of the raising of the widow's son by Elijah at Zarephath, as well as the record of his own translation.[52] Scott points out the difficulty involved in attempting to date with any amount of certainty the Talmudic materials. He notes, however, that

The New Testament period with which we are concerned, fortunately, comes at the beginning of the growth of the Talmud, so that if the material can be arranged in sequence, that which seems to be primary will approximate to the thought of the first century.[53]

This material can be classified into two categories:[54]

1. Primary material—the Mishna, some Talmudic and some Midrashic material. Scott calls the Mishna "practically contemporary (with the New Testament) material."[55]

"The Mishnah is the Oral Law of the rabbinic schools as it had become stereotyped about the end of the second century A.D."[56] It was descended from first century Mishnahs through the collection of Rabbi Akiba (c. 120 A.D.) to Patriarch Rabbi Judah ha-Nasi. Thus, it is almost contemporary with the Gospels. Tractate 'Eduyot 8:7, an exposition of Malachi 4:5,6, says,

> R. Joshua says, "I have it by tradition from R. Johanan ben Zakarr, as he from Hillel, as he from his teacher, as a Halokka of Moses at Sinai, that Elijah will come not to declare (families) clean or unclean, to remove or to bring near, except to remove those who were brought near by force, and to bring near those who were removed by force." R. Judah says, "To bring near only, not to remove." R. Simeon says, "To settle disputes," but the Wise say, "Not to remove and not to bring near, but to make peace forever, as it is said . . . (quoting Mal. 4:5,6)."[57]

Thus Elijah's activity includes: a) the decision of questions about Israelite descent; b) the settlement of religious controversies; and c) the establishment of peace.[58] These are all derived from the Malachi passage about turning the fathers' hearts to the children. Also in the tractates Baba Metsia 1.8; 2.8; c:4,5; Shekalim 2.5 (and Yebamot 102a) Elijah is expected to establish the pure doctrine and to settle disputes over the law (also see I Macc. 2:58): personal disputes are left undecided "until Elijah comes," (Baba Metsia 1.8; 2:8, etc.). For example, someone found a document under his papers and, not knowing what significance it had, he left it alone "until Elijah comes."[59] Included in this category is also other Talmudic and Midrashic material, that is,

> . . . material from the Gemara, or traditional exposition of the Mishnah, which together with the Mishnah, makes up the Talmud. Within the Gemara are included the Baraita (the "external" or non-canonical Mishnah), and Haggadic (homiletic and legendary) material. We have also to draw from the Haggadic commentaries known as the Midrashim.[60]

This material further adds support to the function of Elijah as:

a) raising the dead

> 1) Sota ix. 15 (an addition which appears in some editions of the Mishnah and Talmud): "The Holy Spirit leads to the resurrection of the dead, and the resurrection of the dead comes by the prophet Elijah."
> 2) Yalkut Shim'oni on Psalm 60:9: "If a heretic denies the resurrection, take the prophet Elijah as witness."

3) j. Shabbat i.3 (Jitomir ed., tractate "Shabbat," p. 9 bot.): "Party leads to the resurrection of the dead, and the resurrection of the dead leads to Elijah."

4) j. Shekalim iii. 3 (Jitomir ed., tractate "Shekalim," p. 25): "The resurrection of the dead leads to Elijah, as it is said, 'Behold I will send you Elijah the prophet before the great and terrible day of the Lord come'."

b) purifying the Israelite descent

1) Midrash Shir ha-Shirim Rabba 27:3: "Elijah will come to pronounce clean and unclean."

2) Kiddushin 72b. The Amora Judah in the name of the Amora Samuel speaks of Elijah as purifying Israel from illegitimate admixture.

c) settling religious controversies

1) Menachot 45a. R. Johanan and R. Judah (pupil of Akiba) says: "This section (i.e., of Scripture) Elijah will interpret one day."

2) Pesachim 13a (ch. j. Pesachim iii. 6). In a dispute about doubtful meat, R. Eliezer ben Judah says: "Perhaps Elijah will come and declare it clean."

3) j. Yebamot xii. 1: "If Elijah should come and say what is permitted, he would be listened to."[61]

2. Secondary material—Other Talmudic and Midrashic material. Scott's categorization of primary and secondary material may seem arbitrary. He has attempted to include in "secondary materials" such stories as seem to be of a legendary nature. It cannot with absolute certainty be asserted that none of this material dates back to New Testament times, but "beneath the accretion of legend, may be traced the old ideas which connected the return of the Tishbite with repentance and reconciliation, restoration and resurrection."[62] Examples of this literature are the Pesikta 2, Sanhedrin 109a, 'Abodah Zarah 17b, Berakot 58a, Nedarim 50a, Baba Metsia 85b, Ruth Rabbah 4, Homa 19b, (from *En Jacob*, Sanhedrin 97b, Chagigah 15b, Kiddushin 41a). These examples refer to Elijah as helping someone in trouble or distress, appearing as witness in someone's defense, disclosing celestial mysteries, instruction about Scripture passages, etc.[63]

Also included in this secondary classification are legends and tales of wonder which have embellished the Messianic hope after the period of the Tannaim.[64] Some of these deal with the time and manner of Elijah's coming (j. Pesachim 3.6; Sifra,[65] in Yalkut Shimoni 1.310.1—(collection of Midrashic material of various dates); Pesikta Rabbati, in Yalkut Shimoni 2.32.4 (from Schoettgen, Vol. 2, p. 266); Pesikta Rabbati, 62.1, in Yalkut Shimoni 3.53.3).[66] Another group of these stories includes tasks which will be performed by Elijah in the Messianic age. In Shir ha-Shirim Zuta 38, Elijah will appear with the Messiah and will be asked by the Jews to raise their loved ones from the dead (cf. Mannasseh ben Israel, seventeenth century commentator). Mekilta, tractate Wajissa 5 (Midrash on Exodus 16:33) says that Elijah will bring back three things—a cup of manna, a cup of the lustration water, and a cup of the anointing oil.[67] Deborim Rabbah 3 refers to the coming of Elijah "to console you."[68] Similar to this is the theory of Ruth Rabbah 2:14[69] and Kohelet Rabbah 11:2[70] that Elijah acts as intercessor in heaven for the people.

In apocalyptic circles Elijah is mentioned as the forerunner of the Messiah (I Enoch 90:31; IV Ezra 6:26; also Justin's *Dialogue with Trypho*, c. 8:49). The *Apocalypse of Elijah* also predicts the return of Elijah and Enoch. Their function is to announce the beginning of God's reign.[71] In some sources, Elijah is considered to be the forerunner of God Himself, to prepare the way for the reign of God.[72]

In Hellenistic Judaism, Elijah is also considered a miracle-worker, an intercessor for the elect, a healer of the sick, and a helper for those in trouble.[73]

From this brief survey, four aspects of Elijah's expected activity emerge: repentance, reconciliation, restoration, resurrection. These activies are to prepare Israel for the imminent coming of the Kingdom of God. In all of these traditions—Old Testament, Qumran, and apocalyptic circles—the prophet is seeen against an eschatological background as the servant of redemptive history and eschatological expectation: The prophet is expected to announce and to prepare for the imminent coming of the Kingdom of God.

MOSES

Moses was another of the ancient prophets whom the Jews expected to arise again at the endtime. This belief, although not so prevalent as that in the return of Elijah, arose through the general opinion that Mosaic times would return to Israel.[74] Moses is known as the great prophet of Israel, the Savior of Egypt, the prophet mediator, the author of the Torah. His miracles were seen in connection with God's redemptive plan for Israel.

Later Judaism held Moses in high regard: The more the authority of the Torah increased, the more the respect for its author rose. The *Assumption of Moses* (A.D. 7-30) considers Moses as its central figure: He is the man of the world, his tomb is the whole world (11:8), he is a great angel, the universal Lord of word, the godly prophet of the world, the accomplished scholar of time, the intercessor for the people (11:16f.; 12:6). According to II Baruch 59:3ff. (50-100 A.D.) the secret things of the heavenly realm will be revealed to Moses; in the *Life of Moses,* p. 155f., Moses is declared to be the partner of God; all the elements belong to him; as the friend of God he has joint possession of God's power.[75] Philo (*Sacrifice of Abel,* 8f.; *Life of Moses* I, 158), the Pesikta k. 32(200b) and *Testament of Levi* 8 (109-107 B.C.) speak highly of Moses. The Samaritans also respect him: He is the prophet of God, prophet of the whole world, perfect priest, the first king (Deut. 33:5), intercessor for those in need (G. 72,95,118,184,210,217,223). The task of the returning

Moses was to establish the new age in a national sense (Targum J[1] J[2]; Deut. 33:21; 31:14). Moses was also to be a witness of the nations of the world, to serve the shekinah (Zohar), and to be a companion of the Messiah.[76] Thus, Moses appears in an eschatological setting as the servant of God.

In Exodus 4:16; 7:1 Moses is assigned a role as "God" before Pharoah and Aaron—the presence of the divine is verified by miraculous acts. In Deuteronomy, after Moses' death is recounted, the qualifications of prophet are mentioned: Knowing God face to face, signs and wonders, mighty powers and great and terrible deeds.

> Thus although the Deuteronomist refused to let miraculous performances be the sole criterion for authenticating a prophet like Moses (cf. Deut. 13:15; 18:9-22), it is clear that the signs and wonders are essential for authenticating the special presence of God with the prophet like Moses.[77]

The figure of Moses in Josephus is varied according to the audience which Josephus is addressing: Moses appears as sage, lawgiver, miracle-worker, prophet, and military genius (Jos., *Ant.* iii. 180). In the *Contra Apionem*, Josephus' apologetic interests are quite clear: He presents Moses as the virtuous Lawgiver of the Jews, who excels the Greek heroes.[78] Nowhere in this work does Josephus refer to Moses as miracle-worker.[79] The image of Moses in Josephus' *Antiquities* is more varied.

> Josephus' frequent use of a rationalistic disclaimer in his conclusion of miracle stories (cf. *Antiquities* 1:108; 3:81; 4:158; 10:281; 17:354) must also be regarded as an apologetic nod to the cultured tastes of his audience.[80]

This does not mean that Josephus doubted the reliability of miraculous accounts.[81] Josephus refers to himself as the servant of God ($\delta\iota\alpha\varkappa o\nu o\varsigma$) (*B.J.* iii. 354; iv. 626) and authenticates this claim by his interpretation of dreams and predictions *B.J.* iii. 350-54; 399-408; iv. 622-29; *Life*, 208-09). Josephus, however, subordinates Moses to God in miracle-working.

> While Josephus does not recount the miracles as *Moses'* miracles, he does treat Moses as the lawgiver of the Jews who possesses and displays $\alpha\varrho\epsilon\tau\eta$ and he documents Moses' unique status before God in his roles as lawgiver, prophet, and general by pointing to his $\alpha\varrho\epsilon\tau\eta$.[82]

Thus, although Josephus emphasizes Moses as a sage in order to present him in a favorable light to a skeptical audience, he does recognize the value of miracles for the authentication of status as a prophet.

There were traditions, however, which presented Moses almost totally as a miracle-worker. Moses is treated by Greek and Roman literary authors as the Lawgiver of the Jews but John Gager has recently discovered that:

> On the whole, however, the Moses of the magical documents is a figure unto himself. Here he emerges as an inspired prophet, endowed with divine wisdom and power, whose very name guaranteed the efficacy of magical charms and provided protection against the hostile forces of the cosmos.[83]

Also, in such a tradition as Artapanus represents,[84] Moses is presented as

> ... the leader of an oppressed people who controls the animal cults, strikes terror in the heart of the king, commands the great goddess, Isis, and surpasses the accomplishments of the heroes of romantic Egyptian legends at every turn.[85]

Thus, the nature of miracles as authentication of a prophet's status is viewed differently by different traditions. In literary circles, such as Josephus and Philo represent, Moses is presented as sage, lawgiver, possessor of virtue. In other spheres, miracles play a greater role and Moses is presented as the great miracle-worker, prophet and magician. The writers emphasized the elements which would be most appealing to their audiences. In whatever context Moses appears, it is noteworthy that he appears in connection with the Exodus, the redemption of Israel. Even in the magical traditions, his magic is performed in order to redeem Israel. Thus, even when Moses appears as a magician, the Exodus can be perceived in the background; the miracles are set in an eschatological setting; they have a broader purpose than the exaltation of the performer, rather they are seen in the context of God's redemptive history: The prophet appears as God's agent on earth.

EXAMPLES OF PROPHET FIGURES

The prophet figure can be seen further in Josephus' accounts of the "prophets" in Judea in the first century who organized masses of people while authenticating their claims by promising to work miracles.[86] Of these figures mentioned by Josephus, only two are actually referred to as "prophets," Theudas and the Egyptian.

Theudas arose during the procuratorship of Cuspius Fadus (c. 44-88 A.D.).

> While Fadus was procurator, a certain fraud ($\gamma o \eta s$ $\tau \iota s$ $\alpha \nu \eta \varrho$) named Theudas persuaded the majority of the masses ($\tau o \nu$ $\pi \lambda \epsilon \iota \tau o \nu$ $o \chi \lambda o \nu$) to gather their possessions and follow him to the Jordan river. He claimed to be prophet ($\pi \varrho o \phi \eta \tau \eta s$) and that at his command the river would divide and provide easy passage for them. He misled ('$\alpha \pi \alpha \tau \alpha \nu$) many by saying these things. But Fadus did not allow them to thrive on such folly. He sent a squadron of cavalry against them which fell on them unexpectedly and killed many and took many prisoners. Having captured Theudas himself, they beheaded him and took the head to Jerusalem (Jos., *Ant.* xx. 97-8).

The Egyptian arose during the time of Felix (c. 52 to 55 or 60 A.D.).

> And a certain Egyptian came to Jerusalem at this time claiming to be a prophet ($\pi \varrho o$-$\phi \eta \tau \eta s$). He advised the masses to accompany him to a mountain called the Mount of Olives, which lies opposite the city at a distance of five furlongs. For he claimed that he wanted to show them from there that the walls of Jerusalem would fall at his command, promising to provide entrance to the city through them. When Felix was advis-

ed of this, he commanded his soldiers to take up their arms; and accompanied by a large cavalry and infantry, he rushed from Jerusalem and fell on those with the Egyptian, slaying four hundred and taking two hundred prisoners. The Egyptian himself was not to be found since he had run from the battle. (Jos., *Ant.* xx. 167-72).

Both of these prophet figures attempted to authenticate their claim of charismatic leadership by miracles,[87] but it is significant to note that their miracles were not merely in order to exalt their own person, rather they were to validate their claims of political redemption. Whether political or spiritual, the prophet's miracles were performed in order to indicate redemption for Israel. Thus, the miracles of the prophets had a broader scope than the mere glorification of the miracle-worker; they had redemptive significance.

Significance for the Scene of Jesus

These Messianic expectations were in existence in the minds of the people at the time of Jesus. The disciples voiced these opinions when Jesus asked: "Who do men say that I am?" (Mark 8:27). The disciples' answers reflected these views—Elijah, one of the prophets. Even Peter's confession of Jesus as Messiah may have had political overtones. Jesus modified this statement by ading that the Messiah must die (Mark 8:33).

In the Gospel of John it is said that the people wanted to make Jesus king (John 6) after the feeding of the 5,000. We can see that this miracle recalled other prophet figures who revolted against the political system of Rome (see above in Josephus). This miracle would also recall the Moses expectation.

These ideas were fermenting in the people's minds when Jesus came. An understanding of these ideas sheds light on the people's reactions toward Jesus in the Gospels.

Chapter IX

MUSIC IN ANCIENT ISRAEL

In this chapter, reference is made to historical dates with the following abbreviations:

C.E. — Christian Era

B.C.E. — Before the Common Era (Christian Era)

These reference terms and abbreviations are usually used in Jewish studies. The Common Era, or Christian Era, is the period since the *assumed* year of Jesus' birth.

Chapter IX

MUSIC IN ANCIENT ISRAEL

Music is a topic which is usually overlooked in most books on New Testament backgrounds, probably because music is not a major topic in the New Testament. Most of the mentions of music in the New Testament have to do with singing. For example, when Jesus and the disciples left the upper room to go to the Garden of Gethsemane, they sang a hymn (Matt. 26:30); or Paul and Silas sang in prison (Acts 16:25). Music, however, was a part of the Temple worship and was therefore a part of the scene of the New Testament. Though this chapter relates more to the Old Testament use of music because Jewish Temple worship had its origin in the Old Testament, it can be assumed that the use of music in the New Testament was similar, if not exact. Thus, the understanding of music sheds a unique light on the scene of the life of Jesus.

The musical story of Israel can be traced back to Lamech's son, Jubal, the "father of all those who play the lyre and pipe." It next appears in Ur where Abraham first lived. In that country it was the custom that upon the king's death the court musicians and attendants were traditionally slain and buried with him. From this point onward, music has been attached in some way or other to the children of Israel. Later in history they were commanded to make no "graven images" of their deity and because of this, music, among other things, became very important and took on a deep meaning. It united them as a congregation in singing and faith in God who at least would hear them, they felt, even if they could not see Him. It also united them in one of the deepest and oldest impulses of the human spirit: "To give songful expression to a sense of awe before the terror and the glory of creation."[1]

As time went on, different types of songs evolved from the physical rhythms of daiiy work and from chants by which tribal elders passed on to younger members the lore and teachings of their clan. In this way personal passions came to be expressed in song. Hebrew shepherds following the nomadic pattern of the Near East made primitive instruments similar to those that almost all herdsmen used. Some of these were most likely a reed with holes (flute); a ram's horn with the tip cut away; a hollow gourd and bit of sheep gut (crude stringed instrument); an animal skin strapped over a hollow tree trunk; concussion sticks; and dried gourds filled with seeds and pebbles (percussion instruments).[2]

The next incident significant to the progression of Hebrew musical history is the episode in which Laban asked Jacob the question:

> Wherefore didst thou flee away secretly, and steal away from me; and didst not tell me, that I might have sent thee away with mirth, and with songs, with tabret, and with harp? (Gen. 31:27)

Evidently by this time certain types of instruments were used and accepted in the daily life of the ancient Semitic peoples. When the Israelites submitted to Egypt's high culture they were able to develop and refine their gift of music very rapidly. Four hundred years later when they left they were a people uniquely given to song. Moses taught them to preserve their songs, proverbs and the musical instruments they had brought from Egypt. He can even be regarded as their first music teacher. This most likely took place during the forty years of wandering.

Israelites, in their zealous desire to please God, turned their creative powers full force into the making of music, dances, poetry and songs. Songs at times welled up spontaneously. All a leader had to do was strike up a tune and all would join in. This often became a kind of free prose-poetry. The song found in Exodus 15:1-19 might have come about in such a way.

The women also took an active part. An example of this was Miriam when she took the timbrel in hand and led the women in a dance of joy, caroling to one another the verses that the men sang with Moses (Exod. 15:20-1).

Rothmüller points out that songs also grew out of the national life of the Jewish nation:

> In their exile, all the past achievements of Jewish national and religious life came to be regarded as a cultural heritage which was their one spiritual surety, their one rallying-point in defense of national solidarity... On the return from exile they rallied still more strongly around their traditions, and probably only a few psalms or hymns were written in the ensuing period. Psalms were generally appreciated and sung or recited in public after 500 B.C., but their poetic quality was already declining. The writing of psalms probably came to an end in the days of the Maccabees, in the middle of the second century B.C.[3]

Music of Earlier and Neighboring Civilizations

One problem in determining the shapes and characteristics of the instruments was brought about because the Hebrews could not make any graven images, thus they left no pictorial records of them. Therefore, to understand the music that was to be developed by the Hebrews one must also understand something about the musical development in the countries surrounding them. Another factor involved was trade, which brought about a continuous exchange of goods and articles of luxury. In this way instruments from different countries and cultures were interchanged and the knowledge of their use was disseminated. In Oriental life the finer instruments were considered "objects de luxe" and were among the most desirable articles of trade. The religions of that day also played an important role. "Through the mushrooming of religious groups and sects, all types of hymns, litanies and other sacred songs were created, which eventually were transplanted from one people to another."[4] Undoubtedly, the instruments used in playing these religious songs were also exchanged by different people.

Sumeria — The oldest records of musical organization and system in nations of antiquity are from Sumeria and Egypt. There are many close resemblances between the music of Sumeria and the music of ancient Israel, and at first it was thought that Israel had taken much of its musical art from Sumeria, but in recent times this was found to be erroneous. Although most of the records found in Sumeria concerning musical activities are connected with religious rites and ceremonies, it is also known that they had a vigorous folk music in their culture. Another parallel between Sumeria and ancient Israel is that musicians were employed by the court and nobility in both cultures, though in Israel this occurred much later.[5]

A catalog has been found of Sumerian and Assyrian hymns and secular songs containing poems and songs of all varieties, i.e.: liturgies, royal psalms, festival songs, lamentations, poems of victory and heroic acts, popular songs for workmen and shepherds, and numerous love songs for both sexes. Also, as in Israel, they had schools of music at the largest temples in which the young clergy were trained systematically in musical liturgy.[6]

The musical service at these temples was performed by "liturgists" (*kalū*) and "psalmists" (*narū*), whose functions were administering the daily sacred ceremonies and providing a vocal background for them. In these temples the most prominent object was the temple tower or *ziggurat,* crowned by a small room or chapel containing a bed and a gold table. Galpin describes it, "Here, in the meeting place of earth and heaven, the chosen priestess by night received the revelation of the god."[7] This oracle was delivered by the priest accompanied by the sounds of the "cross-strung" harp (*zag-sal*) or of the lyre (*al-gar*). This custom was continued by the Hebrew prophets and psalmists who "opened their dark sayings upon the harp."[8]
who "opened their dark sayings upon the harp."[8]

The prime example of the importance of music in these temples is found in the Temple of Ningirsu at Lagash where a special officer was in charge of the singers. Another had the function of supervising the preparation of a choir made up of both male and female singers. Sacred singers had their own guilds.

...they became at last a learned community, a kind of college, which studied and edited the official liturgical literature... We have... considerable liturgical literature of the learned college attached to the Temple of Bel in Babylon.[9]

When Sumeria was invaded by foreign conquerors who burned the houses and the Temples of Lagash and carried the inhabitants into captivity, the laments that were composed were very similar to some of the Hebrew psalms which were also written in times of national disaster.

Canaan — Prior to the occupation of the Hebrews, the land of Canaan had no civilization of its own. This was most likely because this narrow strip of land was too much of a crossroad of the ancient world to develop its own culture. Most of the music that was used in this area was for pagan ceremonies in the form of worship. We are informed about the character of these ceremonies in the description of the incident at Mt. Carmel—I Kings 18:26-28.

> The delirious ecstacy, the invocations (i.e. "singing") accompanied by savage dances and noisy music, were the outstanding features of the ceremonies of the priests of Ba'al. They give us a vivid picture of the orgiastic character of this kind of ritual music.[10]

As the Israelites became more and more developed in their music, their spirituality and ethically higher religion also took effect and prevailed over the wicked pagan worship of Canaan. These qualities carried them into a victory over the wicked crude forms of the heathen cults. This was the start of the transformation of music of pagan rites into the spiritually loftier music of the Hebrews. Because of their many qualities they were able to create their own music and withstand the surrounding pagan musical influence which so encompassed them at the beginning of their quest of what would later become the land of Israel. Israel brought from Egypt and the desert the joy of singing, a vivid fantasy in music, as well as a wealth of old songs. The Hebrew music prevailed despite its undeveloped form. It succeeded in rapidly overcoming pagan preponderance and in finding its own form of musical expression. Hebrew musical culture came into bloom relatively soon after the conquest of Canaan, approximately in Samuel's time. Its development was rapid, for by the time of David and Solomon there were highly organized musical institutions. Israel learned to preserve its musical culture from the dangerous and disintegrating inroads of foreign influence.[11]

The Bible as an Historical Source of Jewish Music

The information on music in the Bible is far more eloquent and meaningful than all other records of antiquity concerning music, except those of the Greeks.

The musical references of the Bible are almost the first records in the history of mankind that afford a comprehensive insight into the musical culture of a people of high Antiquity . . .

In Israel's early history, music has been mostly an implement for superstition and magic. In the intermediate stage it was the necessary background for religious rites. Only in its further development it became a possession of the entire people. At this stage, it was deeply rooted in the people's consciousness, it was no more a mere accessory of religion, or the privilege of a single class, but the common property of a whole nation. Music became a people's art, in the broadest sense of the word.[12]

Because music was a people's art the authors who wrote about it took for granted that their readers had a genuine knowledge of and were thoroughly familiar with all the musical matters of that day; therefore, they considered it unnecessary to give long descriptions and minute details of the instruments about which they wrote. The importance of music can be seen very early in the Bible. Genesis 4:20-22 tells of music being one of three fundamental professions.

In primeval times music was completely subjected to the daily functions of the people. This represents the pure and exclusive form of "music for practical use" or "utilitarian" music ("Gebrauchsmusik").[13] In the course of time, music was given higher importance as it became a part of religious ceremony. This was an important step in the development of Israel.

Other Historical Sources of Jewish Music

1. Two books of Flavius Josephus (37 ca. 100 C.E.), *Wars of the Jews,* and *Antiquities of the Jews.*

2. Numerous historical and philosophical essays of Philo of Alexandria called Philo Judaeus (ca. 20 B.C.E.-ca. 40 C.E.)

3. Writings of Tacitus (ca. 55-ca. 117 C.E.)

4. Writings of Diodorus Siculus (1st century B.C.E.)

5. Writings of Athenaeus (ca. 200 C.E.)

6. Works of Nicolas Damascenus (ca. 100 B.C.E.)

7. Early rabbinical literature, such as the Mishnah, Gemara, Tosefta, the Babylonian and Palestinian Talmud, and the Targumim, the Aramaic versions of the biblical text.

8. The collection of Jewish legends and tales, the Midrashim, also contains quite a number of references to music.[14]

For musicological research the value of the early rabbinic literature is rather uneven. They tried to clarify obscure passages of biblical text and explain obsolete musical terms. Some of these expressions are rather useful but others are of little help. The aim of the rabbinic writers was to preserve and expound tradition and in this way their work was very helpful. Many musical terms, notions, and much musical tradition would be lost without their retrospective care. A good example of this is the rabbinical literature of the early Diaspora which is very important. It shows that the Israelites never entirely gave up their music after the destruction of the Temple in spite of all the severe religious prohibitions.

> As a sign of mourning for the ravaged sanctuary, all musical activity was supposed to be abandoned. This interdiction was carried out in one field only, where the spiritual leaders of the dispersed people retained their full sway: in the religious service. Instrumental music, as part of the ceremony, ceased to exist with the downfall of Jerusalem. Singing, however, as practiced in the Synagogue, never was seriously threatened by rabbinic prohibitions.[15]

The Jews of the Diaspora saved their secular music, especially its intimate forms: The music at home, and the singing of *zemirot* in the family.

Besides religion, music was the only stimulus for the Jew's inner life. History has proven that he never gave up this comfort to his soul even for a short period.

Another source of Jewish music is the writings of the early Church Fathers. All music referred to by the patristic literature is related (directly or indirectly) to Israel. The reason for this is that the early Christian church was the immediate successor to the Jewish religion and, therefore, incorporated the sacred ceremonies of the Temple or Synagogue without change. Vocal music was also an important element in the sacred service of the Temple and continued to be important later during the time of the Apostolic Christians, e.g., singing of psalms, hymns, spiritual songs, and responses, with or without instrumental accompaniment.[16]

In this way it can be seen that what was important to the Church Fathers must have been an important element previously to the Jews in their sacred worship.

Visual Musical Illustrations

Written sources provide good information, but authentic reproductions concerning Jewish music are very scarce. Following are two good examples of visual illustrations:

1. "On the Arch of Triumph in Rome, erected to the glory of the emperor Titus after the destruction of the Temple of Jerusalem, are shown the sacred silver trumpets (*ḥaẓoẹrot*), together with the sacred vessels of the sanctuary, which Titus carried away as booty in his triumphal procession.

2. "A coin of Bar-Kokba issued during the war of liberation against the emperor Hadrian (132-135 C.E.), shows a pair of trumpets; they are designed in such a shortened and clumsy fashion that it is somewhat difficult to reconstruct their original shape...."[17]

The importance of the coin is that it was issued by a victorious national hero and had a sacred symbol of the Jewish religion on it. (Note: Bar-Kokba's revolt was the first successful revolt of Judaism against a powerful oppressor after the destruction of their national existence.) Stamping of the coins was a visible sign of the urge for national survival. On the coins, two instruments were represented. This is an unmistakable sign that they are sacred trumpets.

Other coins of Bar-Kokba show the biblical *kinnor* in several varieties. The design depicted is crude, the strings are represented by thick lines showing mostly three, five, or six strings. The stringed instruments reproduced on the coins show great similarity to the Greek *lyra* or *kithara* which might be later forms of the Israelite instruments designed from actual Greek patterns.

Depicted on a vase (about 1025 B.C.E.) found at Megiddo, is an early form of the *kinnor,* probably that of David's time. It shows curved side-arms, a straight, horizontal cross bar, protruding on both sides, to which four strings are attached. The *kinnor* originally had ten strings, but the vase, like the coins, shows it with less. This instrument is very much like a lyre on a wall-painting found in Tomb 38 at Thebes (ca. 1420 B.C.E.). Both have a square sounding board, curved side-arms and the same cross bar protruding on both ends. The only difference is that the Egyptian one shows seven strings.

The instrument that was found on the vase at Megiddo is a reproduction of the Egyptian lyre. There is no absolute way of knowing whether the lyre was brought along by the Israelites from Egypt or whether it was imported earlier by the Canaanites and found by the Israelites. There is even a chance that the Egyptian lyre might have served as a model for the Jewish *kinnor* or even have been used by David himself and introduced by him into the Temple music.[18]

There is also in a fresco of a sepulchural grotto at Beni-Hassan, in the tomb of a prince named Nehera-si-num-hotep, who lived in the epoch of the Pharaoh Amenemhet II of the 12th Dynasty (1938-1904 B.C.E.) a mural in which a prince is approached by a procession of nomads asking permission for settling in Egypt. In the mural is depicted a Semitic lyre-player holding an instrument of eight strings under his right arm. He manipulates them partly with his bare left hand while his right hand plucks the strings with the aid of a plectrum. There is a chance that his left hand is perhaps "stopping" the strings. "The body of the instrument is a square board, having an opening at the upper part, which apparently serves as a hole in the resonance body. This instrument was considered to be the prototype of the Hebrew *kinnor*."[19]

Depicted on an ivory from Megiddo, dated approximately 1200 B.C.E., is what might also be a possible model of the Jewish *kinnor*. Pictured on the ivory is a Canaanite king sitting on a throne drinking from a bowl while one of his musicians entertains him by playing on a lyre. The instrument has nine

Whistle—from Birs Nimrûd, Babylon,
(*Formerly Royal Asiatic Society, London*)

Double Reed-pipes—from the Older
Cemetery, Ur; *c.* 2800 B.C. *(University
Museum, Philadelphia)*

Shell Horn—From Nineveh; *c.* 700 B.C.
(*British Museum*)

Illus. 11

Flutes, Pipes and Horns

Large Timbrel—Nippur Figurine; *c.*
2000 B.C. *(University Museum,
Philadelphia)*

Harpist; *c.* B.C.-1785 B.C. *(Rijkmuseum,
Leyden)*

Illus. 12

A musician, probably a Canaanite or Phoenician, plucking
the strings of a lyre. Detail from an ivory plaque found in
Megiddo, Northern Palestine; *c.* 1200 B.C. (*Palestine
Archaeological Museum, Jerusalem*)

Illus. 13

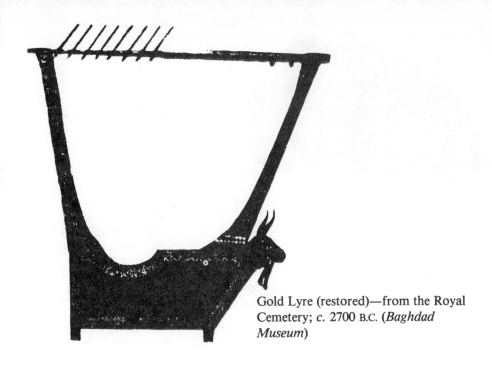

Gold Lyre (restored)—from the Royal Cemetery; *c.* 2700 B.C. (*Baghdad Museum*)

Boat-shaped Lyre—from the Royal Cemetery; *c.* 2700 B.C. *(University Museum, Philadelphia)*

Illus. 14

Lyres from Ur

Small Bow-shaped Harp—from a vase, Bismya; *c.* 3200 B.C. (*Istanbul Museum*)

Line Drawing of the same Bow-shaped Harp—from Bismya; *c.* 3200 B.C. (*E. J. Banks,* Bismya)

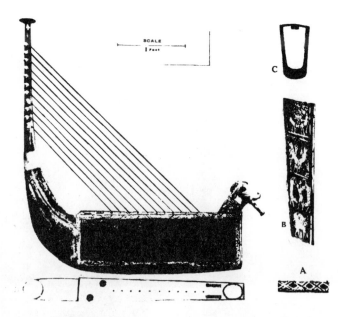

Large Bow-shaped Harp (restored)—from the Royal Cemetery, Ur; *c.* 2700 B.C. (*British Museum*)

A,B. Border and terminal plaque of soundboard (enlarged).
C,D. Section and contour of body (restored).

Illus. 15   Bow-shaped Harps

Bow-shaped Harp—from stone slab, Khafage; *c.* 3000 B.C. (*University Oriental Institute, Chicago*)

Bow-shaped Harp and Clappers—from an archaic seal, Ur; *c.* 2800 B.C. (*University Museum, Philadelphia*)

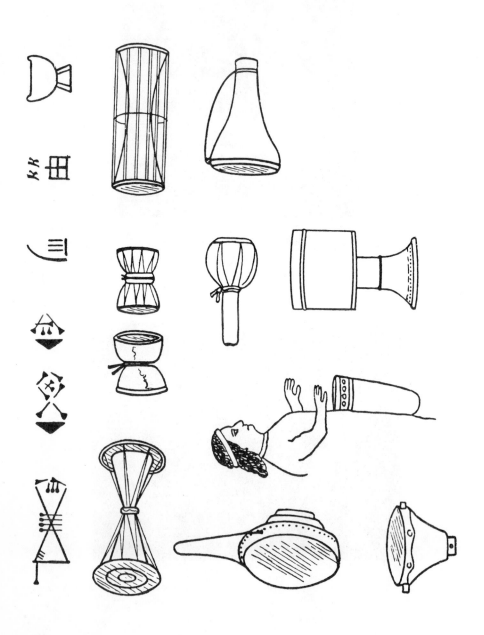

Illus. 16   Percussion Instruments

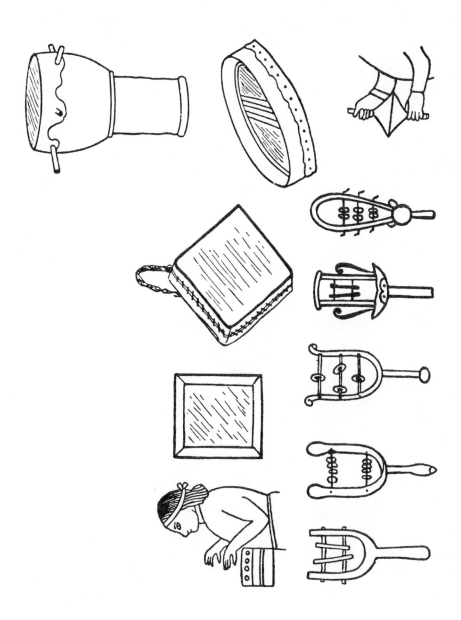

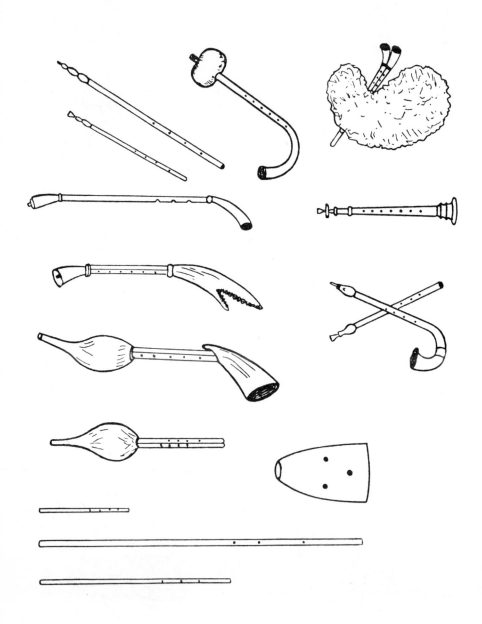

Illus. 17   Wind Instruments

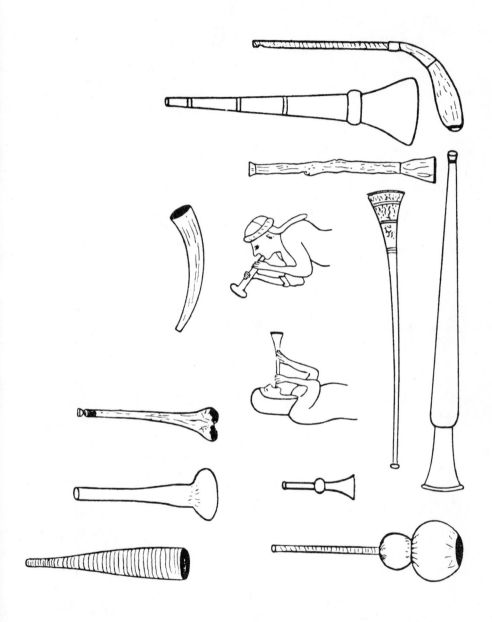

Illus. 18

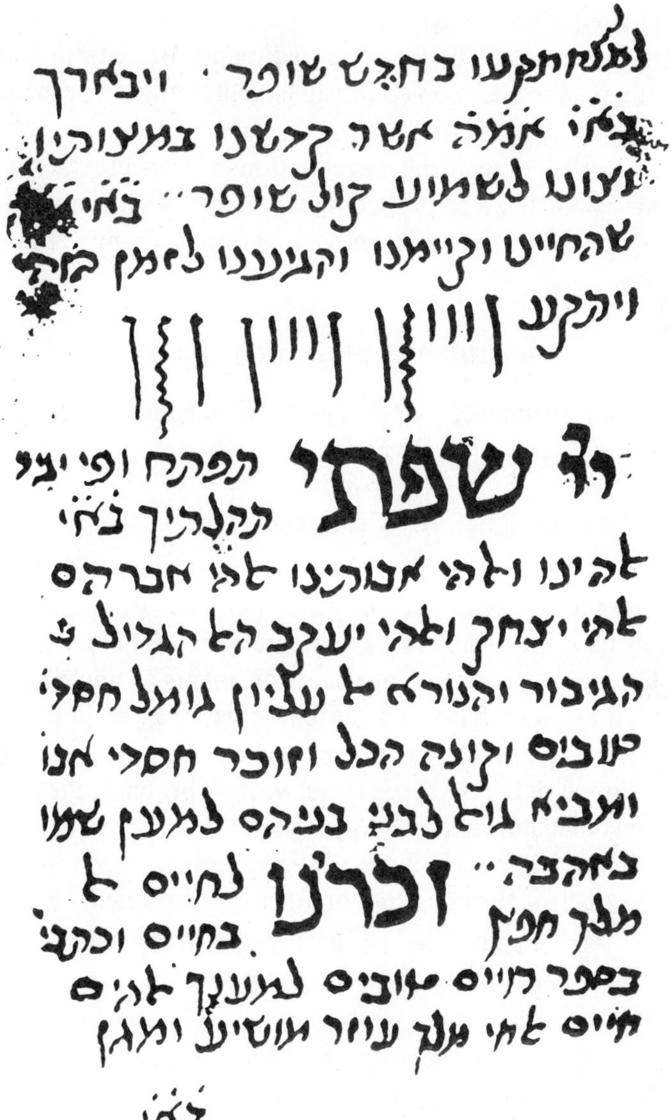

These may be the oldest known *shofar*-calls in a Hebrew manuscript from the 13th century, the *Codex Adler* (in the Jewish Theological Seminary of America, New York, cat. No. 932).

Illus. 19

strings strung horizontally and is plucked with the fingers of the left hand. The large resonance body is held under the left arm of the player. There is no way of finding out what the right hand is doing because it is hidden behind the corpus of the instrument. This is undoubtedly a pre-Israelitic instrument and, therefore, might have been copied by the Israelites or have been an influence on the form of the Jewish lyre that was to come.

The last discovery of pictorial reproductions of ancient Israel recovered so far was at Megiddo. It was a bronze figure (35 cm. high), most likely representing a Jewish flute-girl. The above-mentioned examples are the only findings to date.

Instruments of the Bible B.C.E.

The biblical instruments — B.C.E. — are divided into three categories:
I. Strings
II. Winds
III. Percussion

The family of stringed instruments were most important in the musical practice of the ancient Hebrews. The winds were the next important, and the percussion instruments were the least integral part of the music.

The Bible mentions sixteen musical instruments as having been used in Ancient Israel. Daniel refers to six more that were played in King Nebuchadrezzar's court. Their names characterized them as non-Jewish instruments. In the third chapter of the Book of Daniel we have probably the sole specimen of Babylonian or Chaldean music. We will not take up the problem of the text of Daniel here but will merely discuss the instruments mentioned.[20]

Materials used for the construction of these instruments are:

hazozerot were made of beaten silver (Num. 10:2). They were blown by priests and used in sacrificial ceremony, in war and in royal coronations.[21]

shofar was made from the horn of a ram or wild goat.

keren was made from the horn of a neat.

meziltayim (cymbals) were made of brass.

stringed instruments were made of wood.[22]

There was to be no playing of instruments on the Sabbath except for accompaniment for singing at worship.

Stringed and wind instruments, when not in use, were wrapped in napkins or kept in special receptacles. Different kinds of receptacles were made for *kinnorot* and *nebalim*. Wind instruments were kept in either "cases for pipes" or "bags for pipes." There was a distinction made in the regulations for cleanliness as to whether an instrument could be laid in the case from above or from the side.

I. STRINGED INSTRUMENTS[23]

A. *Kinnor*[24] — The invention was ascribed to Jubal. It was "David's harp," the preferred instrument in Israeli music. The word has two plural forms, one masculine, *kinnorim*, one feminine, *kinnorot*, which is an unexplainable peculiarity not found with any other name of instrument.

The Bible mentions *kinnor* in forty-two places. Biblical scribes do not reveal anything about the shape of the *kinnor* and there are no authentic pictures found in Hebrew antiquities. Opinions about its nature are controversial.

Modern research says that *kinnor* was not a harp-like instrument or type of lute with long-necked fingerboard, but an instrument similar to the Greek *kithara*.

Kithara and *lyra* represent basically the same type of instrument. *Kithara* was the larger of the two, had lower tones and more voluminous sound, had larger side-arms, mostly hollow and produced an increased resonance. The players hung *kithara* with a strap around shoulders while marching. *Lyra* was smaller and more delicate in type. Side-arms were mostly of one piece, fixed directly upon the sounding box.

B. *Nebel*[25] — This stringed instrument was used for accompaniment of singing, and is mentioned twenty-seven times in the Bible. Plural of the word is *nebalim*. The original meaning of the word is "to inflate," "to bulge." In Hebrew, *nebel* (or *nevel*) is also the term for leather bottles and other bulky vessels, also pots made of clay.

This instrument had twelve strings and was plucked with fingers; the sounding box was on the upper part. It was lower pitched than the *kinnor*, also larger and had a stronger sound. The strings were made from entrails (*meyav*) of sheep. It was an upright, portable harp which might have been in various sizes. The basic form has not been modified much at all through the centuries.

The inventors of the instrument were the Phoenicians, who were inhabitants of Sidon.

C. *'Asor* — This instrument is found only three times in the Old Testament—Psalms 33:2; 92:3; 144:9—and the word is derived from a root meaning "ten." In all three passages *'asor* is connected with another instrument. Some people think that since *'asor* means "ten" it was connected with other instruments and meant they had ten strings.

It is still undecided whether or not it is a separate instrument or connected in some other way to instruments with which it is mentioned.

D. *Gittit* — This instrument is found in headings of Psalms 8, 81, and 84. Literal meaning is "that from Geth." It might refer to an instrument that could have originated in Geth (Gath) where David stayed for some time.

The *Gittit* was a sort of lute; the Targum translates it "on the zither."

E. *Sabbeka* — References to this instrument are Daniel 3:5, 7, 10, 15. It is mentioned as one of the instruments played at Nebuchadrezzar's court. It is generally agreed that this is identical with the Greek *sambykē* and the Roman *sambuca*.

It was a horizontal angular harp, similar to the triangular, four-stringed, high-pitched *sambykē* of the Hellenes.

F. *Pesanterin* — References to this instrument are Daniel 3:5, 7, 10, 15. This instrument was also played at Nebuchadrezzar's court. Not much is known about its characteristics except that it must have been a stringed instrument with probably eight strings stretched above a slightly arched sound-box. The box had ten small round openings—sound holes—and the player struck the strings with a rather large stick.

G. *Kathros* — References: Daniel 3:5, 7, 10, 15. This instrument was also played at Nebuchadrezzar's court. *Kathros* (or *kithros*)—the name of this instrument does not give any clue to what it was like—its form or its character. The name indicates an instrument of the most varied type. The Greek kithara and Roman *cithara* were lyres.

The origin of the word points to the Far East. *Kithros* could have come from another part of the Mediterranean Sea and been exchanged in trade. The instruments Daniel mentions are not of the family of instruments used by the Israelites in Palestine, but are exotic types used for pagan worship.

H. *Neginot* — General meaning of the term *bineginot* or *'al-neginot* is to sing to the accompaniment of stringed instruments, but also simply "song." However, *neginot* is frequently interpreted as a musical instrument.

References are Psalms 4, 6, 54, 55, 61, 67, 76; Lamentations 3:14; 5:14; Isaiah 38:20; Psalms 77:7; Job 30:9.

Early Bible translators already show the discrepancies with regard to the meaning of this word. Nevertheless, the root of the word refers to its meaning. *Neginot* derives from the verb *naggen* "to touch," "to strike"—indicating clearly the manner of playing stringed instruments. This probably refers to stringed instruments for the accompaniment of singing.

I. *Shushan*—References: Psalms 45, 60, 69, 80 contain the word *shushan*. From *Rashi* some expounders think the word has a double meaning—an instrument of six strings in the shape of a lily. It is most likely not an instrument at all, but a popular song whose melody has been utilized for these psalms.

II. WIND INSTRUMENTS[26]

A. *'Ugab* — *'Ugab* is one of two instruments mentioned in the earliest musical reference in the Bible (Gen. 4:21), their initial use having been attributed to Jubal who was the "father" of the musical profession. This word is also used in Job 21:12, 30:31, and Psalms 150:4.

Not enough is known about it to make an absolute statement, but most likely the word "*'ugab*" did not refer to a specific instrument but rather to a whole family of some type. This seems to be indicated in Psalms 150:4. "Praise Him with stringed instruments (*minnim*) and the pipe (*'ugab*). "Stringed instruments" is used here as a collective term, and because of the parallelistic construction of biblical poetry it makes it almost certain that *'ugab* refers here to the family of wind instruments.

B. *Ḥalil*—plural is *ḥalilim* — This instrument occurs six times in the Old Testament—I Samuel 10:5; I Kings 1:40; Isaiah 5:12; 30:29; Jeremiah 48:36, twice in last mentioned passage. It is of Asiatic origin. Babylonians had used it mainly for lamentations. (It was some type of flute, maybe even a double-reed mouthpiece).

Use of *ḥalilim* in early ritual is confirmed in several biblical passages—I Sam. 10:5 in which *ḥalil* is mentioned as one of the instruments played by "a band of prophets."

Use in religious ceremonies is directly referred to in Isaiah 30:29: "Ye shall have a song ... and gladness of heart, as when one goeth with the pipe (*ḥalil*) ..."

Ḥalil, 'ugab and *'abub* are the three words found in the Bible which indicate wind instruments, individually as well as collectively. The timbre of the *ḥalil* is shrill and penetrating, similar to oboe-type, blown with a mouthpiece of reed.

This instrument is one of joy and gaiety and was played at all merry occasions, such as festivals, banquets, popular entertainments, coronations, etc. At the Feast of Tabernacles wealthy people frequently hired *ḥalil*-players for domestic entertainment. In contrast, the tone could also be mournful and wailing and was appropriate for funeral ceremonies, too. Its shrill tone could also create a state of ecstasy.

C. *Nekeb* — This is not a musical instrument — just thought to be by some.

D. *Neḥilot* — The expression *'el ha-neḥilot*" is used only once in the Bible, in the heading of Psalm 5. This expression is probably an instruction for accompanying Psalm 5 with woodwinds (pipes), whereas, with most psalms stringed instruments were usually used, or especially called for.

E. *'Alamot* — It is not certain whether this is a musical instrument or not.

F. *Maḥol* — This instrument is thought to be used in the Bible as a musical instrument at certain times. In the superscriptions of Psalms 53 and 88 *'al mahalot* refers to musical renditions of these Psalms, indicating the accompaniment with woodwinds. (Nothing conflicts with this theory.)

G. *Mashroḳita* — The *Mashroḳita* was among the instruments of Nebuchadrezzar's court (Dan. 3:5, 7, 10, 15). The word could be derived from Hebrew *sharaḳ* "to hiss," "to whistle," but it is generally assumed that it refers to a foreign instrument, one of the instruments that were considered "exotic."

There are some insurmountable difficulties in trying to find out exactly what this instrument was like, so for want of a better, more definite solution we will identify it with the *syrinx* which had a row of pipes of different length, which produced a hissing sound. This peculiarity seemed to justify the derivation of the word from the Hebrew *sharaḳ*.

H. *Sumponyah* — This instrument is not mentioned in the Hebrew text of the Bible. It appears in the Book of Daniel among instruments played in Nebuchadrezzar's orchestra (3:5, 10, 15). It is not certain at all if this was a wind or stringed instrument or if it was an instrument at all. Some musicologists still think it was a type of bagpipe.

I. *Ḥazoẓerah*—plural *ḥazoẓerot* — This instrument was a long straight trumpet built by the Israelites after Egyptian models. It was in Egypt during the reign of Tut-Ankh-Amen. Two of these, a silver and a bronze, were found in his tomb. Trumpets were also used by the Assyrians, as bas-reliefs show us.

The *ḥazoẓerah* was one ell long, its straight tube somewhat wider than *ḥalil* and widened at the lower end into a bell. The mouthpiece was rather broad. The form was identical with today's signal trumpets, called "herald's trumpets." The *ḥazoẓerah* was made of metal, either bronze or, for sacred trumpets, beaten silver.

God commanded Moses to make two trumpets (Num. 10:2). The sounding of the *ḥazoẓerah* was the exclusive privilege of Aaron's descendants (Num. 10:8). Players were called *ḥazoẓerim* and they played the sacred trumpets. Unlike pagan worship (with instruments) Israelites blew trumpets not to awaken their god-like pagans, but "for a memorial before your God." (Num. 10:10).

Trumpets (secular) were used to gather the congregation, to cause camps to set forward, to invite princes for a gathering, to sound alarms in danger, to give signals when going to war; (religious) for religious feasts, the New Moon, daily burnt and peace offerings and all important ritual ceremonies. The Old Testament mentions *ḥazoẓerah* twenty-nine times.

J. *Shofar*—plural *shofarot*[27] — The *shofar* is still used in the Jewish liturgy and is the only instrument of Ancient Israel that survived the millennia in its original form. The Hebrews took over the *shofar* from the Assyrians. The word is derived from *shapparu* (Assyrian) meaning "wild goat" and is made of a ram's horn. The original form of the shofar was a curved one like that of the natural ram's horn.

The Year of the Jubilee is like the New Year in the blowing of the *shofar* and in the Benedictions. The *shofar* blown in the Temple was made from the horn of a wild goat, straight, with its mouthpiece overlaid with gold. Later when the *shofar* was blown on New Year's day, this was to remind God symbolically of his promise given to Abraham, Isaac and Jacob. The blowing on other days was also symbolic in that the faithful should remember the ram Abraham sacrificed in the place of his son.

The *shofar* was the only instrument permitted to be blown after the burning of the sanctuary in Jerusalem, all music being prohibited as a sign of mourning.

The primitive *shofarot* were made by cutting off the tip of the natural horn or boring a hole into it; therefore there was no mouthpiece and only crude sustained tones could be produced. The *shofar* with a mouthpiece represents a more developed form of the instrument, but even then the tones were limited to two or maybe three in number.

If *shofarot* were damaged, they could be used again only if they were expertly repaired. They were not to be painted over with colors, but ornaments and inscriptions could be carved on them.

The *shofar* was blown only by priests and Levites on special occasions, in secular events by laymen, children and by women in cases of emergency, and was frequently blown on other than ritual occasions.

The *shofar* is mentioned most frequently in the Bible—seventy-two times. By this we know its great importance in the religious and secular life of the Jewish people.

Examples of religious use:

1. Transfer of the ark of the covenant by David (II Sam. 6:15).

2. Renewal of the covenant by King Asa (II Chron. 15:14).

3. Announcement of the New Moon (Ps. 81:3).

4. Thanksgiving to God for His miraculous deeds (Ps. 98:6; 150:3).

Examples of secular festivities:

1. Absalom's accession to the throne (II Sam. 15:10).

2. Solomon's anointment as king (I Kings 1:34).

3. Jehu's accession to the crown (II Kings 9:13).

The *shofar* was the regular signal instrument in times of war for assembling the warriors, attacking the enemy, pursuing the vanquished or announcing the victory. The *shofar* played a decisive role in the seige of Jericho.

Of all the Jewish instruments used in the sacred service the *shofar* is the only one that has survived; because the Jews have maintained their religious institutions and their musical tradition.

K. *Ķeren* — The literal meaning of the word *ķeren* is "firm," "solid." It refers to the hard horn of the neat in contrast to the soft flesh of the bovine cattle.

It is implied that the *ķeren* was made from animal horn and was powerful, that is, loud. It also served as a signal instrument; it was made entirely of neat horn and had no metal parts. It is not connected in biblical text with the sacred service and, therefore, it is assumed it was used exclusively as a secular instrument.

L. *Yobel* — This term appears for the first time in the Bible in Leviticus 25:9-54. It was used especially for announcing the Year of Jubilee. The *yobel* was much louder than the *shofar* or *ķeren*; therefore, it was bound to have a larger shape. It had a wide resounding bell of metal that could be put on and taken off and functioned like a megaphone. The description of Moses' ascension of Mt. Sinai (Exod. 19:13, 16, 19) indicated that such a larger horn type with a resounding bell was used.

The characteristic feature of the *yobel* was the metal sound bell that, no doubt, was put together of several parts. The adquate translation of *yobel* would be "horn of the Jubilee," or "high-sounding horn."

III. PERCUSSION—SHAKING AND RATTLING INSTRUMENTS[28]

A. *Tof*—plural *tuppim*[29] — This is a collective term for all kinds of hand-drums of the ancient Hebrews. The form of this instrument is not given in the Scriptures so we have to rely on analogies with similar instruments of other ancient Oriental people and on pictorial reproductions provided by the antiquities of Egypt and Assyria.

The *tof* consisted of a wooden or metal hoop covered with an animal skin and was played with either the fingers or the clenched fist. There is no indication it was played with sticks. It was the most primitive, common instrument of ancient Israel and could be played easily by anybody.

In Israel the *tuppim* were played by the girls and women and occasionally by the men, and were used much for dancing. They were the symbol of *joy*.

The *tof* was used in religious ceremonies in the early history of the Jews. Dancing, singing and playing are the three elements with which they glorified God.

B. *Meziltayim, Zelzelim*[30] — The only percussion instruments admitted unreservedly in the sacred service were the bronze cymbals which were named in the plural form—*meziltayim*.

The Egyptian cymbals had a broad, flat rim and a large bulge in the center. They were held upright and played sideways. The Jewish *zelzelim* were no doubt similar. According to Josephus they were large bronze plates played with both hands. The cymbals of the Temple were made of brass "to sound aloud" (I Chron. 15:19).

These instruments are found for the first time in the Bible at the transfer of the ark of the covenant to Jerusalem (II Sam. 6:5). At the institution of the regular sacred music the *meziltayim* acquired an important ritual function, being played by three precentors heading a group of singers and leading their groups by beating the cymbal. They were often played by the Temple Levites.

Jewish song was not metrical like our Western music; therefore, marking of the beats with cymbals, as we know it, could not be applied in the music of the Temple. The sounding of the cymbals was the signal for starting the choir-singing in later Jewish ceremonies. Cymbal-playing Levites are mentioned at the rededication of the Temple by Hezekiah (II Chron. 29:25).

C. *Shalishim*—This word appears only once in the Bible (I Sam. 18:6) and it is not certain whether it is even an instrument—it is very vague. By analogy with Ugaritic (+⌞+) — metal (meaning three) they could be symbols or metal bowls.[31]

D. *Mena'ane'im* — This word appears in biblical text only in II Samuel 6:5. It originates from the verb *nu'a* which means "to shake," "to move about." They are a shaking instrument, like the Egyptian *sistrum,* though not quite so richly adorned. They consisted of a metal frame, inserted with rods and carrying loose rings. The frame had a handle which the player held to shake the instrument, thereby creating a tinkling sound.

These instruments were possibly taken over from Egypt or Babylonia.

E. *Pa'amonim* (derived from the verb *pa'am*, meaning "to strike") — In Exodus 28:33,34 and 39:25,26 it signifies the little bells attached to the lower seam of the high priest's purple garment. These bells were made of gold and had a bright sound which was just loud enough to indicate the whereabouts of the high priest. Since bells proper were used only in seventh century B.C.E., these must have been metal platelets. Later, they were substituted by actual bells.[32]

F. *Mezillot* — This is mentioned in Zechariah 14:20 and is rendered generally as "bells" which were hung upon horses. The Jewish *mezillot* must have been larger and more compact than the dainty *pa'amonium* on the high priest's garment, because they were supposed to carry an inscription on them — "Holy Unto The Lord."

The *pa'amonim* and *mezillot* were not musical instruments as we consider such. They did not serve musical or artistic aims; their purpose was to exert an extra-musical effect by their sound.

Music in the Temple at Jerusalem

From the composition of the orchestra of the first Temple it can be seen that Israel accepted and adapted the same type arrangement of religious orchestra as was used in Egypt at its cultural height. There is a legend that when Solomon married Pharoah's daughter she brought with her 1,000 varieties of instruments. This seems to have some validity and is based on historical facts, for the instruments used in the first temple and the arrangement of its orchestra was similar to those in Egypt.[33]

Instruments used in the first Temple were:[34]

    I. Strings
       A. *Nebel*
       B. *Kinnor*

   II. Non-Musical Wind Instruments
       A. *Shofar*
       B. *Chatzotzerah*

  III. Musical Wind Instruments
       A. *'Ugav*
       B. *Halil*
       C. *'Alamoth*

  IV. Percussion
       A. *Tof*
       B. *Meziltayim*
       C. *Pa'amonim*

The instruments used in the second Temple were perhaps not quite so elaborate, but there is no reason to expect that the order and method of worship through music had drastically changed. Thus, these instruments were probably heard by Jesus and the disciples since they attended the Temple on several occasions, especially at the time of the Feasts. Music was undoubtedly important to Jesus himself, since he led the disciples in a hymn on the way to his betrayal at the Garden of Gethsemane (Mark 14:26).

AFTERWORD

A major element in comprehending literature is an understanding of the author's world view and the historical setting in which the literature was produced. *Before the Times*, by using both original material and well-respected secondary sources, has attempted to help bridge the distance between the twentieth-century reader and the literature which records the birth and teachings of Christianity.

Many individuals, although familiar with both the Old and New Testaments, find the three centuries preceding the world into which Christ was born confusing and vague. On the one hand, *Before the Times* has helped provide a basis by which the New Testament world, and the forces which shaped it, can be better understood. More significant, perhaps, is the realization that the birth of Jesus and the Christian message occurred at a time which included elements that facilitated its almost universal influence on the western world. Was this a mere accident of time? To one prominent New Testament writer the time at which the birth of Christ occurred was not simply a fortuitous event.

> "But when the fulness of the time was come, God sent forth his Son, made of a woman, made under the law, to redeem them that were under the law, that we might receive the adoption of sons. And because ye are sons, God hath sent forth the Spirit of his Son into your hearts, crying, Abba, Father. Wherefore thou art no more a servant, but a son; and if a son, then an heir of God through Christ." (Galatians 4:4-7)

"But when the fulness of the time was come . . ." Saint Paul wrote these word to the church at Galatia during the latter half of the first century. Although directed to a local congregation the content and implications of his statement are in no way provincial but have had profound significance for millions of Christians throughout the world. The birth and life of Jesus Christ can be summarized as redemptive events which offer believers a unique relationship with God and the hope of eternal life.

Perhaps the words of Paul "in the fulness of time" could be viewed as a rhetorical element to introduce his christology. Such a view, however, would seem to miss the richness and the complexity of the situation in which the birth of Christianity occurred. As the preceding chapters have so graphically shown, forces and events involving the Jewish, Greek and Roman cultures all contributed to setting the stage upon which the redemptive act of Christ could be carried out and communicated to the world.

The Jews were a chosen people. To Abraham the promise was given that he would be the father of a great nation and that many throughout the centuries would call him "blessed." Although born and nurtured in a polytheistic Mesopotamian culture, Abraham responded to the voice of God and left his home in Ur of Chaldees to seek a land promised by God. Significant was the physical move, but more significant was Abraham's shift from the belief in many gods to a monotheistic position, a belief not found in either the Egyptian or Mesopotamian cultures which dominated Abraham's world. From the nation that Abraham produced came the great lawgiver, Moses, and the Torah, which preached equality and respect for all persons, taught justice, and declared that there was one God, whose name was "I am that I am." The God of Abraham and Moses was the Being from whom all that exists partakes of being. Although conquered, oppressed and enslaved in the intervening centuries before "the fulness of time," and dispersed throughout the near eastern and western worlds, Jews with their love of the Torah and their reverence for God held to their monotheistic faith.

Among the ambitions of Alexander the Great, who lived more than 300 years before the birth of Christ, was "one language and one world." His armies swept across the world like a flame of fire, and with his conquest the Greek language became the *lingua franca,* and common language, and Greek culture became dominant. Although his empire was fragmented soon after his death, the Greek language and Hellenistic culture continued to be influential and widespread.

After Alexander came Julius Caesar with ambitions to conquer the world. Extending from the western end of the Mediterranean Sea to the Euphrates River in the Near East, the Roman world was organized into a great empire. Efficiently administered by means of provinces and districts closely supervised by local governors and backed by superior military power, the Roman world was generally peaceful during the reign of Caesar Augustus, who ruled when Jesus Christ was born in a small village of the Roman province of Judea called Bethlehem.

For Saint Paul, the redemptive event of Christ's life occurred in "the fulness of time." Through the dispersion of the Jews the concept of monotheism so central to their belief had been introduced to cultures far beyond Jerusalem. The principles of the Torah had become widely known through the translation of the Old Testament into Greek, the common language of the world after Alexander's conquest. Roman emphasis on law and order and their system of roads, which were paved, well drained, and usually patrolled had provided a means of safe travel across the Roman empire. Access to cities and avenues of communication had been greatly improved.

In this setting Christianity was born. Beginning with the teachings of Jesus, who proclaimed salvation, forgiveness and peace, it rapidly expanded through the missionary efforts of those who had themselves experienced redemption and subsequent peace in their lives.

As this book has shown, this rapid expansion can be explained in part by the many forces in Judaism and Greek and Roman culture which prepared the world for its reception. Without the concept of monotheism, the teachings of the Torah and the Messianic hope, and the many contributions of the Greeks and Romans to language, law, administration, travel and other elements of the culture of Jesus' day, the message of redemption would not have found the fertile soil so necessary to its reception and propagation.

In the larger context, Paul's expression "when the fulness of time was come God sent forth his Son," must be regarded as an insightful grasp of the factors which provide the milieu for the coming of Christ and an affirmation of God's sovereignty. From the teachings of Jesus, many times in obscure villages in Judea, Galilee and Samaria, grew the Christian faith, which has touched and transformed the lives of millions during the past two millenia. One cannot help but ask whether, if the birth of Christ had occurred several hundred years earlier or later, its impact and influence would have been the same.

To Christians the sacrifice of Christ is looked to as the act which brings them redemption and eternal life, but in a sense this is only the beginning. There is yet to be a culmination which will result in a completion of the redemptive work begun at Calvary. This culmination can be viewed on two levels. The first is an intensely personal level which involves the end of one's life in its present state and in Saint Paul's words results in the Christian's "being present with the Lord." The second is the level of universal longing spoken of in Scripture and awaited by many believers of the three monotheistic faiths—Judaism, Christianity, and Islam. This aspect of the culmination will occur with the coming of One who will establish world peace and provide universal justice and love.

Although throughout the centuries Christianity has provided many individuals with the answer to the question of life's meaning, the circumstances of our world still make this question painfully relevant. Today, many individuals are filled with uncertainty, suspicion and fear. While some are preoccupied with material gain and a philosophical emphasis that often stresses self love and the treatment of others merely as a means to a selfish end, others find themselves bewildered by what appears to be a kind of aimlessness and lack of direction in the world order. Believers, too, are not exempt from the pressures and anxieties of living in the twentieth century. Comfort can be found, however, in the realization that, viewed from a much broader perspective, the Messianic concepts discussed in this book suggest a "fulness of times" to come when all the promises of God to the patriarchs, Israel, the Church and the world left unfulfilled at his first advent will then be realized.

As Saint Paul held that Christ's first coming was not a fortuitous event but was long prepared for by the working of a sovereign will among many nations throughout a long history, so believers may hold that today's events, though often appearing to occur aimlessly or in contradiction to a divine will, are working toward the ends that God has decreed; and that they will bring about a world of righteousness and peace for all nations. This Messianic hope has supported millions of believers living in a world that often appears to be dominated by actions that are directly opposed to the concepts and values of Judaism and Christianity.

On an individual level there is comfort in the concept that events which occur in one's life that are deemed to be negative may, given a larger perspective, have been part of a process which will lead one to fulfillment and provide a greater understanding of the meaning of life. Taken in a larger context, perhaps centuries from now, one will look back and see that the events that today are swirling around us in apparent aimlessness and chaos were those very events that were designed to culminate in the "fulness of times" hoped for by multitudes of believers.

This book has in several ways shown the sovereignty of God in the events preceding and accompanying Christ's birth. A close reading of its pages in an effort to see the Hand of God at work in world events will surely strengthen the believer's faith for the future. The reader will find that faith points in two directions. It points first to the past, to a world of recorded events and concrete acts which help to produce and to nourish faith. It points also to the future which is both conditioned and created by the past.

Gary R. Moncher
Oakland, California

APPENDIX

APPENDIX

TABLE OF JEWISH WEIGHTS AND MEASURES,

PARTICULARLY OF THOSE MENTIONED IN JOSEPHUS'S WORKS.

Of the JEWISH *Measures of* LENGTH

	Inches.	Feet.	Inches.
Cubit, the standard,	21	1	9
Zereth or large span,	10.5	0	10½
Small span,	7	0	7
Palm or hand's breadth,	3.5	0	3½
Inch or thumb's breadth,	1.16	0	1.16
Digit or finger's breadth,	0.875	0	0.875
Orgyia or fathom,	84	7	0
Ezekiel's Canneh or Reed,	126	10	6
Arabian Cannah or pole,	168	14	0
Schœnus, line or chain,	1,680	140	0
Sabbath-day's journey,	42,000	3,500	0
Jewish mile,	84,000	7,000	0
Stadium or furlong,	8,400	700	0
Parasang,	252,000	21,000	0

Of the JEWISH *Measures of* CAPACITY.

	Cub. Inches.	Pints or Pounds.
Bath or Epha,	807.274	27.83
Corus or Chomer,	8,072.74	278.3
Seah or Saton,	269.091	9.266
Ditto, according to Josephus,	828 28	28.3
Hin,	134.54	4.4633
Ditto, according to Josephus,	414.12	14.3
Omer or Assaron,	80.722	2.78
Cab,	44.859	1.544
Log,	11.21	0.39
Metretes or Syrian firkin,	207	7.125

Of the JEWISH WEIGHTS *and* COINS.

	£	s.	d.
Stater, Siclus, or shekel of the sanctuary, the standard,	0	2	6
Tyrian coin, equal to the shekel,	0	2	6
Bekah, half of the shekel,	0	1	3
Drachma Attica, one-fourth,	0	0	7½
Drachma Alexandrina, or Darchon, or Adarchon, one-half,	0	1	3
Gerah, or Obolus, one-twentieth,	0	0	1½
Manch, or Mna—100 shekels in weight, 21,900 grains Troy,			
Maneh, Mna, or Mina, as a coin—60 shekels,	7	10	0
Talent of silver—3000 shekels,	375	0	0
Drachma of gold, not more than	0	1	1
Shekel of gold, not more than	0	4	4
Daric of gold,	1	0	4
Talent of gold, not more than	648	0	0

TABLE OF THE JEWISH MONTHS

IN JOSEPHUS AND OTHERS, WITH THE SYRO-MACEDONIAN NAMES JOSEPHUS GIVES THEM, AND THE NAMES OF THE JULIAN OR ROMAN MONTHS CORRESPONDING TO THEM.

Hebrew Names.	Syro-Macedonian Names.	Roman Names.
(1) Nisan.	Xanthicus.	March and April.
(2.) Jyar.	Artemisius.	April and May.
(3.) Sivan.	Dæsius.	May and June.
(4.) Tamuz.	Panemus.	June and July.
(5.) Ab.	Lous.	July and August.
(6.) Elul.	Gorpiæus.	August and September.
(7.) Tisri.	Hype. beretæus.	September and October.
(8.) Marchesvan.	Dius.	October and November.
(9.) Casleu.	Apellæus.	November and December.
(10. Tebeth.	Audynæus.	December and January.
(11.) Shebat.	Peritius.	January and February.
(12.) Adar.	Dystrus.	February and March.

Veadar, or the Second Adar, intercalated.

964

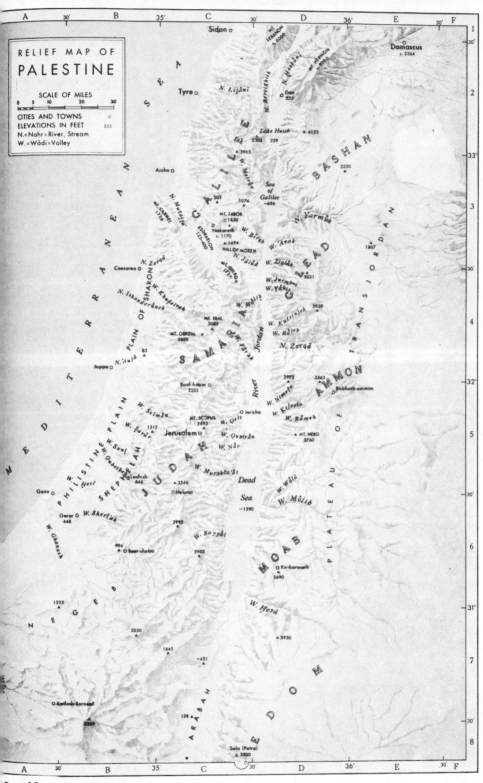

RELIEF MAP OF
PALESTINE

SCALE OF MILES

0 5 10   20   30

CITIES AND TOWNS   o
ELEVATIONS IN FEET   555
N.= Nahr = River, Stream
W.= Wâdi = Valley

Sidon o

MT. LEBANON
▲ 6090

MT. HERMON
▲ 9190

Damascus
c. 2264

S   E   A

Tyre o

N. Lîṭânî

N. Berrishtha

BASHAN

Dan
555

Lake Huleh
2300 229

▲ 4123

2320

Accho o

▲ 3963

G
A
L
I
L
E
E

W. Melek

N. Na'mein

Sea
of
Galilee
−696

N. Yarmuk

MT. CARMEL
1740

502

1074

MT. TABOR
± 1850

N. Jalūd

W. Bîreh

1807

ESDRAELON
125−300

Nazareth
c. 1170

W. 'Arab

G
I
L
E
A
D

N. Zerqa

Caesarea o

▲ 1694

HILL OF MOREH

W. Ziglâb

MT. GILBOA
1696

2221

W. Jurm
W. Yâbis

N. Iskanderûneh

P
L
A
I
N

O
F

S
H
A
R
O
N

W. Khudeirah

W. Mâlih

3930

W. Kufrinjeh

MT. EBAL
3085

W. Far'ah

W. Râjeb

MT. GERIZIM
2890

N. Zerqa

S
A
M
A
R
I
A

Jordan

85

N. 'Aujā

Joppa o

Baal-hazor o
3333

River

2972

3563

AMMON

W. Nimrîn

W. Kelt

Rabbath-ammon

W. Selmân

MT. SCOPUS
2693

Jericho o

W. Rāmeh

1317

W. Sarâr

W. Qelt

MT. NEBO
2760

P
H
I
L
I
S
T
I
N
E

P
L
A
I
N

W. Sanṭ

Jerusalem o

W. Qumrân

W. 'Anā

T
R
A
N
S
J
O
R
D
A
N

Gaza o

W. Qubeibeh

W. Nâr

W. Sureir

Ḥesī

J
U
D
A
H

W. Murabba'ât

Dead

W. Wâlā

o Lachish
846

▲ 3346

Sea
−1290

W. Mōjib

Gerar o
448

o Hebron

W. Sherī'a

2992

W. Sayyâl

994

o Beer-sheba

2103

M
O
A
B

Kir-haraseth
3690

1225

P
L
A
T
E
A
U

O
F

N
E
G
E
B

2050

W. Hesā

1645

3930

−451

A
R
A
B
A
H

o Kadesh-barnea

2389

E
D
O
M

128

Sela (Petra)
c. 3800

Map 10

205

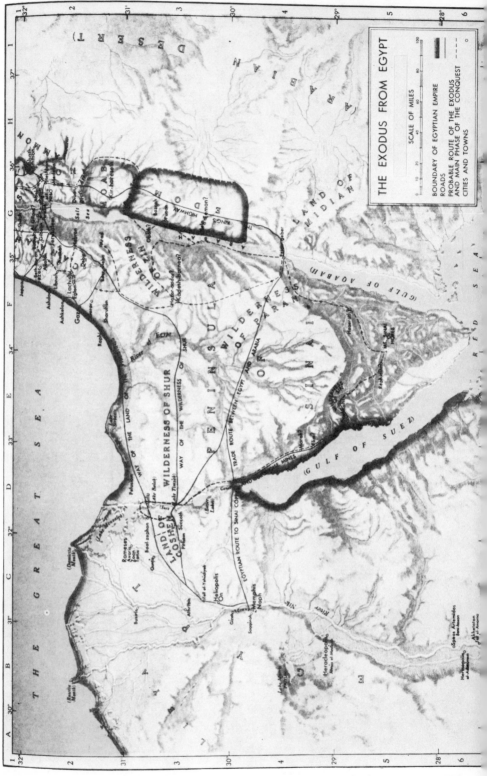

THE EXODUS FROM EGYPT

206

Map

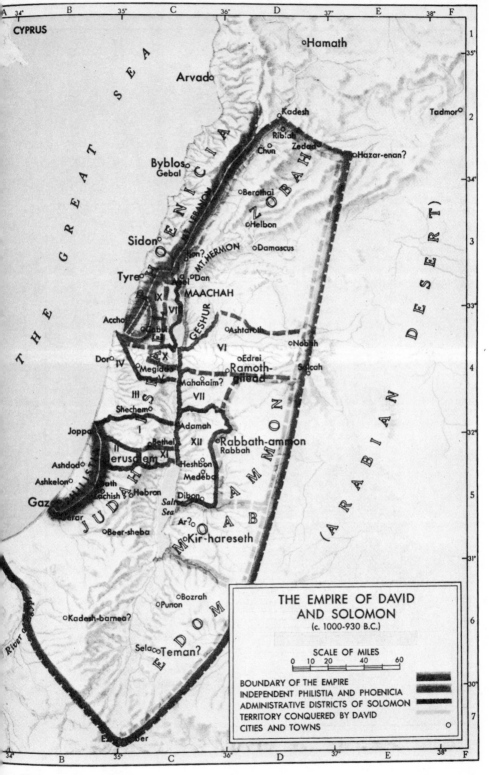

CYPRUS

THE GREAT SEA

Hamath

Arvad

Kadesh
Riblah
Chun   Zedad
                Hazar-enan?

Byblos
Gebal

Berothai

ZOBAH

Helbon

Sidon   Damascus

MT. HERMON
Ijon?   Dan
Tyre   MAACHAH
          IX
          VIII   GESHUR
Accho
        Gabul
                Ashtaroth
        X   VI   Nobah
Dor   IV   Edrei   Salcah
    Megiddo   V   Mahanaim?   Ramoth-gilead
        III
    Shechem   VII
                Adamah
Joppa   I   Rabbath-ammon
        Bethel   XII   Rabbah
Ashdod Jerusalem XI
Ashkelon   Heshbon   AMMON
        Gath   Medeba
Gaza Lachish Hebron   Dibon
    Gerar   Salt
                Sea   MOAB
        Beer-sheba   Ar?
                Kir-hareseth

JUDAH

PHILISTIA

PHOENICIA

(ARABIAN DESERT)

River of Egypt

Bozrah
Kadesh-barnea?   Punon

EDOM
        Sela   Teman?

Ezion-geber

THE EMPIRE OF DAVID
AND SOLOMON
(c. 1000-930 B.C.)

SCALE OF MILES
0 10 20   40   60

BOUNDARY OF THE EMPIRE
INDEPENDENT PHILISTIA AND PHOENICIA
ADMINISTRATIVE DISTRICTS OF SOLOMON
TERRITORY CONQUERED BY DAVID
CITIES AND TOWNS

Map 12

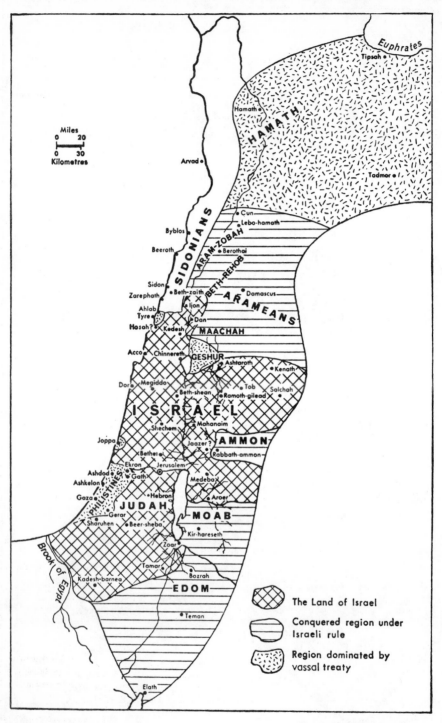

Map 13

The Kingdom of David.

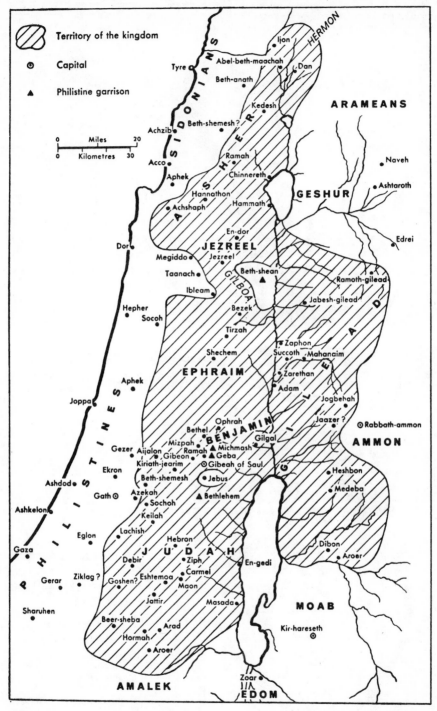

Map 14

The Kingdom of Saul.

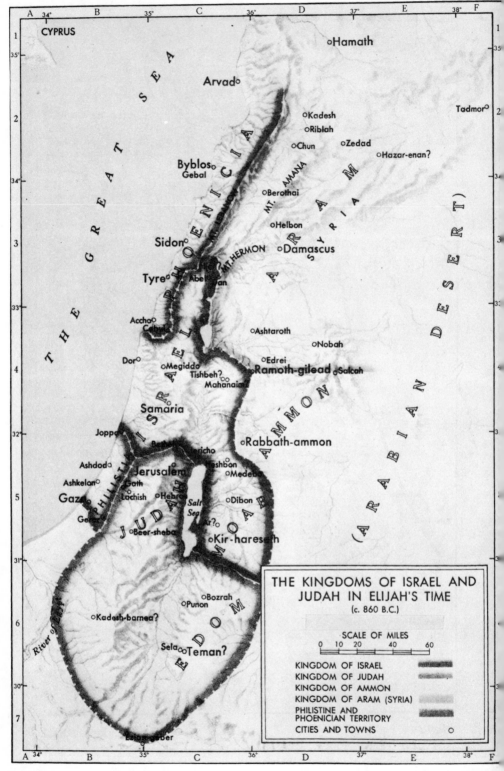

THE KINGDOMS OF ISRAEL AND
JUDAH IN ELIJAH'S TIME
(c. 860 B.C.)

SCALE OF MILES
0   10   20   40   60

KINGDOM OF ISRAEL
KINGDOM OF JUDAH
KINGDOM OF AMMON
KINGDOM OF ARAM (SYRIA)
PHILISTINE AND
PHOENICIAN TERRITORY
CITIES AND TOWNS   o

CYPRUS

THE GREAT SEA

PHOENICIA

Hamath

Arvad

Kadesh
Riblah
Chun   Zedad
                    Hazar-enan?
Tadmor

Byblos
Gebal

MT. AMANA
Berothai

Helbon

Sidon   Damascus
MT. HERMON
Tyre   Abel-...
                              A R A M   S Y R I A

Accho
Cabul   Ashtaroth
                    Nobah
Dor   Edrei
Megiddo   Ramoth-gilead   Salcah
Tishbeh?
Mahanaim

ISRAEL   A M M O N

Samaria

Joppa   Rabbath-ammon

Ashdod   Jericho
Ashkelon   Jerusalem   Heshbon
Gaza   Gath   Medeba
Lachish   Hebron
Geth   Salt   Dibon
          Beer-sheba   Sea   M O A B
Ar?
Kir-haresh

JUDAH

PHILISTIA

(ARABIAN DESERT)

Bozrah
Punon
Kadesh-barnea?

E D O M

Sela Teman?
River of Egypt

Ezion-geber

210

Map 1

THE KINGDOM OF JUDAH
IN ISAIAH'S TIME
(c. 700 B.C.)

SCALE OF MILES
0   10   20   40   60

ASSYRIAN EMPIRE
KINGDOM OF JUDAH
KINGDOM OF EDOM
KINGDOM OF MOAB
KINGDOM OF AMMON
INDEPENDENT TYRE
ASSYRIAN PROVINCES   DU'RU
CITIES AND TOWNS   o

Map 16

211

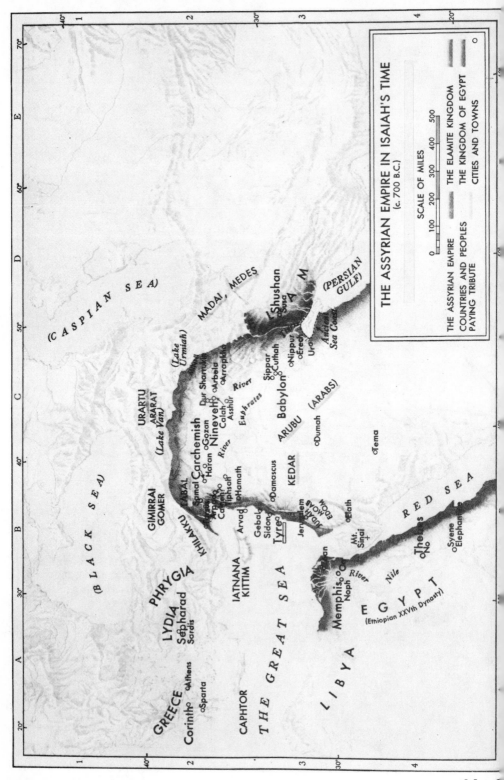

THE ASSYRIAN EMPIRE IN ISAIAH'S TIME
(c. 700 B.C.)

SCALE OF MILES

0   100   200   300   400   500

THE ASSYRIAN EMPIRE

COUNTRIES AND PEOPLES
PAYING TRIBUTE

THE ELAMITE KINGDOM

THE KINGDOM OF EGYPT

CITIES AND TOWNS

(CASPIAN SEA)

BLACK SEA)

THE GREAT SEA

RED SEA

GREECE

Corinth○ ○Athens

○Sparta

LYDIA

Sepharad

Sardis○

PHRYGIA

KHILAKKU

GIMIRRAI
GOMER

URARTU
ARARAT
(Lake Van)

TUBAL

Simal○

Carchemish

○Gozan

○Haran

○Arpad

Calneh○

○Hamath

Arvad○

Gebal○

Sidon○

Tyre○

Nineveh○

Calah○

Asshur○

Dur Sharrukin○

○Arbela

○Arrapkha

River

Euphrates

River

Tigris

Sippar○

Cutah○

Babylon○

○Nippur

Erech○

Ur○

Ancient
Sea Coast

(PERSIAN
GULF)

Shushan
Susa

ELAM

MADAI, MEDES

(Lake Urmiah)

Damascus○

KEDAR

(ARABS)

ARUBU

○Dumah

○Tema

Jerusalem○

JUDAH

MOAB

EDOM

○Elath

Mt.
Sinai

IATNANA
KITTIM

CAPHTOR

Memphis○

Noph○

○On

Nile   River

EGYPT

(Ethiopian XXVth Dynasty)

LIBYA

Thebes○
No

Syene○
Elephantine

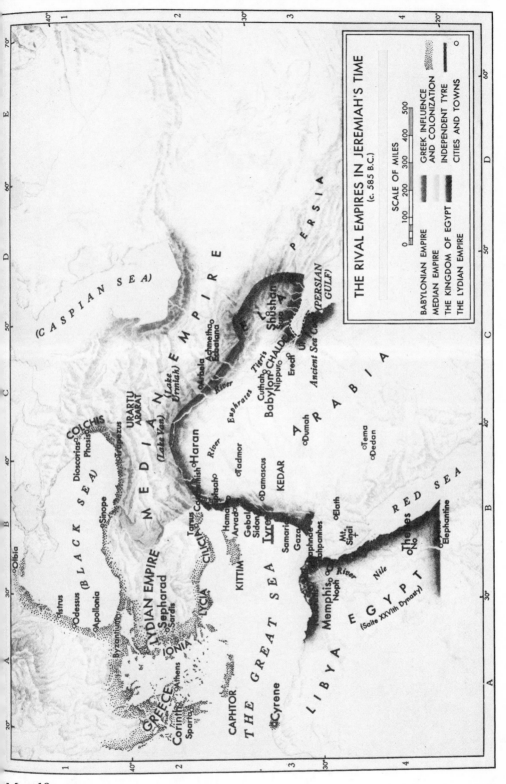

THE RIVAL EMPIRES IN JEREMIAH'S TIME
(c. 585 B.C.)

SCALE OF MILES
0   100   200   300   400   500

BABYLONIAN EMPIRE
MEDIAN EMPIRE
THE KINGDOM OF EGYPT
THE LYDIAN EMPIRE

GREEK INFLUENCE
AND COLONIZATION
INDEPENDENT TYRE
CITIES AND TOWNS

(CASPIAN SEA)

MEDIAN EMPIRE

PERSIA

ELAM

CHALDEA

URARTU
ARARAT

COLCHIS

(Lake Urmiah)
(Lake Van)

Achmetha
Ecbatana

Ashtabad

Shushan
Susa

(PERSIAN GULF)

Tigris River

Euphrates River

Cuthah
Babylon
Nippur
Eredu
Ur

Ancient Sea Coast

BLACK SEA

Dioscorias
Phasis

Tyanus
Trapezus

Sinope

Olbia
Istrus
Odessus
Apollonia

Byzantium

Sepharad
Sardis

LYDIAN EMPIRE

IONIA

GREECE
Corinth
Sparta

Athens

CAPHTOR

Cyrene

THE GREAT SEA

LIBYA

Carchemish
Haran

Tagus
Cilicia

KITTIM

LYCIA

Pelusa

Tadmor

Hama
Gebal
Sidon
Arvad

Samaria
Gaza

Tyre

Daphnae
Tahpanhes

Memphis
Noph

Mt. Sinai

Elath

Damascus

KEDAR

ARABIA

Dumah

Tema
Dedan

RED SEA

Thebes
No

Elephantine

Nile River

EGYPT
(Saite XXVIth Dynasty)

Map 18

213

A | 34° | B | 35° | C | 36° | D | 37° | E | 38° | F

CYPRUS

THE GREAT SEA

Arvad
ARVAD

Hamath

HAMATH

Tadmor

Tripolis
TRIPOLIS

Riblah
Chun
Zedad
Hazar-enan?

Byblos
Gebal

ROYAL PARK

MASSYAS

Berothai
MT. AMANA

Sidon
SIDON

Helbon

Ijon?
MT. HERMON
Damascus

Tyre
TYRE

Abelo
Dan

GELIL
HA-GOIM

QARNAIM

HAURAN

Acchao

Ashtarotho

Nobah

Dor
DOR

Ramoth-gilead
Edrei

Salcah

GILEAD

Samaria
SAMARIA

AMMON

Joppa

Rabbath-ammon

Bethele

Ashdod
ASHDOD

JUDAH
Jerusalem

Heshbon
Medeba

Ashkelo
Gaza

Lachish
Beth-zur
Hebra

Salt Sea

MOAB

Beer-sheba

IDUMAEA

ARABS

Kadesh-barnea?

River of Egypt

Elath?

THE PROVINCE OF JUDAH
IN NEHEMIAH'S TIME
(c. 440 B.C.)

SCALE OF MILES
0   10   20   40   60

BOUNDARY OF THE
PERSIAN EMPIRE

PROVINCES OF THE
FIFTH PERSIAN SATRAPY

○   CITIES AND TOWNS

(ARABIAN DESERT)

Map I

MANASSEH

Tell Qasileh •   Aphek • → Eben-ezer •   Tappuah •

Gath-rimmon? •   Lebonah •

Joppa ⊙   Azor •   Ono •   ⊙ Shiloh

I S R A E L

EPHRAIM   Baal-hazor •

Lod •   Bethel •   Ophrah •

Gimzo •   Mizpah •

Beth-horon •   Upper • Michmash •

Gittaim •   Lower •   Beth-aven •

Eltekeh •   Gezer • Shaalbim • Gibeon •   Ramah • ▲ Geba

Jabneel •   Gibbethon •   Aijalon • Chephirah •   Beeroth • Almon •

Kiriath-jearim •   Gibeah • Anathoth •

Ekron ⊙   Timnah •   Eshtaol •   Mozah • → Nob BENJAMIN

Zorah •   Jebus ⊙

Ashdod ⊙   Beth-shemesh •   Manahath •

Gath ⊙   Azekah •   Zanoah •

Jarmuth •   Hushah •   ▲ Bethlehem

Ashkelon ⊙   Sochoh •   Etam •

Achzib? • Adullam •   Netophah •

Libnah •   Keilah • Gedor •   Tekoa •

Moresheth-gath? •   Beth-zur •

Mareshah •   SHELAH   Nezib •   Halhul •

Gaza ⊙   Eglon • Lachish •   J U D A H   Hebron ⊙

Adoraim •   En-gedi •

KENAZ   Ziph •

Yurza •   Gerar • Ziklag? •   Debir •   Juttah •

Goshen? •   Anab • Sochoh •   Carmel •

Eshtemoa • Maon •

Madmannah •   K A L E B

Sansannah •   Jattir Anim •   Masada •

Sharuhen •   KENITES

Beer-sheba •   Arad •

SIMEON   Hormah •

JERACHMEEL

Aroer •

⊙   Capital.

▲   Philistine garrison.

→   Philistine campaign

0   Miles   20

0   Kilometres   30

Map 20   The Philistine Cities and the Areas of their Expansion.

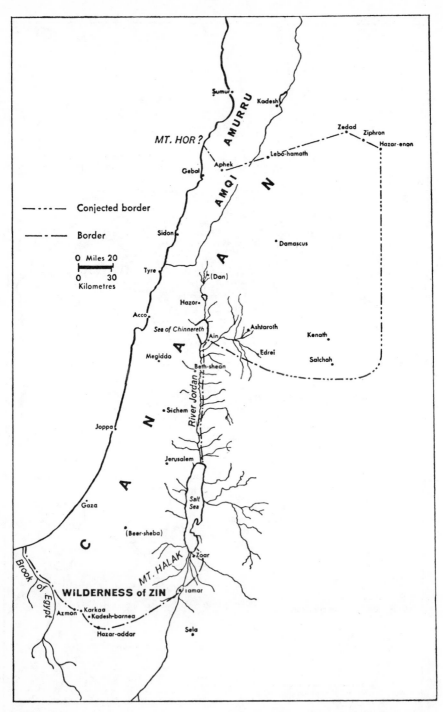

Map 21   The Borders of the Land of Canaan.

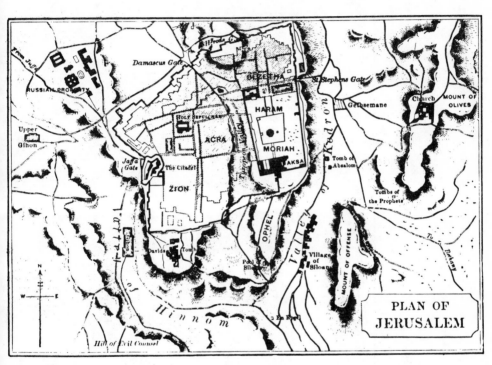

Map 22

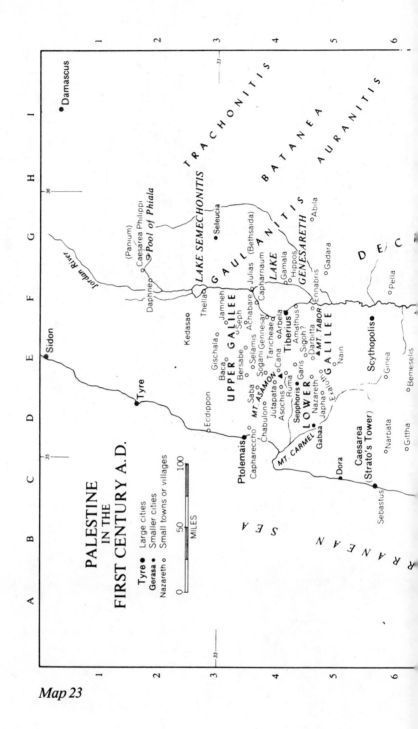

PALESTINE
IN THE
FIRST CENTURY A.D.

Tye ● Large cities
Gerasa ● Smaller cities
Nazareth ○ Small towns or villages

MILES
0   50   100

Damascus

Sidon

Tyre

Jordan River

(Panum)
Caesarea Philippi
Pool of Phiala

TRACHONITIS

Daphne

LAKE SEMECHONITIS

BATANEA

Seleucia

G A U L A N I T I S

AURANITIS

Kedasa

Thella

Jamneh
UPPER GALILEE
Seph
Baca
Gischala
Selamis
Achabare
Julias (Bethsaida)
Capharnaum
LAKE
Gamala
GENESARETH
Abila

DEC

Ecdippon

Bersabe
Saba
Sogani
Gennesar
MT. ASAMON
Jutapata
Taricheae
Cana
Arbela
Hippos
Gadara
Pella

Chabulono
Asochis
Ruma
Garis
Amathus
Ennabris

Caphareccho
Sepphoris
Sigoh ?
Tiberius
Darbitta
MT. TABOR

Ptolemais

LOWER GALILEE
Nazareth
Exaloth
Nain

Gabaa
Japha
Ginea

MT. CARMEL

Scythopolis

Benesenis

Dora

Caesarea
(Strato's Tower)

Narbata

Gittha

Sebastus

M E D I T E R R A N E A N   S E A

Map 23

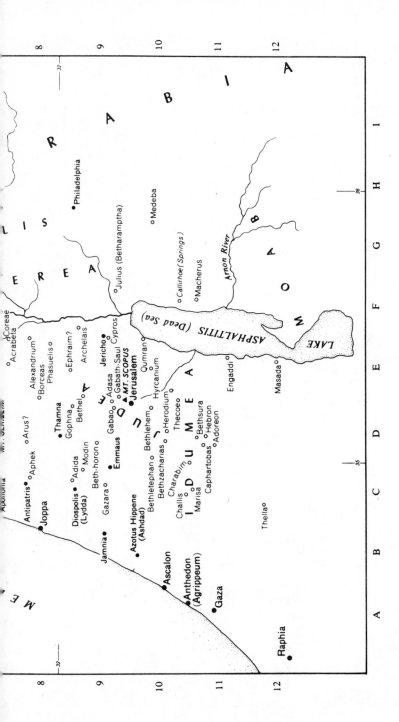

219

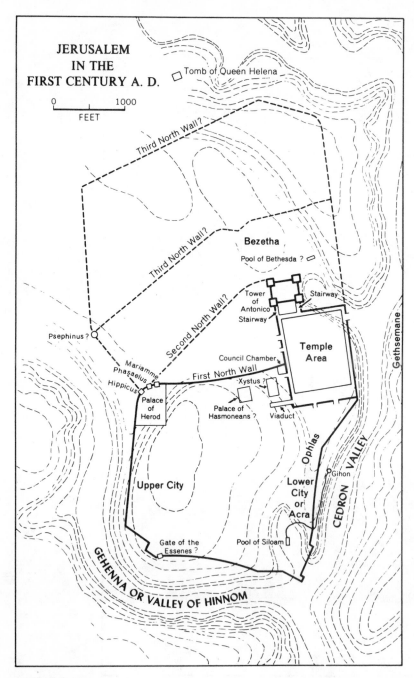

JERUSALEM
IN THE
FIRST CENTURY A. D.

Tomb of Queen Helena

0   1000
FEET

Third North Wall?

Third North Wall?

Bezetha

Pool of Bethesda ?

Second North Wall?

Tower
of
Antonico
Stairway

Stairway

Temple
Area

Gethsemane

Psephinus ?

Mariamme
Phasaelus
Hippicus

Council Chamber

First North Wall

Xystus ?

Palace
of
Herod

Palace
of
Hasmoneans ?

Viaduct

Ophias

Gihon

CEDRON VALLEY

Upper City

Lower
City
or
Acra

Gate of the
Essenes ?

Pool of Siloam

GEHENNA OR VALLEY OF HINNOM

Map 24

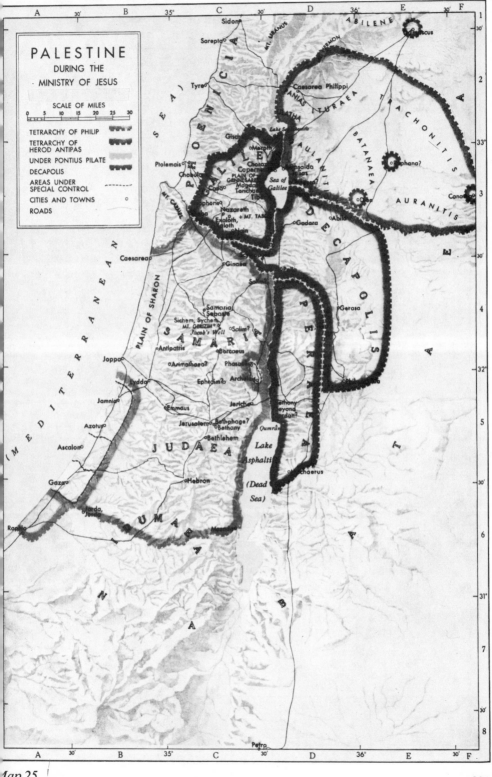

PALESTINE
DURING THE
MINISTRY OF JESUS

SCALE OF MILES

TETRARCHY OF PHILIP
TETRARCHY OF
HEROD ANTIPAS
UNDER PONTIUS PILATE
DECAPOLIS
AREAS UNDER
SPECIAL CONTROL
CITIES AND TOWNS
ROADS

Map 25

221

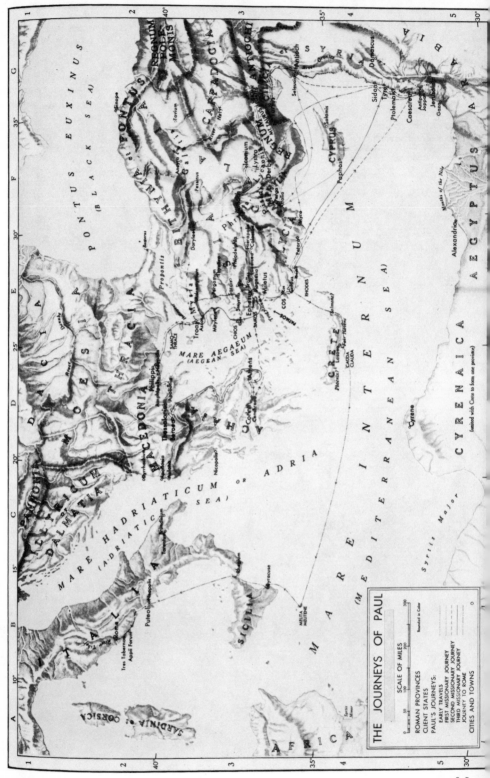

222

Map

REFERENCES

REFERENCES

Chapter I

1. Harold Lamb, *Alexander of Macedon,* pp. 101-04
2. The Delphian Course:, *The World's Progress,* Vol. 2, p. 358.
3. *ibid.* p. 371.
4. Jacob Abbott, *Alexander the Great,* p. 94.
5. Sir William Woodthorpe Tarn, *Hellenistic Civilisation,* p. 60.
6. *ibid.* p. 58.
7. Abbott, pp. 94ff.
8. William H. McNeill, *History of Western Civilization —
   A Handbook,* p. 108.
9. Abbott, pp. 134-35, 138.
10. E.W. Marsden, *Greek and Roman Artillery,* p. 101.
11. Abbott, pp. 178-80ff.
12. *ibid.* p. 160.
13. Lamb, pp. 39-43.
14. Tarn, p. 50.
15. *ibid.* p. 51.
16. *ibid.* p. 147; The Delphian Course, p. 370.
17. Tarn, pp. 145-48.
18. *ibid.* p. 146.
19. The Delphian Course, p. 370.
20. Tarn, p. 148.
21. *ibid.* p. 146.
22. *ibid.*
23. *ibid.* p. 250.
24. *ibid.*
25. *ibid.* pp. 250f; The Delphian Course, p. 371.
26. Edward McNall Burns, *Western Civilizations, p. 188.*
27. *McNeill, p. 110.*
28. *ibid.* Tarn, p. 250.
29. Lamb, p. 36-37.
30. Abbott, p. 24.
31. Lamb, pp. 276, 343-44; McNeill, p. 104.

32. Lamb, p. 443-44.
33. McNeill, p. 106; The Delphian Course. p. 370.
34. Abbott, pp. 17f; 180f.
35. Burns, p. 188.
36. Tarn, pp. 302-04; Lamb, p. 366.
37. McNeill, p. 115; Tarn, p. 307.
38. Tarn, p. 295.
39. Burns, p. 199.
40. Tarn, p. 269.
41. The Delphian Course, p. 370.
42. McNeill, p. 113.
43. The Delphian Course, p. 372.
44. *ibid.*
45. McNeill, p. 115.
46. The Delphian Course, p. 371.
47. McNeill, pp, 108-116.
48. The Delphian Society, p. 371.
49. Tarn, p. 339.
50. McNeill, p. 104.
51. Tarn, p. 333.
52. *ibid.* p. 79.
53. *ibid.* pp. 79ff.
54. McNeill, p. 116.
55. Tarn, p. 360.
56. *ibid.*
57. McNeill, p. 111.
58. *ibid.* pp. 111-112.
59. *Merrill C. Tenney, ed., The Zondervan Bible Dictionary,* pp. 324f.

Chapter II

1. E. E. Levinger, *The Story of the Jews,* pp. 43-44.
2. *ibid.* p. 44
3. *ibid.* p. 45
4. D. S. Russell, *The Jews from Alexander to Herod,* pp. 17-18.
5. Sidney Tedesche, *The First Book of Maccabees* (Jewish Aprocryphal Literature, Vol. I), pp. 18-19, 73-79.
6. Moshe Pearlman, *The Maccabees,* p. 50.
7. *ibid.* pp. 60-61.
8. Elias Bickerman, *The Maccabees,* p. 14.
9. *ibid.* p. 17.
10. Pearlman, p. 77.
11. Bickerman, pp. 18-20.
12. Pearlman, p. 250.
13. William Reuben Farmer, *The Maccabees, Zealots and Josephus,* pp. 132-33.
14. *ibid.* p. 138.
15. *ibid.* pp. 140-41.

Chapter III

1. Max I. Dimont, *Jews, God, and History,* pp. 85-88, 93-94.
2. Paul Goodman, *History of the Jews,* pp. 41-44.
3. D. S. Russell, *The Jews from Alexander to Herod,* pp. 80-102.
4. *ibid.* p. 85.
5. *ibid.* pp. 86-89.
6. *ibid.* p. 87; Cecil Roth, *History of the Jews,* p. 94-95
7. Russell, p. 87; Roth, pp. 94f.
8. Russell, p. 88; cf. Dimont, p. 90f.
9. Jackson, F. J. Foakes, *Josephus and the Jews,* p. 132.
10. Dimont, pp. 85-88.
11. Jackson, p. 133-34.
12. Russell, p. 90.
13. Roth, p. 95.
14. Jackson, p. 133-34.
15. Russell, pp. 90, 95-96.
16. Roth, p. 97.
17. Russell, pp. 91-92.
18. *ibid.* p. 95.
19. Roth, pp. 97-98.
20. Jackson, p. 43.
21. *ibid.* pp. 131-36; Russell, pp. 100-102.
22. Elma Ehrlich Levinger and Rabbi Lee J. Levinger,
    The Story of the Jew, pp. 50.
23. P. M. Raskin, "The Eternal Riddle" in Levinger (title page.

Chapter IV

1. George Foot Moore, *Judaism in the First Centuries of the Christian Era,* Vol. I, p. 59.
2. *ibid.*
3. D. S. Russell, *The Jews from Alexander to Herod,* p. 160.
4. Eduard Lohse, *The New Testament Environments,* p. 77.
5. Bruce Metzger, *The New Testament, Its Background, Growth and Content, p. 40.*
6. *Werner Foerster, From the Exile to Christ,* p. 65.
7. *ibid.* p. 66.
8. F. F. Bruce, *New Testament History,* p. 72; also cf. Robert M. Grant, *A Historical Introduction to the New Testament,* p. 257; Metzger, p. 40.
9. Lohse, p. 77; cf. Russell, p. 162.
10. Russell, p. 163, for Manson's theory.
11. Moore, p. 60.
12. Russell, p. 162-63.
13. Bo Reicke, *The New Testament Era,* p. 156.
14. Victor Tcherikover, *Hellenistic Civilization and the Jews,* p. 259.
15. Metzger, p. 41-2; cf. Kaufmann Kohler, "Pharisees," *The Jewish Encyclopedia,* Vol. IX, (1905), p. 665.
16. For a more detailed history see Reicke, pp. 161-62.
17. *ibid.* p. 160.
18. *ibid.* pp. 160-61.
19. Russell, pp. 160-61.
20. Lohse, p. 77.
21. *ibid.* pp. 77-78.
22. Moore, pp. 58-59.
23. David M. Rhoads, *Israel in Revolution,* pp. 36-37.
24. Jacob Nuesner, *A Life of Yohanan Ben Zakkai,* pp. 37, 39.
25. *ibid.* p. 36.
26. Bruce, p. 80.
27. Rhoads, pp. 34-35.
28. Neusner, p. 35.
29. Bruce, p. 80.
30. Neusner, p. 41.
31. *ibid.* p. 64.
32. Reicke, p. 163.
33. Neusner, p. 34.
34. *ibid.*
35. *ibid.* pp. 20-21, 38.

36. *ibid.* p. 64.
37. Lohse, p. 43.
38. Neusner, pp. 157ff.
39. Morton Smith, "Palestine Judaism in the 1st Century," *Israel, Its Role in Civilization,* p. 76; cf. Josephus, *Antiquities.*
40. Nuesner, p. 169.
41. *ibid.* p. 196-97.
42. *ibid.* p. 171.
43. *ibid.* p. 66.
44. Lohse, pp. 78-79; Reicke, p. 157.
45. Reicke, pp. 157-58.
46. Russell, p. 161.
47. Bruce, p. 79; cf. Josephus, *Antiquities,* . xviii. 1, 3.
48. See Lohse, pp. 80-81.
49. Rhoads, p. 34; cf. Josephus, *Antiquities.* xiii. 10, 6.
50. Grant, p. 259.
51. Lohse, pp. 78-79.
52. *ibid.* p. 81.
53. Russell, p. 164.
54. Lohse, pp. 81-82; see Rhoads for a discussion of whether the Pharisees were a religious or a political party, pp. 34-39.
55. Neusner, pp. 53-54.
56. *ibid.* p. 55.
57. Bruce, p. 79.
58. Neusner, p. 80.
59. cf. Everett Harrison, *A Short Life of Christ,* pp. 123ff.
60. Neusner, p. 43.
61. Pirke Aboth, iii. 19; cf. Bruce, p. 80.
62. Tcherikover, p. 253.
63. Neusner, p. 23; Metzger, p. 42; Russell, p. 156.
64. Lohse, p. 74; Moore, p. 69.
65. Rhoads, pp. 39-40.
66. Russell, p. 157.
67. *ibid..*
68. Reicke, pp. 153-54.
69. *ibid.* p. 153.
70. Bruce, p. 74.
71. Russell, p. 158.
72. Tcherikover, p. 262.
73. Lohse, p. 76.

74. Rhoads, p. 41.
75. *ibid*. p. 42; cf. Lohse, p. 77.
76. Neusner, p. 198.
77. Russell, p. 159; cf. also Moore, p. 68.
78. Lohse, p. 76; also see Josephus, *Bell* ii. 166; Rhoads, p. 41.
79. Rhoads, p. 41.
80. Neusner, p. 197.
81. Russell, p. 158.
82. Lohse, p. 76.
83. Rhoads, p. 40, cites Günther Baumbach, "Das Sadduzaerverständnis bei Josephus Flavius und im Neuen Testament", *Kairos* 13 (1971):27.
84. Rhoads, p. 40.
85. Russell, p. 159.
86. Reicke, p. 156.
87. Tcherikover, p. 253.
88. Metzger, pp. 40-41.

Chapter V

1. Gaster, Theodor H., "Samaritans." *The Universal Jewish Encyclopedia,* IX (1943), 335.
2. *ibid.*
3. *ibid.*
4. Gaster, p. 337.
5. *ibid.*
6. *ibid.*
7. *ibid.*; Gaster, p.336.
8. *ibid.*
9. *ibid.*
10. *ibid.*
11. *ibid.*
12. *ibid.*
13. *ibid.*
14. John Macdonald, *The Theology of the Samaritans,* p. 49.
15. *ibid.*
16. Macdonald, p. 67.
17. *ibid.*
18. *ibid.*
19. *The Interpreter's Dictionary of the Bible,* p. 194.
20. *ibid.*

Chapter VI

1. F. F. Bruce, *New Testament History, p. 85.*
2. *ibid.*
3. *ibid.* p. 82
4. D. S. Russell, *The Jews from Alexander to Herod,* p. 164.
5. C. F. Pfeiffer, *Between the Testaments,* pp. 116-17.
6. Bo Reicke, *The New Testament Era,* pp. 169-70.
7. Bruce, p. 82.
8. Russel, p. 166.
9. *ibid.*
10. *ibid.* p. 165.
11. Bruce, p. 90.
12. *ibid.*
13. Reicke, p. 173.
14. Russell, p. 165.
15. Bruce, pp. 90-91.
16. Russell, pp. 172-73.
17. Reicke, pp. 168-69
18. *ibid.* p. 169.
19. Père de Vaux, *L' Archaeologie et les Manuscrits de la Mes Morte,* pp. 100ff.
20. Reicke, p. 172.
21. Yigael Yadin, *The Message of the Scrolls,* p. 182.
22. *ibid.* p. 185.
23. *ibid.* pp. 185-86.
24. Renan, quoted by Pfeiffer, p. 118.
25. E. Schurer, quoted by Pfeiffer, p. 118.
26. Bruce, p. 92.

Chapter VII

1. Frank M. Cross, Jr., *The Ancient Library of Qumran and Modern Biblical Studies,* pp. 1-21.
2. R. K. Harrison, *The Dead Sea Scrolls,* p. 1-2.
3. Charles F. Pfeiffer, *The Dead Sea Scrolls,* pp.11- 12.
4. *ibid.,*p. 12.
5. Josef T. Milik, *Ten Years of Discovery in the Wilderness of Judaea,* p. 11.
6. Andre Dupont-Sommer, *The Dead Sea Scrolls,* p. 9.
7. D. Barthelemy and J. T. Milik, *Qumran Cave I* (Discoveries in the Judaean Desert I), part I, chap. I, by G. Lankester Harding, pp. 3-7; F. F. Bruce, *Second Thoughts on the Dead Sea Scrolls,* p. 13; Cross, p. 4.
8. Bruce, p. 13.
9. Barthelemy and Milik, p. 5.
10. Cited by Bruce, pp. 13-14.
11. Dupont-Sommer, p. 10.
12. Harrison, pp. 3-4.
13. Yigael Yadin, *The Message of the Scrolls,* pp. 32f.
14. Harrison, pp. 3-4.
15. Yadin, pp. 16-19, 23.
16. *ibid.* p. 23.
17. Harrison, p. 4, cites Sukenik's diary.
18. Yadin, p. 25.
19. *ibid.* p. 26-30.
20. Dupont-Sommer, p. 13; cf. Harrison, p. 5.
21. John C. Trever, *The Untold Story of Qumran,*pp. 17-18; Yadin, p. 30.
22. Bruce, p. 16.
23. Trever, pp. 21-22, 25.
24. *ibid.* p. 22, 25.
25. *ibid.* p. 23, 27.
26. *ibid.* pp. 22-27.
27. William Sanford LaSor, *The Dead Sea Scrolls and the Christian Faith,* p. 15; Trever, pp. 59-60.
28. Millar Burrows, *The Dead Sea Scrolls,* p. 12.
29. Trever, pp. 66-67.
30. *ibid.* pp. 72-75.
31. *ibid.* pp. 77-78, 83.

32. Burrows, p. 8.
33. Harrison, p. 7.
34. *ibid.*; Burrows, p. 15; John C. Trever, *The Dead Sea Scrolls, A personal Account,* p. 79.
35. Trever, *The Dead Sea Scrolls,* pp. 83-89.
36. Burrows, p. 17.
37. Harrison, p. 7.
38. Yadin, p. 36.
39. Harrison, p. 7.
40. Yadin, pp. 37-38.
41. Harrison, p. 25.
42. Yadin, pp. 36-37.
43. *ibid,* pp. 40-1, 45; Harrison, pp. 25.
44. Harrison, p. 25.
45. Yadin, p. 52.
46. *ibid.* p. 36.
47. Barthelemy and Milik, pp. 6-7.
48. Dupont-Sommer, p. 17.
49. Barthelemy and Milik, pp. 3-4.
50. Pfeiffer, p. 17.
51. Milik, p. 45; cf. Pfeiffer, p. 17, who says that there is no linguistic resemblance to Gomorroh in the name "Qumran."
52. Milik, p. 15.
53. *ibid.* pp. 15-16.
54. Harrison, pp. 10-11.
55. Barthelemy and Milik, p. 3.
56. Cross, p. 11.
57. *ibid.* pp. 12-13.
58. Harrison, p. 12.
59. Cross, p. 14.
60. Harrison, p. 12.
61. Cross, pp. 14-15.
62. Harrison, pp. 13-14.
63. Cross, p. 16.
64. *ibid.* pp. 18-19.
65. Milik, pp. 16-17.
66. Cross, p. 26.
67. *ibid.* p. 20; Milik, pp. 16-18.
68. Cross, pp. 20-21.
69. Harrison, p. 16.
70. *ibid.*

71. Cross, p. 27.
72. Pfeiffer, p. 19.
73. See Yadin, pp. 60-65 for his theory.
74. John D. Trever, *The Dead Sea Scrolls,* pp. 206-07.

Chapter VIII

1. Joseph Klausner, *The Messianic Idea in Israel,* p. 7; Sigmund Mowinckel, *He That Cometh,* pp. 3-5.
2. Mowinckel, p. 5.
3. *ibid.* p. 7.
4. Klausner, p. 11; Mowinckel, p. 340.
5. Klausner, pp. 15-16.
6. *ibid.* pp. 17-20.
7. *ibid.* pp. 17-18.
8. Mowinckle, p. 62.
9. *ibid.* p. 66.
10. *ibid.* p. 74.
11. *ibid.* p. 78.
12. *ibid.* p. 68.
13. Klausner, pp. 19-20.; Joseph A. Fitzmyer, *Essays on the Semitic Background of the New Testament,* pp. 115-126.
14. Klausner, pp. 21-30.
15. John M. Allegro, *The Dead Sea Scrolls,* p. 167.
16. *ibid.* p. 168.
17. *ibid.* pp. 168-69.
18. William Sanford LaSor, *The Dead Sea Scrolls and The Christian Faith.* p. 152; Millar Burrows, *More Light on the Dead Sea Scrolls,* pp. 297-311 for a survey of the positions.
19. Thurman Coss, *Secrets from the Caves,* p. 101; LaSor, p. 153-54.
20. Coss, p. 100.
21. Burrows, pp. 297-311; LaSor, pp. 152-56; Frank M. Cross, Jr., *The Ancient Library of Qumran and Modern Biblical Studies,* pp. 165-73.
22. LaSor, p. 155; cf. Karl Georg Kuhn, "Die beiden Messias Aarons und Israels," *NTS* 1 (1954-55): 178.
23. LaSor, p. 156.
24. *ibid.* pp. 156-57.
25. LaSor, p. 157. See pp. 157-63 for a discussion of Messiah in IQ28a; the passage which mentions the eschatological Messiah is restored almost completely in spite of manuscript damage. Also see Josef T. Milik, *Ten Years of Discovery in the Wilderness of Judaea,* pp. 123-28, for a discussion of the emendation.
26. LaSor, pp. 123-28; see Milik for an opposing view—that Messiah is eschatological; see also Burrows, p. 152, for the view that is generally

accepted that in QL "Messiah" occurs as a title; Burrows, p. 264, says "the word 'anointed' or 'Messiah' is clearly used for one who is to come at the end of the present age."

27. Mowinckel, p. 281.
28. Oscar Cullman, *The Christology of the New Testament,"* pp. 114-16.
29. Mowinckel, p. 282.
30. *ibid.* p. 284; R. Meyer, *Der Prophet aus Gailiaa,* pp. 70ff.; E. Meyer, *Ursprung und Anfänge des Christentums,* II, pp. 402ff.
31. F. P. Buhl, *Det israelitiske Folkes Historie,* pp. 437ff.; Mowinckel, p. 285.
32. Mowinckle, p. 311, 314.
33. Klausner, p. 465-66.
34. *ibid.* p. 459.
35. Mowinckel, pp. 326-29.
36. *ibid.* p. 335.
37. *ibid.* p. 303.
38. *ibid.* p. 304-06.
39. David Tiede, *The Charismatic Figure as Miracle Worker,* p. 197; cf. also S. G. F. Brandon, *Jesus and the Zealots, pp. 112-13.*
40. Brandon, pp. 112-13, cf. 100, 108-09.
41. Tiede, pp. 202f.
42. Cullmann, pp. 15-16; Paul Volz, *Die Eschatologie der Judischen Gemeinde in neutestamentlicher Zeitalter,* pp. 193ff.
43. Cullman, pp. 15-16. Cullman maintains that although these are Jewish-Christian writings, they can be used as sources for the Judaism of the New Testament era.
44. Ferdinand Hahn, *the Titles of Jesus in Christology,* p. 359; Cullmann, p. 19; Volz, p. 200; see A. Merx, *Der Messias oder Ta'ab der Samaritaner.*
45. Cullmann, p. 19; Hahn, p. 359.
46. Coss, pp. 99-100; Burrows, pp. 310-11.
47. Burrows, pp. 329-32. cf. Millar Burrows, J. C. Trever, and W. H. Brownlee, *The Dead Sea Scrolls of St. Mark's Monastery,* Vol. I, *The Isaiah Manuscript, the Habakkuk Commentary, pp. xix-xxiii.*
48. Volz, p. 194.
49. R. B. Y. Scott, "The Expectation of Elijah," *The Canadian Journal of Religious Thought,* p. 490; Howard Temple, *The Mopsaid Eschatological Prophet,* p. 3.
50. *ibid.*
51. *ibid.* Teeple, p. 4.

52. Scott, p. 492. An example of belief in return of the dead are found in W. C. Allen, *A Critical and Exegetical Commentary on the Gospel According to St. Matthew (The International Commentary)* on Matthew 14:2, p. 157; Teeple, p. 6, says that the idea that Elijah would raise the dead did not exist till the Palestinian Talmud (Shabbut 3c; 5th century A.D.) and in some Midrash.

53. Scott, pp. 492-93.

54. For this classification we are indebted to Scott, p. 493.

55. *ibid.* For the same view see Dr. W. M. Christie, *JTS* (July 1925); H. St. John Thackeray, *The Relation of St. Paul to Contemporary Jewish Thought, pp. 25-27.*

56. Scott, p. 493.

57. See Volz, pp. 195f.

58. Scott, p. 493; also see Teeple, p. 4.

59. cf. Volz, p. 196; H. L. Strack-P. Billerbeck, *Kommentar zum Neun Testament aus Talmus Midrasch* IV, pp. 794ff.; Louis Ginzberg, *Eine unbekannte judische Sekte* (1922): 304ff. E. T. *The Legends of the Jews* (1910-39); Scott, pp. 493-95; Teeple, pp. 3, 5.

60. Scott, p. 494.

61. *ibid.* pp. 494-97.

62. *ibid.* p. 497.

63. cf. Scott, pp. 493-94. See Volz, p. 196; Louis Ginsberg, "Elijah," *The Jewish Encyclopedia,* Vol. V (1907), pp. 126-27, for further examples.

64. See Klausner, pp. 391ff.

65. Midrash on Leviticus quoted in C. Schoettegen, vol ii, p. 534.

66. J. Theodor, "Pesikta Rabbati," and "Yalkut Shimoni," *The Jewish Encyclopedia.* Vol VIII (1907), PP. 561-62 and 568-69.

67. Ginzberg, "Elijah," *The Jewish Encyclopedia,* pp. 126-27.

68. Schoettegen, vol. ii, p. 226; Joachim Jeremias, "Ηλιας", *TDNT* 2, p.930.

69. Ferdinand Wilhem Weber, *Judische Theologie Auf Grund des Talmud und verwandter Schriften gemeinfasslich dargestellt, p. 282.*

70. Volz, p. 192

71. Teeple, p.5; Volz, p.200; R. Meyer, *Der Prophet;* Scott, p. 498.

72. Volz, p. 200.

73. Dieter, Georgi, *Die Gegner des Paulus im 2 Korintherbrief: Studien zur Religiosen Propaganda in der Spatantike,* pp.148, 216; Jeremias, *TDNT* 2, p. 930; Theodore J. Weeden, *Mark: Traditions in Conflict,* p. 58.

74. Volz, p. 194
75. *ibid*. p. 195.
76. Teeple, p. 46.
77. Tiede, p. 103.
78. cf. Tiede, for discussion of Josephus' audience, pp. 207ff.
79. Tiede, p. 212; cf. John G. Gager, "The Figure of Moses in Greek and Roman Pagan Literature," who has observed that in pagan and in literary circles Moses is evaluated as lawgiver, even if they are aware of his reputation as miracle-worker (Unpublished dissertation, Harvard University, 1968).
80. Tiede, p. 215; cf. H. St. John Thackery, *Josephus, the Man and the Historian,* p. 57, and Josephus, *Antiquities,* p. 52 n.b.; also Gerhard Delling, "Josephus and das Wunderbare," *NT* 2 (1958): 305.
81. Cf. Delling, pp. 305-09; George W. MacRae, "Miracle in the Antiquities of Josephus, *"Miracles: Cambridge Studies in Their Philosophy and History,* pp. 136-42; Tiede, pp. 216f.
82. Tiede, p. 230; cf. pp. 227f.
83. Gager, p. 312; cf. Tiede, p. 104
84. cf. J. Freudenthal, *Hellenistische Studien.* Haft 1 and 2: *Alexander Polyhistor,* pp. 143-74. For Eusebius' text of Artapanus on Moses. cf. Tiede, Appendix II, p. 321; cf. Felix Jacoby, *Die Fragmente der Griechischen Historiker,* pp. 1957ff.
85. Tiede, p. 177
86. Not all of these figures were Zealots, Tiede, p. 197; cf. Brandon, *Jesus and the Zealots,* who refers to these non-Zealots as para-Zealots.
87. Tiede, pp. 198, 200ff.

Chapter IX

1. Alfred Sendrey and Mildred Norton, *David's Harp,* p. 2-3.
2. *ibid.* p. 3.
3. Aron Marko Rothmuller, *The Music of the Jews,* p. 72.
4. Alfred Sendrey,*Music in Ancient Israel,* p. 35.
5. Francis Galpin, *The Music of the Sumerians, Babylonians and Assyrians,* p. 51-2; Sendrey, p. 36.
6. Sendrey,
   p. 36-7.
7. *ibid.* p. 37; Galpin, p. 53
8. Galpin, p. 53.
9. Sendrey, p. 37.
10. *ibid.* p. 59
11. *ibid.*
12. *ibid.* p. 60.
13. *ibid.* p. 61.
14. *ibid.* pp. 62-63.
15. *ibid.*
16. *ibid.* p. 63-644.
17. *ibid.*
18. *ibid.* p. 65, 68-69.
19. *ibid.*pp. 69-70
20. See Galpin, pp. 66-69 for a fuller explanation of these.
21. *Encyclopedia Judaica,* p. 563.
22. Sendrey, p. 264.
23. *ibid.* pp. 266-307.
24. Sendrey, pp. 266-68, 71; also Boehm, "Music," *Encyclopedia Judaica,* p. 563-64.
25. Sendrey, pp. 278-82, 89-92; also Boehm, "Music," *Encyclopedia Judaica,* p. 564.
26. Sendrey, pp. 307-342.
27. Boehm, "Music," *Encyclopedia Judaica,* p. 565; Sendrey, pp. 342-64, 65-71.
28. Sendrey, pp. 371-389.
29. Boehm, "Music," *Encyclopedia Judaica,* p. 565; Sendrey, pp. 372-75.
30. Boehm, "Music," *Encyclopedia Judaica,* p. 564; Sendrey, pp. 375-81.
31. Boehm, "Music," *Encyclopedia Judaica,* p. 564; Sendrey, p. 381.

32. Boehm, "Music," *Encyclopedia Judaica*, p. 564; Sendrey, p. 385.

33. Abraham Idelsohn, *Jewish Music in Its Historical Development*, pp. 7-8.

34. *ibid*. p. 8.

BIBLIOGRAPHY

BIBLIOGRAPHY

Abbott, Jacob. *Alexander the Great.* New York: Circle Publishing Co., n.d.

Allegro, John M. *The Dead Sea Scrolls; a Reappraisal.* Hammondsworth, Middlesex: Penguin Books, 1956.

Allen, Willoughby Charles. *A Critical and Exegetical Commentary on the Gospel According to St. Matthew.* (The International Critical Commentary) New York: C. Scribner's Sons. 1957.

Barthelemy, D., and Milik, Josef T. *Qumran Cave I (Discoveries in the Judean Desert I).* Oxford: Clarendon Press, 1955.

Baumbach, Günther. *"Das Sadduzäerverständnis bei Josephus Flavius und im Neuen Testament."* Kairos 13 (1971): 27.

Bible. *The Holy Bible Containing the Old and New Testament.* KJV. New York: American Bible Society, 1970.

Bible. *New American Standard Bible.* Carol Stream, Ill.: Creation House, 1973.

Bible. *The New Oxford Annotated Bible with the Apocrypha.* Edited by Herbert G. May and Bruce M. Metzger. RSV. New York: Oxford University Press, 1973.

Bickerman, Elias. *From Ezra to the Last of the Maccabees.* New York: Schocken Books, 1962.

The Maccabees: An Account of Their History from the Beginnings to the Fall of the House of the Hasmoneans. New York: Schocken Books, 1947.

Boehm, Yohanon, "Music." *Encyclopedia Judaica,* XII (1971), 563-66.

Brandon, Samuel G. F. *Jesus and the Zealots: A Study of the Political Factor in Primitive Christianity.* New York: C. Scribner's Sons, 1967.

Bright, John. *A History of Israel,* 2nd edition. Philadelphia: Westminster Press, 1972.

Bruce, Frederick F. *New Testament History.* Garden City, N.Y.: Anchor Books, Doubleday, 1972.

Bruce, Frederick F., ed. *Second Thoughts on the Dead Sea Scrolls.* Grand Rapids: Wm. B. Eerdmans, 1956.

Buhl, F. Peter William. *Det israelitiske Folkes Historie.* Copenhagen: 1922, 1936.

Burns, Edward McNall. *Western Civilization,* 6th ed. New York: W. W. Norton, 1963.

Burrows, Millar. *Burrows on the Dead Sea Scrolls.* Grand Rapids: Baker Book House, 1978.

The Dead Sea Scrolls. New York: Viking Press, 1955.

More Light on the Dead Sea Scrolls, New York: The Viking Press, 1958.

Burrows, Millar; Trever, John C.; and Brownlee, William H., editors. *The Dead Sea Scrolls of St. Mark's Monastery, Vol. I: The Isaiah Manuscript, and the Habakkuk Commentary.* New Haven: American Schools of Oriental Research, 1950.

Coggins, R. J. *Samaritans and Jews.* Atlanta, Ga.: John Knox Press, 1975.

Coss, Thurman. *Secrets from the Caves.* New York: Abingdon Press, 1963.

Cross, Frank M., Jr. *The Ancient Library of Qumran and Modern Biblical Studies* (The Haskell Lectures 1956-57). New York: Doubleday, 1958.

Cullman, Oscar. *The Christology of the New Testament,* rev. ed. Translated by Shirley C. Guthrie and Charles A. M. Hall. Philadelphia: Westminster Press, 1964.

Delling, Gerhard. "Josephus und das Wunderbare." NT 2 (1958): 305.

The Delphian Course: World's Progress, Vol. I. Chicago: The Delphian Society, 1913.

Dimont, Max I. *Jews, God and History.* New York: New American Library, 1962.

DuPont-Sommer, André. *The Dead Sea Scrolls: A Preliminary Survey.* Translated by E. Margaret Rowley. New York: Macmillan Co., 1952.

The Essene Writings From Qumran. Gloucester, Mass. Peter Smith, 1973.

Encyclopedia Judaica, Vol. 12. New York: Macmillan, 1971.

Farmer, William Reuben. *The Maccabees, Zealots and Josephus.* New York: Columbia University Press, 1956.

Fitzmyer, Joseph A. *Essays on the Semitic Background of the New Testament.* London: Scholar's Press, 1974.

Foerster, Werner. *From the Exile to Christ*. Philadelphia: Fortress Press, 1964.

Freudenthal, J. *Hellenistische Studien*. Haft 1 and 2: *Alexander Polyhistor*. Breslau: Verlag von H. Skutsch, 1875.

Gager, John G. "The Figure of Moses in Greek and Roman Pagan Literature." unpublished dissertation, Harvard University, 1968.

Galpin, Francis William. *The Music of the Sumerians and Their Immediate Successors, the Babylonians and Assyrians*. New York: Da Capo Press, 1970.

Gaster, Theodor H. "Samaritans." *The Universal Jewish Encyclopedia*, IX (1943), 335-39.

Georgi, Dieter. *Die Gegner des Paulus im 2. Korintherbrief: Studien zur Religiösen Propaganda in der Spätantike*. (Wissenschaftliche Monographien zum Alten und Neuen Testament, 11.) Neukirchen-Vluyn: Neukirchener Verlag, 1964.

Ginzberg, Louis. *Eine unbekannte jüdische Sekte*. E.T. *The Legends of the Jews*. Philadelphia: The Jewish Publication Society of America, 1911-40.

"Elijah." *The Jewish Encyclopedia*, Vol. V (1907), 126-27.

Goodman, Paul. *History of the Jews*. rev. and enl. by Israel Cohen. New York: E. P. Dutton, 1953.

Grant, Robert M. *A Historical Introduction to the New Testament*. New York: Simon & Schuster, 1972.

Hahn, Ferdinand. *The Titles of Jesus in Christology*. New York: World Publishing Co., 1969.

Harrison, Everett F. *A Short Life of Christ*. Grand Rapids: Wm. B. Eerdmans, 1968.

Harrison, R. K. *The Dead Sea Scrolls*. New York: Harper & Bros., 1961.

Idelsohn, Abraham. *Jewish Music In Its Historical Development*. New York: Schocken Books, 1967.

The Interpreter's Dictionary of the Bible, Vol. 4, edited by George Arthur Buttrick. Nashville: Abingdon Press, 1962.

Ishak, Priest Amram. *The History and Religion of the Samaritans*, Jerusalem: Greek Convent Press, n.d.

Jackson, F. J. Foakes. *Josephus and the Jews*. Grand Rapids: Baker Book House, 1977.

Jacoby, Felix. *Die Fragmente der Griechischen Historiker*. Leiden: E. J. Brill, 1957.

Jeremias, Joachim. "Ηλιας." *TWNT* II: 930-35. E.T. *TDNT* 2:928-41. Grand Rapids: Wm. B. Eerdmans, 1964.

Josephus, Flavius. *The Works of Flavius Josephus*. Chicago: Thompson & Thomas, 1901.

Kahen, Hasanein Wasef. *The Samaritans: Their History, Religion, Customs*. Nablus, Israel: 1974.

Klausner, Joseph. *The Messianic Idea in Israel: From Its Beginning to the Completion of the Mishnah*. New York: Macmillan Company, 1955.

Kohler, Kaufmann. "Pharisees." *The Jewish Encyclopedia,* IX (1905), 665.

Kuhn, Karl Georg. "Die beiden Messias Aarons und Israels." *NTS* 1 (1954-55): 178.

Lamb, Harold. *Alexander of Macedon*. Garden City, N.Y.: Doubleday, 1946.

LaSor, William Sanford. *The Dead Sea Scrolls and the Christian Faith*. Chicago: Moody Press, 1962.

The Dead Sea Scrolls and the New Testament. Grand Rapids: Wm. B. Eerdmans, 1972.

Levinger, Elma Ehrlich, and Levinger, Rabbi Lee J. *The Story of the Jews*. New York: Berhman's Jewish Book Shop, 1928.

Lohse, Edward. *The New Testament Environment*. Translated by John E. Steely. Nashville: Abingdon Press, 1976.

Macdonald, John. *The Theology of the Samaritans*. Philadelphia: Westminster Press, 1964.

McNeill, William H. *History of Western Civilization: A Handbook,* rev. and enl. Chicago: University of Chicago Press, 1969.

MacRae, George W. "Miracle in the Antiquities of Josephus" in Charles F. D. Moule, ed., *Miracles: Cambridge Studies in Their Philosophy and History*. London: A. R. Mowbray, 1965.

Manson, Thomas William. *The Servant-Messiah: A Study of the Public Ministry of Jesus*. Grand Rapids: Baker Book House, 1977.

Marsden, E. W. *Greek and Roman Artillery*. Oxford: Clarendon Press, 1969.

Merx, Adalbert. *Der Messias oder Ta'eb der Samaritaner*. Giessen: A. Töpelmann, 1909.

Metzger, Bruce M. *The New Testament: Its Background, Growth and Content.* Nashville: Abingdon Press, 1965.

Meyer, Eduard. *Ursprung und Anfänge des Christentums,* i-iii. Stuttgart und Berlin: J. G. Cotta, 1921.

Meyer, R. *Der Prophet aus Galiläa.* Buchges: Darmstadt, Wissenschaftliche, 1970.

Milik, Josef T. *Ten Years of Discovery in the Wilderness of Judaea,* translated by J. Strugnell. Naperville, Ill.: A. R. Allenson, 1959.

Montgomery, James A. *The Samaritans,* rev. ed., 1968, repr. of 1907 ed. New York: KTAV Publishing House, 1968.

Moore, George Foot. *Judaism in the First Centuries of the Christian Era: The Age of the Tannaim,* Vol. I. New York: Schocken Books, 1971.

Mowinckel, Sigmund Olaf. *He That Cometh.* Translated by G. W. Anderson. New York: Abingdon Press, 1954.

Neusner, Jacob. *A Life of Yahanan Ben Zakkai: Ca. 1-80 C.E.* Leiden: E. J. Brill, 1970.

Pearlman, Moshe. *The Maccabees.* London: Weidenfeld and Nicolson, 1973.

Pfeiffer, Charles F. *Between the Testaments.* Grand Rapids: Baker Book House, 1959.

The Dead Sea Scrolls. Grand Rapids: Baker Book House, 1962.

Purvis, James D. *The Samaritan Pentateuch and the Origin of the Samaritan Sect.* Cambridge, Mass.; Harvard University Press, 1968.

Reicke, Bo Ivar. *The New Testament Era.* Philadelphia: Fortress Press, 1968.

Rhoads, David M. *Israel in Revolution: 6-74 C.E.* Philadelphia: Fortress Press, 1976.

Roth, Cecil. *A History of the Jews.* New York: Schocken Books, 1961.

Rothmüller, Aron Marko. *The Music of the Jews,* new and rev. ed. Cranbury, N.J.: A. S. Barnes, 1975.

Russell, David S. *The Jews from Alexander to Herod.* London: Oxford University Press, 1967.

Scott, R. B. Y. "The Expectation of Elijah." *The Canadian Journal of Religious Thought,* Vol. 3, No. 6 (Nov.-Dec. 1929): 490-502.

Sendrey, Alfred. *Music in Ancient Israel.* New York: Philosophical Library, 1969.

Sendrey, Alfred, and Norton, Mildred. *David's Harp: The Story of Music in Biblical Times.* New York: The New American Library, 1964.

Smith, Morton. "Palestinian Judaism in the First Century" in Moshe Davis, ed., *Israel, Its Role in Civilization, Part II, Ch. 4.* New York: Arno Press, 1977.

Strack, Herman L., and Billerbeck, Paul. *Kommentar zum Neuen Testament aus Talmund Midrasch,* Vol. IV. Munich: Beck Verlag, 1922-65.

Tarn, William Woodthorpe. *Hellenistic Civilisation.* Chicago: Meridian Books, 1961.

Tcherikover, Victor. *Hellenistic Civilization and the Jews.* New York: Atheneum, 1970.

Tedesche, Sidney. *The First Book of Maccabees* (Jewish Apocryphal Literature, Vol. I). New York: Harper & Bros., 1950.

Teeple, Howard M. *The Mosaic Eschatological Prophet.* Philadelphi: Society of Biblical Literature, 1957.

Tenney, Merrill C. *The New Testament Times.* Grand Rapids: Wm. B. Eerdmans, 1965.

Tenney, Merrill C., ed. *Zondervan Bible Dictionary.* Grand Rapids: Zondervan Publishing House, 1963.

Thackeray, H. St. John. *Josephus: The Man and the Historian.* New York: Jewish Institute of Religion Press, 1929.

The Relation of St. Paul to Contemporary Jewish Thought. New York: Macmillan, 1900.

Theodor, J. "Pesikta Rabbati" and "Yalkut Shimoni." *The Jewish Encyclopedia,* Vol. VIII (1907), 561-62; 568-69.

Tiede, David Lenz. *The Charismatic Figure as Miracle Worker.* SBL Dissertation Series, Number 1. University of Montana: Missoula, Montana, 1972.

Trever, John C. *The Dead Sea Scrolls, A Personal Account.* Grand Rapids: Wm. B. Eerdmans, 1977.

The Untold Story of Qumran. Westwood, N.J.: Fleming Revell, 1965.

Vaux, Roland de (Père). *L'Archeologie et les manuscrits de la Mer Morte* (Schweich Lectures of the British Academy, 1959). London: Oxford University Press, 1961.

Volz, Paul. *Die Eschatologie der Judischen Gemeinde in neutestamentlicher Zeitalter.* Tubingen: J. C. B. Mohr (Paul Siebeck), 1934.

Weber, Ferdinand Wilhem. *Judische Theologie auf Grund des Talmud und verwandter Schriften gemeinfasslich dargestellt,* 2nd ed. Leipzig: Dorffling & Franke, 1897.

Weeden, Theodore J. *Mark: Traditions in Conflict.* Philadelphia: Fortress Press, 1971.

Yadin, Yigael. *The Message of the Scrolls.* New York: Simon & Schuster, 1957.